Economic Microfoundations of Strategic Management

"I have often said that there is more work that calls for research on the micro-foundations of strategic management then there is actual work on the micro-foundations of strategic management. Foss and Foss help address this gap by building a framework for understanding why some firms outperform others rooted in a deep understanding of contracting and property rights—a great contribution."

—Jay Barney, *Residential Professor of Strategic Management, Lassonde Chair of Social Entrepreneurship, Eccles School of Business, The University of Utah*

"Foss and Foss have revitalized the strategy and organizations literatures by reminding us that property rights are central to production and exchange. In the tradition of pioneering thinkers like Ronald Coase, Armen Alchian, Harold Demsetz, and Yoram Barzel, they link the emergence, definition, and enforcement of property rights to incentives, information, governance, and innovation. This book is essential reading for economists, management scholars, and others seeking to understand firms and markets."

—Peter G. Klein, *Caruth Chair of Entrepreneurship, Hankamer School of Business, Baylor University, and Faculty Director of Baylor's Baugh Center for Entrepreneurship and Free Enterprise*

Kirsten Foss · Nicolai J. Foss

Economic Microfoundations of Strategic Management

The Property Rights Perspective

palgrave
macmillan

Kirsten Foss
Norwegian School of Economics
Bergen, Norway

Nicolai J. Foss
Copenhagen Business School
Copenhagen, Denmark

ISBN 978-3-031-12912-4 ISBN 978-3-031-12910-0 (eBook)
https://doi.org/10.1007/978-3-031-12910-0

This Palgrave Macmillan imprint is published by the registered company Springer Nature Switzerland AG
The registered company address is: Gewerbestrasse 11, 6330 Cham, Switzerland

Preface and Acknowledgments

This book is a collection and synthesis of our joint work since the mid-1990s on property rights economic and how it furthers the study of various (macro) management phenomena, in particular strategy. It integrates a number of our articles. While we have not included any of these articles in unchanged form, often text portions from these articles have been recycled (or only tweaked) and we grateful to the following publishers for their permission to do this. The papers that we particularly draw on are (chronologically ordered):

1. Kirsten Foss, Nicolai J. Foss, and Peter G. Klein. "Uncovering the Hidden Transaction Costs of Market Power: A Property Rights Approach to Strategic Positioning." *Managerial and Decision Economics*, 39: 306–319 (2018).
2. Kirsten Foss, Nicolai J. Foss, and Peter G. Klein. "Managerial Authority in the Coasian Firm: An Entrepreneurial Interpretation." In Claude Mènard and Elodie Bertrand, eds. *The Elgar Companion to Ronald Coase*. Edward Elgar (2016).

3. Kirsten Foss and Nicolai J. Foss. "Coasian and Modern Property Rights Economics." *Journal of Institutional Economics*, 11: 391–411 (2015).
4. Kirsten Foss and Nicolai J. Foss. "Understanding Opportunity Discovery and Sustainable Advantage: The Role of Transaction Costs and Property Rights," *Strategic Entrepreneurship Journal*, 2: 191–207 (2008).
5. Kirsten Foss and Nicolai J. Foss. "Value and Transaction Costs: How the Economics of Property Rights Furthers the RBV," *Strategic Management Journal*, 26: 541–553 (2005).
6. Kirsten Foss and Nicolai J. Foss. "Assets, Attributes and Ownership," *International Journal of the Economics of Business*, 8: 19–37 (2001).
7. Kirsten Foss. "Organizing Technological Interdependencies: A Coordination Perspective on the Firm." *Industrial and Corporate Change*, 10: 151–178 (2001).

We are grateful to many colleagues who have offered comments on our work on property rights over the years. These include, in alphabetical order, Esben Sloth Andersen, Christian G. Asmussen, Jay Barney, Yoram Barzel, Eric Brousseau, Thrainn Eggertson, Teppo Felin, Eirik Furubotn, Geoff Hodgson, Chihmao Hsieh, Michael Jacobides, Peter G. Klein, Henrik Lando, Richard N. Langlois, Lasse Lien, Joseph Mahoney, Richard Makadok, Uskali Mäki, Claude Ménard, Will Mitchell, Peter Møllgaard, Jackson Nickerson, Pavel Pelikan, Sylvia Saes, Stephane Saussier, Nils Stiglitz, Anne Yvrande, and Decio Zylbersztajn.

Intellectually, our greatest debt is to Yoram Barzel. Yoram has been a true trailblazer in property rights economics, cultivating his own distinct and highly generative approach. No one has, in our opinion, dug deeper into the intricacies of property rights. We are happy to dedicate this book to Yoram.

Bergen, Norway
Copenhagen, Denmark

Kirsten Foss
Nicolai J. Foss

Contents

List of Figures

List of Tables

1

Strategy and Property Rights

On the morning of January 24, 1848, a carpenter, James Marshall, was busy constructing a water-powered sawmill for John Sutter on the bank of a river near the Sierra Nevada mountains. While working on the mill project, he noticed some shiny flecks in the waterbed. Various tests confirmed that the flecks were gold. One of the most famous episodes in economic history, the California gold rush, started May 12, 1848, when Sam Brannan made public Marshall's earlier discovery of gold (Clay & Wright, 2005; Umbeck, 1977a, 1977b). The news were quickly disseminated nationally as well as internationally, leading to in an influx of about 300,000 people traveling to California to search for gold.

At the start of the gold rush, gold was essentially "free for the taking" (Clay & Wright, 2005), that is, unowned or "open access" property. While goldfields were primarily located on land owned by the US government, it did not define and enforce any property rights to the gold, and the mining activity was basically unregulated. However, in this relative legal anarchy property rights were established. Specifically, a de facto (if not de jure) delineation of property rights emerged from interaction among miners, based in miners adhering to a basic "finders-keepers"

K. Foss and N. J. Foss, *Economic Microfoundations of Strategic Management*, https://doi.org/10.1007/978-3-031-12910-0_1

ethics, and ultimately supported by the threat of the use of "equalizers" (i.e., revolvers) and other means of physical enforcement.

It is meaningful to talk of "property rights" here, because what emerged were generally recognized (among the relevant miners) rights to control certain resources (i.e., particular pieces of land). Miners would invest in making sure that other miners respected these rights, for example, through the acquisition of firearms and signaling their willingness to use armed force. They would undertake such investments for the obvious reason that resource control was valuable, that is, associated with potential net future payments from the gold that was mined and subsequently sold. These "property" or "control" rights may not be exactly what a legal scholar may think of as a right; yet, from an economic point of view it makes sense to think of them as de facto property rights, or what PRE scholar Yoram Barzel (1997) calls "economic rights."

Of course, in the California gold rush such economic rights were far from perfectly secure. Thus, when a miner discovered a particularly rich piece of land, he would try to mine it in secret and as quickly as possible. This implied that substantial parts of the wealth generated by the gold land dissipated, as miners allocated resources to spying, rushing, crowding, and investing in enforcing their de facto property rights (Umbeck, 1977a). As more miners entered the gold fields, land became scarcer and more valuable on the margin, which in turn increased the pace of the race and drove up the costs of privately protecting rights. Such value-reducing externalities implied that the initial legal anarchy gradually increasingly gave way to contractual institutions, so that formal property rights to mineral land were completely developed by 1850. Small mining firms emerged as teams were established to realize scale economies in cooking, etc.

Our basic claim in this book is that in many respects the study of firm strategy may benefit from thinking of it as a gold rush. Thus, consider competitive strategy, that is, how firms seek out valued positions in their markets, and establish them and defend them. Having a favorable positions means having an offering that customers value highly as compared to those of the competition. Firms may seek to protect such positions in numerous, including protecting the underlying resources that establish the position, but also through adjusting price, location, customer service, décor, functions, and so on. Such positions are like desired gold-rich positions along the American River at Coloma (where Marshall originally discovered gold) which miners sought to protect through secrecy, speed (mining before and quicker than others), the threat of violence, and so on. Like the miner's positions along the river, competitive positions are sought out and defended. This goes beyond analogy: There is a real sense in which competitors in the market seek to de facto delineate property right, not just to value-generating resources but also the income streams these yield, that are (de facto or *de jure*) not delineated by the state and its legal machinery (Bush & Mayer, 1974).

The positions that get established, that is, the de facto property rights that will exist, are determined by the resources invested in establishing them (we can think of these as transaction costs) and by the relative capabilities of the competitors as they scramble for positions in markets or goldfields. Competitors monitor each others' actions, and try to infer strategies and underlying capabilities, for example, by trying out new strategies and observing and analyzing competitor reactions. These are costly processes, and the relevant costs needs to be factored into the costs of strategies and weighed against the benefits of these strategies (i.e., the income stream from occupying a given position in the market—or a goldfield). Both the gold rush and the more ordinary competitive contexts are fraught with uncertainty and transaction costs. Luck plays a major role in shaping outcomes.

Of course, the analogy is limited in that the gold rush example is a race for delineating *use* rights to certain resources (i.e., gold fields), whereas most of the phenomena studied in competitive strategy research concern delineating *income* rights to rent streams, with use rights to resources being taken more or less as given. Still, it is fruitful to think of strategy as concerning the discovery of a source of a significant expected rent stream—which may not be legally protected—and overcoming the associated transaction costs of seizing it; raising the (transaction) costs of rivals while lowering own costs; keeping value dissipation at bay, for example, by credibly signaling to competitors that they will be resisted, etc. It is also a way of thinking that is fairly uniquely associated with property rights economics (henceforth, PRE). In other economics-based approaches to strategy we don't find, for example, the concern with transaction costs and value dissipation that is characteristic of PRE.

Accordingly, the basic aim of this book is to argue that the PRE has the potential to further our thinking about some of the core issues in strategy (*aka* strategic management *aka* business policy). Here is a different way of thinking about the relevance of the PRE for strategy, one that focuses on resources rather than competitive interaction (as in the above gold rush example). In general, PRE highlights the control over assets or resources as the key to the understanding of processes of value creation and appropriation, and, ultimately, competitive advantage. Understanding the role of resource control in these processes ultimately means understanding the incentives that individuals face with respect to providing effort, accumulating human capital, helping others, getting new ideas, formulating new business projects, and bargaining for their share of the value they have helped to create—all behaviors that have a direct bearing on core issues of value creation, value appropriation, and competitive advantage. In this logic, we address core strategy issues in a bottom-up manner, starting with individuals and the resources that have access to and can more or less control.

Much thinking in strategy views the core strategy issues in a very different light. Thus, large swaths of strategy research see competitive advantage as determined by "resources," "capabilities," "competences," "dynamic capabilities," etc. that are often not related to individuals and their choices in any transparent manner. Partly in response to critique of this exact point, scholars have begun trying to understand how, for example, "capabilities" relate to the mental representations of top managers (e.g., Levinthal, 2011; Teece, 2007). However, the alternative approach is to begin from individuals and their choices and interaction and then see how far this can get us with respect to some of the core issues in strategy, such as understanding how capabilities actually emerge from choices and behaviors (Abell et al., 2008). This is the approach taken in this monograph. This microfoundational approach is given actual content by means of the PRE. Since our argument is still unusual we will flesh out the microfoundations in greater detail in the next chapter. We continue by discussing the PRE more broadly in the context of the evolution of the strategy field.

Property Rights Economics in the Conversation of Strategy Researchers[1]

The Importance of Strategy Research

Strategy is one of the most exciting fields of management research. It a major research field, it has very direct practice relations and implications, and frontier strategy research is challenging and rigorous, theoretically as well as empirically. While the field is a rather direct importer of advances in economics, sociology, and psychology, as well as an importer of methods (in particular, econometric methods), it has also developed a number distinct cumulative theories, such as the resource-based view (Barney, 1991; Peteraf, 1993; Wernerfelt, 1984) or the dynamic capabilities approach (Teece, 2007; Teece et al., 1997).

The field is taken up with the truly major—and in the context of management research: macro—questions: Why are some companies more successful than other companies, and what can they do sustain or revitalize such success? They are obviously major questions to firms. But, they are also major questions from the point of view of management as a practice. There is a sense in which other management questions—such as, how can we best design our HRM practices? Our logistics? Our internal organization? Our supply chain?—are subordinate to these strategy questions. Like its close cousin, organization theory, strategy offers a holistic perspective on the enterprise. Ultimately, the various functions, total resource portfolio, collection of processes, etc. of a company are economically justified only to the extent that they contribute to the survival of the company, that is, at least the company breaks even. Indeed, strategy is part of "macro" management theory (as a comparison, the psychology-based "organizational behaviour" field is the quintessential "micro" field).

The questions why some companies are more successful than other companies, and what they can do to sustain or revitalize such success are also truly major questions from the point of view of the rest of society. Firm-level value creation, the entrepreneurial actions firms engage in to

[1] Apologies to Mahoney and Pandian (1992).

reach high levels of sustained value creation, what is the role of innovation in renewing such value creation, and how created value is split between the firm's various stakeholders is of obvious societal relevance. These issues are the heart of contemporary discussions of dynamism and innovation, whether the market dominance of big established companies is transitory, and whether inequality is rooted in how value is split among the firm's stakeholders.

For example, established firms are engines of societal value creation—an elementary insight often overlooked in the current enthusiasm for start-up activity. But, the reason start-up activity is needed ultimately is that some (in fact, just a few) start-ups will eventually become established growing firms that generate jobs and revenue on a stable, long-run basis. To become such engines of long-run value creation, jobs, etc., firm performance needs to be based on some kind of resources that confer an advantage—a basic insight of the strategy research field.

More efficient firms are also likely to outcompete less efficient rivals. So, efficiency may drive the concentration of industries (Brozen, 1977; Demsetz, 1973; Oi, 1983), in particular when, as is the case of the new breed of tech "superstar firms" (Autor et al., 2020), network externalities are present. Thus, in a modern-day version of the classical antitrust debates of the 1970s (e.g., Brozen, 1977; McGee, 1977), critics of such firms argue that efficiency may turn into dominance, and dominance can be "abused" (Khan & Vaheesan, 2017). Establishing dominance, or at least a strong market position, and keeping through the creation of various barriers is a staple of traditional industrial organization economics (e.g., Scherer & Ross, 1990)—but it is also a key theme in some core theories of what strategy scholars call "competitive strategy." Thus, the early thinking of the perhaps still most influential strategy scholar, Michael Porter (1980, 1981), is directly based on this kind of economics. Indeed, as has often been remarked, Porter turned antitrust's concern with reducing market power that increases prices and profits on its head, advising companies to seek those positions where they can exercise profitable market power.

Economics and Strategy

The above observations illustrate how economics has helped to frame some of the core issues in strategy as the field has evolved since the 1960s (Rumelt et al., 1994). This book continues this established tradition. We address what we consider the core or "classical" issues in firm strategy research—notably value creation, value appropriation, how "market power" approaches (such as the positioning approach of Porter, 1980) relate to "efficiency" approaches (such as the resource-based view; Barney, 1991), and the meaning of the "firm" in strategy research. We examine and discuss in a non-technical manner much of the economics underpinning of these concepts and ideas. Last, but not least, we bring some perhaps unusual economics to bear on strategy issues, namely the PRE.

Economics has decisively informed strategy research for more than four decades. The basic reason is not hard to discern: Economics has overlapping themes with strategy, notably competition/rivalry, and trying to do as well as possible ("maximize utility (profit)" given scarcity and the actions of others with whom one somehow interacts. Not surprisingly, many of the elemental concepts of strategy research are straight out of the (micro)economics textbook (e.g., concepts of profits, values, opportunity costs, rents, market structure, etc.). When strategy began to emerge as an academic discipline toward the end of the 1970s, it was in no small measure aided by the presence of a body of work available that could be imported and tweaked to fit the purposes of strategy. The first such direct import-with-tweaks manifests in the work of Michael Porter (1980, 1981), which was explicitly based on the 1950s and 1960s industrial organization economics. Strategy research also made use of advances in game theory, both in its non-cooperative (Ghemawat, 1991) and cooperative (Brandenburger & Stuart, 1996) manifestations.[2] Ideas on real options from economic finance theory have been used to rigorously conceptualize the value of strategic flexibility and of waiting. Chicago-UCLA price theory and thinking on industrial organization

[2] The focus on-cooperative game theory is on the moves players should rationally make and the resulting equilibria. The focus of cooperative game theory is on the value created by coalition of players and how much value each player can appropriate.

(e.g., Demsetz, 1973) was imported to strategy and tweaked to become the "resource-based view" (Barney, 1991; Lippman & Rumelt, 1982; Peteraf, 1993). So-called evolutionary economics, deriving directly from Nelson and Winter (1982) and more distantly from Schumpeter (1911, 1942), has strongly shaped strategy research on capabilities and dynamic capabilities (e.g., Teece et al., 1997; Winter, 2003). We, along with other strategy scholars (e.g., Kim & Mahoney, 2002, 2005; de Avila Monteiro & Zylbersztajn, 2012), argue that PRE now needs to be added to the repertoire of strategy scholars.

The Distinctiveness of This Book

Books on firm strategy tend to fall into two groups that address very different audiences. The first group are highly eclectic textbooks that pull together multiple tools and frameworks with often widely different origins. If you are or have been a business school student, you have been exposed to the genre. A typical example is Johnson, Whittington, Scholes, Angwin, and Regnér's *Exploring Strategy*, now in its 11th edition (strategy textbooks also tend to have ever-expanding author lists!). The other group consists of highly practitioner-oriented books that typically jump inductively from what one or a few companies seem to have done right to general success recipes, or, more modestly (and validly), offer potentially useful analogies for managerial decision-making in similar situations. At least some of these books are based on high-level research and offer compelling narratives and tight, logical reasoning. An example is Richard P. Rumelt's *Good Strategy, Bad Strategy: The Difference and Why It Matters* (Rumelt, 2011). Of course, the academic, journal-based literature is quite different from these two genres, as the interest lies in theorizing and measuring specific mechanisms that drive outcomes such as persistent above-normal profits. No journal article will usually seek to address as many different subjects as we do in this book.

This book lies somewhat in-between the usual book and the usual article in strategy. It is book-like in that we address a number of relatively different subjects. It is, however, also journal-like in that the book, in contrast to the usual strategy textbook, is informed by a specific perspective which runs through all the chapters of the book, namely PRE. We argue that this body of thinking, rooted in microeconomics, has a unique potential to further thinking about the core issues of strategy. This uniqueness stems from (1) the adoption of a highly "micro" unit of analysis, namely the individual property right; (2) the tight linking of this unit to individual action and interaction; (3) examining how the definition, exchange, capture and protection of property rights are costly processes; and (4) arguing that attempts to reduce these costs shape a host of social phenomena and practices, including contracts, business practices, firms, and formal and informal institutions.

PRE applies these ideas in such a way that they span all levels of analysis, including those that are of interest to strategic management scholars. Its insights into the definition, exchange, capture, and protection of property and the costliness of these processes speak directly to key processes in strategy of creating new value and protecting it. Since our claim that PRE has a great potential to generate new insight is a strong one, and since PRE is relatively unknown to most students, researchers, and scholars with an interest in strategy, we will spend the remainder of this introductory chapter placing the PRE in the context of the economics underpinning of strategy research and also characterize PRE itself.

Property Rights and Other Approaches in Strategy Research

As mentioned already, strategy research has drawn liberally from a number of influences in economics (Kim & Mahoney, 2005). These include industrial economics in the Bain-Mason tradition, the UCLA-Chicago brand of price theory and industrial economics, game theory, but also financial economics, contract and transaction cost economics, labor economics, and other currents in economics. These continue to shape the discourse in the strategy literature, along with advances on the data side (big data sets and more micro data have become available) and on the side of empirical research methodology (not just the advances in econometrics often summarized as the "credibility revolution," but also, for example, machine learning techniques). Thus, from one perspective PRE is just one more addition of an established body of thinking in economics to strategy thinking.

However, PRE is worth adding, because it is different. PRE spans several levels of analysis, informing highly "micro" work on, for example, the nature of transaction costs (Barzel, 1985) and the economics of contracting (e.g., Cheung, 1968), as well as highly "macro" work on the nature of the state (Barzel, 2002), comparative systems (i.e., "capitalism versus socialism") (Pejovich, 1990) and the causes of economic growth (e.g., North, 1990), with work on, for example, the consequences of price controls (Cheung, 1974) or how measurement costs shape the organization of industry (Barzel, 1982) occupying more intermediate levels of analysis.

Historically, PRE has developed in parallel with, and has sometimes intersected, a number of the economic approaches that have shaped strategy. In particular, PRE is related to the brand of price theory and industrial economics that developed from the 1950s and into the 1980s in the economics departments at the University of California-Los Angeles and University of Chicago (e.g., Demsetz, 1973; Friedman, 1976; Stigler, 1966), to transaction cost economics (Williamson, 1975, 1985, 1996), and to the modern (formal) economics of contracts (Grossman & Hart, 1986; Hart & Moore, 1990; Holmström, 1979). Like these approaches, PRE is first and foremost a "micro" approach that starts from a careful analysis of individual choice in terms of constrained optimization and builds from this analysis to offer predictions regarding how agents will choose to structure their interaction.

However, the PRE goes beyond these related approaches in a number of key ways. First, as we shall argue its emphasis on "micro"—in particular truly accounting for *all* the relevant constraints on choice that individuals face—goes beyond the emphasis in, for example, transaction cost economics and contract theory. For example, some economists who work on contracts and ownership analyze situations in which some property rights (i.e., contractual stipulations) simply cannot be enforced by a court of law (or any other mechanism). Therefore, these will not be put into the contract, which is therefore left "incomplete." On the other hand, ownership rights to assets are assumed to be perfectly enforceable. While such "asymmetrical" assumptions (Foss & Hallberg, 2014) may make mathematical modeling and reasoning in general much simpler, it risks leading the analyst astray. For example, ownership rights are never fully enforceable, and this may be relevant for analyzing contractual arrangements. A PRE theorist will typically argue that therefore this real-life fact should be included in the analysis. (The additional complication that follows from this may be one reason that PRE research is often verbal rather than formal/mathematical.) This consistent emphasis on micro in the sense of accounting for all relevant constraints that agents face is a feature that is generative of new insight, including new insight in classic strategy issues.

Second, the basic unit of analysis of PRE differs from the units of analysis of its theoretical close relatives. Approaches often derive their names from their unit of analysis, such as *transaction* cost economics or *contract* economics. *Property rights* economics is no different in this respect. Thus, PRE starts from an understanding of property rights—the de facto rights that individuals hold over assets with respect to making use of these in various ways, deriving income from them, selling them, and so on. It asserts that what happens at the level of units in firms, firms themselves, industries, even the level of the whole economy can ultimately be broken down to property rights issues—that is, issues such as, who are the holders of which property rights to which assets? How well do these holders of property rights make use of their property rights? How well do they protect them? How do formal and informal institutions influence the cost of trading, capturing, and protecting such property rights? And so on.

Ultimately, the reason that property rights matter is that they structure people's incentives to make decisions to consume, produce, invest, save, buy, and sell—in short, all sorts of economic decisions, including those decisions that are of interest in strategy. We are, in effect, making the argument that PRE constitutes important microfoundations for strategy and that is a key reason that it needs to enter the conversation of strategy scholars to a larger extent. We define microfoundations and elaborate on the microfoundational nature of PRE in Chapter 2.

The notion of a property right is mainly known to strategy students and scholars from the context of intellectual property rights—that is, government defined and protected rights to intellectual creations, such as inventions or literary works. Intellectual property rights, which indeed offers many particularly vivid illustrations of the delineation, capture, and protection of legal rights to intellectual assets. However, property rights can be held to any (attribute of an) asset and thus are not limited to intellectual creations. And they are not necessarily dependent on delineation and enforcement by government. From the economic perspective, property rights can exist in a situation without government (i.e., anarchy) and even without law. Less extremely, property rights may exist when government enforcement is non-existent, weak, or ineffective, as we shall later explain. From an economic perspective, property rights are rather the effective ability to derive utility from access to an asset based on some kind of *control*. The idea of control of assets or resources is more probably more intuitive to strategy scholars than the notion of property rights, and in the context of strategy, the PRE is indeed very much an inquiry into the consequences of resource control for value creation and appropriation.

Property Rights Economics: New Old Insights

A basic reason why notions of "property rights" and "property rights economics" may sound somewhat alien to even economics-trained strategy scholars is that PRE is seldom taught as a distinct part of the curriculum in economics classes or economics programs. Modern strategy scholars are much more likely to be familiar with industrial economics and its foundation in non-cooperative game theory, as well as cooperative game theory. But, part of the ignorance is also, perhaps somewhat paradoxically, caused by the relative success of property rights economics: Many of the key property rights ideas have been absorbed into the economic mainstream and have thus in a sense lost their distinctiveness. For example, a key notion in PRE, the so-called Coase Theorem (Coase, 1959, 1960) (which we discuss in Chapter 3) is taught in many undergraduate programs, sometimes even in the first year of teaching, and is certainly taught in classes on resource/environmental/ecological economics. Another now entirely mainstream notion, namely transaction costs, was also initially developed by property rights economics, notably Coase (again), Alchian, Demsetz, Cheung, and others. Thus, Coase was the recipient of the 1991 Nobel Prize "for his discovery and clarification of the significance of transaction costs and property rights for the institutional structure and functioning of the economy" (Kungl. Vetenskapsakademien, 1991).

Relatedly, examining how institutions and politics shape economic growth has become an important part of economics. While modern economists may prefer to cite so-called modern political economy (e.g., Acemoglou, 2003; Persson & Tabellini, 2000) as sources, one of the key pioneers in this inquiry was economic historian and property rights economist, Douglass North, another recipient of the Nobel Prize (1990). Much of the groundwork regarding how property rights shape incentives and thus contribute to economic growth and dynamism was done by Harold Demsetz in the 1960s and Yoram Barzel in the 1970s. Other Nobel laureates, notably Ellinor Ostrom, James Buchanan, and Oliver Williamson, have been influenced by PRE in their work. One of the two 2016 recipients of the Nobel Prize, Oliver Hart (the other was Bengt Holmström), explicitly received the award for his work on property rights, although as we show in Chapter 4, his take on property rights is in key respects different from that of, for example, Coase, Demsetz, and Barzel (see also Foss & Foss, 2000b; Foss & Klein, 2016).

While property rights ideas are thus decades old as well as highly influential in economics, the explicit application of the PRE to strategy is rather recent (beginning with Foss, 2003; Foss & Foss, 2000a, 2005, 2008; Kim & Mahoney, 2005, 2010; Mahoney & McGahan, 2007; de Avila Monteiro & Zylberstzajn, 2012, 2015).[3] In Chapter 5, we cover the application of PRE to the core strategy issue of value creation and appropriation, and also show how resources—that is, bundles of property rights to productive assets—are best thought of as endogenous rather

[3] However, the history of applying transaction cost economics to strategy has a long history (e.g., Oxley, 1999; Rumelt et al., 1991; Teece, 1986).

than exogenous. In Chapter 6, we further show how PRE ideas are applicable to the understanding of competition and competitive strategy. The reason that PRE matters to strategy fundamentally is that it places *control* central.

While there are different notions of property rights in economics, all coalesce around the notion of effective control, that is, what an individual can do with resources she owns or otherwise has access to in order to maximize her well-being or "utility." In turn, such control provides incentives. The more one can do with an asset (e.g., in terms of servicing customer segments) and the larger the extent to which one can appropriate the economic fruits of using the asset, the stronger the incentives to use the asset in a value-creating ("efficient") manner. Thus, asset control speaks directly to issues of value creation and appropriation.

However, control needs to be acquired and it needs to be protected. Thus, abstracting from obtaining control by means of theft or borrowing, access to already owned assets is secured by purchasing, renting, or leasing the asset, that is, through some kind of (more or less costly) market transaction from another individual involving either the transfer of titles to property or the transfer of use rights through some contractual arrangement. Once access to the asset has been secured, it has to be protected against other individuals' capture. Such capture is motivated by the desire to appropriate the income stream associated with the asset ranges from direct theft over opportunistic holdup (i.e., a forced renegotiation of deals involving the asset so as to appropriate parts of the value created by the asset; Hart, 1995; Williamson, 1996) to competitive imitation (Giachetti et al., 2017). Individuals will spend resources on capture. Conversely, individuals who hold property rights to assets will spend resources on protecting assets against capture (Barzel, 1997).

To offer a mundane example, the United States has witnessed what has been described as a de facto decriminalization of retail theft, following a strong increase in shoplifting, particularly from 2020 to 2021 (Hogan, 2022), which is not unrelated to officials in major cities apparently instructing police to not arrest people for shoplifting. In other words, property rights have become less secure because they are legally less well enforced. Stores have tried to protect their income streams against the resulting capture (i.e., shoplifting) by raising prices, and larger stores invest in protecting their property rights by means of private security. The result is a new equilibrium with lower overall value creation (as value is dissipated both because of higher prices and higher costs of protecting property rights), closed stores, and smaller stores being at a disadvantage relative to larger stores (that can better spread out the fixed costs of private security on their transactions).

While the example may be mundane it illustrates the fundamental capture and protection dynamics that emerge when transaction costs—here, the costs of capturing and protecting property rights—change. It also illustrates the real consequences such changes have. These ideas are directly applicable to understanding competition and competitive strategy. As the costs of capturing and protecting property rights are core examples of transaction cost, PRE helps to place transaction cost ideas centrally in strategy.

As in the example, resources will be dissipated on capture and protection activities until an equilibrium is reached in which the marginal costs and benefits of capture and protection activities are equalized across all relevant individuals. In extreme cases, all created value could be fully dissipated. Rational forward-looking agents will seek to avoid such outcomes. They will choose contracts, governance structures, and formal and informal institutions that can keep value-dissipating processes at bay. However, since contracts, organizations, and institutions are costly to devise, run, and maintain, transaction costs are ubiquitous. The above is essentially a nutshell presentation of the PRE. In the rest of this chapter, we will further indicate how PRE matters to strategy and related areas, such as the theory of the firm and entrepreneurship.

Relevance to Strategy and Overview of the Book

The unique combination of insights in PRE is (1) taking the individual property right as the unit of analysis; (2) linking it to individual action and interaction (i.e., property rights are fundamentally about control in the context of social interaction); (3) examining how the definition, exchange, capture, and protection of property rights are costly processes;

and (4) arguing that attempts to reduce these costs shape a host of social phenomena and practices, including contracts, business practices, firms, and formal and informal institutions. These features make the PRE capable of furthering the microfoundations of strategy in ways no other approach can. Here are some of the core strategy phenomena that we argue that PRE illuminates in new, interesting ways (to be considered in greater detail in the rest of the book).

Value Creation

While strategy scholars often think of new value creation in terms of dramatic acts of product innovation (which may increase consumers' willingness to pay), process innovation (which lowers the costs of providing products and services), or business model innovation (which recombines the fundamental elements of enterprise), much actual firm-level value creation efforts are quite mundane. Thus, sorting the products one offers (or purchases) in a better way, improving how one monitors or incentivizes employees or making improved contracts with customers or suppliers are examples of actions that can create much value by reducing transaction costs and providing better incentives. For example, the courier multinational giant United Parcel Service (UPS) is famous for the extremes to which it goes in terms of its data-driven monitoring of drivers and trucks (Blank, 2021; Hullinger, 2015). Thus, on board monitoring equipment means that UPS is capable of tracking the mechanical performance of all of its trucks and their location, as well as speed, and braking behavior, including every time a truck starts or stops, the opening and closing of doors, etc. Such information is used as inputs into route optimization, that is, minimizing not only route length but also the stops and starts required to deliver packages. Moreover, the characteristics of routes (e.g., speed limits) can be optimally matched with different vehicles to save on energy costs. Driver behaviors can be compared in order to optimize driver behaviors. Even seemingly small gains add up very considerable, given the sheer size of UPS (revenues of more than 85 billion USD in 2020). Thus, a saving of one minute/day/driver increases profit by $14.5 million over the course of a year (Hullinger, 2015). In the terminology of PRE, such gains result from UPS being able at delineating and protecting various attributes of some of its key assets, namely its trucks.

Positioning Theory and Barriers to Strategizing

Market power (i.e., the ability to raise price above marginal cost) and bargaining power (i.e., how much one can potentially capture of the value from a transaction) are central constructs in competitive strategy. Both inform positioning research which, based on industrial organization economics, is focused on building, protecting, and exercising market and bargaining power. These ideas are at the heart of well-known frameworks such as the Porter (1980) 5-forces framework. Bargaining power is highlighted in cooperative game theory approaches to strategy (Brandenburger & Stuart, 1996, 2007).

However, position research, like its industrial organization ancestor, does not explicitly include transaction costs.[4] The problem is that conclusions from positioning analysis are sensitive to transaction costs. The Coase Theorem implies that the absence of transaction costs means the absence of inefficiencies, including the kind of inefficiencies assumed in positioning research (i.e., reduced output due to the ability to set prices at "non-competitive" levels). The idea is that absent costs to making and enforcing deals, all value-increasing trades will be made and agents will trade any inefficiency away. The broader implication is that if relevant transaction costs are sufficiently low, parties made worse off by the exercise of market and bargaining power may be able to negotiate, bargain, form coalitions, and otherwise contract around the focal firm's attempts to appropriate monopoly profits. Hence, the presence and size of transaction costs matter critically to competitive strategy.

[4] Cooperative game theory has recently begun to consider transaction costs in the form of "frictions" (Chatain & Zemsky, 2011).

The Theory of the Firm, Learning, and Entrepreneurship

In the last three chapters of the book (save for the Conclusion chapter), we touch on the closely related issues of the firm, learning, and entrepreneurship. Our reasoning starts from a novel interpretation of Coase's seminal article, "The Nature of the Firm" (Coase, 1937). In this article, Coase defines the firm in terms of the authority relation and the open-ended employment contract. This has been criticized by PRE scholars, who have argued that managerial authority is an epiphenomenon as (allegedly) the boss does not hold more power over employees than a customer holds power over, say, a grocer (Alchian & Demsetz, 1972). Coase's view has also been criticized on the ground that it neglects the one-person enterprise (which is a correct critique) (Demsetz, 1991). We argue, however, that Coase's reasoning is entirely consistent with PRE (cf. also Barzel & Kochin, 1992), and that the particular advantage of the authority relation is that it is a low-cost way of allocating use rights in the presence of incomplete contracts. Managers specialize in learning the shadow prices (or opportunity costs) of resource uses and this helps to explain the centralization of managerial authority in firms as well as the boundaries of firms. We unfold this view in Chapters 7 and 8.

New value creation stems from entrepreneurial acts. If entrepreneurs succeed and can somehow protect their ideas, acquire relevant complementary assets, and so on, initial acts of entrepreneurship may turn into sustained competitive advantages. Thus, entrepreneurship is of inherent interest from a strategy perspective. Entrepreneurs are only interested in pursuing those ideas that can somehow be kept proprietary (or sold, which requires that property rights to the ideas can be defined and enforced). In other words, the appropriability concerns highlighted in so much of the technology management and entrepreneurship literatures are fundamentally property rights issues.

Entrepreneurs often experiment with resource combinations. They may have to combine and recombine resource before they "get it right." However, these processes dissipate resources in the form of transaction costs as the entrepreneur (and those she has hired) tries to assess whether resources have characteristics that make them combinable at a profit. Thus, property rights and transaction costs shape paths of entrepreneurial exploration of new resource combinations. In Chapter 9, we elaborate on this basic idea and show how it contributes to the extant entrepreneurship literature.

References

Abell, P., Felin, T., & Foss, N. J. (2008). Building micro-foundations for the routines, capabilities and performance link. *Managerial and Decision Economics, 29*, 489–502.

Acemoglu, D. (2003). Why not a political Coase theorem? Social conflict, commitment, and politics. *Journal of Comparative Economics, 3*, 620–652.

Alchian, A. A., & Demsetz, H. (1972). Production, information costs, and economic organization. *American Economic Review, 62*, 772–795.

Autor, D., Dorn, D., Katz, L. F., Patterson, C., & van Reenen, J. (2020). The fall of the labor share and the rise of superstar firms. *Quarterly Journal of Economics, 135*, 645–709

Barney, J. B. (1991). Firm resources and sustained competitive advantage. *Journal of Management, 17*, 99–120.

Barzel, Y. (1982). Measurement costs and the organization of markets. *Journal of Law and Economics, 25*, 27–48.

Barzel, Y. (1985 [2005]). Transaction costs: Are they just costs? Reprinted in C. Mènard (Ed.), *Controversies and challenges in the new institutional economics*. Edward Elgar.

Barzel, Y. (1997). *Economic analysis of property rights* (2nd ed.). Cambridge University Press.

Barzel, Y. (2002). *A theory of the state*. Cambridge University Press.

Barzel, Y., & Kochin, L. (1992). Ronald Coase on the nature of social cost as a key to the problem of the firm. *Scandinavian Journal of Economics, 94*, 19–31.

Blank, Z. (2021). *More than just route planning: How UPS drivers optimize their routes*. https://www.getstraightaway.com/blog-posts/more-than-just-route-planning-how-ups-drivers-optimize-their-routes

Brandenburger, A. M., & Stuart, H. W. (1996). Value-based business strategy. *Journal of Economics and Management Strategy, 5*, 5–24.

Brandenburger, A. M., & Stuart, H. W. (2007). Biform games. *Management Science, 53*, 537–549.
Brozen, Y. (1977). The concentration-collusion doctrine. *The Antitrust Law Journal, 46*, 826–863.
Bush, W., & Mayer, L. (1974). Some implications of anarchy for the distribution of property. *Journal of Economic Theory, 8*, 401–412.
Chatain, O., & Zemsky, P. (2011). Value creation and value capture with frictions. *Strategic Management Journal, 32*, 1206–1231.
Cheung, S. N. S. (1968). Private property rights and sharecropping. *Journal of Political Economy, 76*, 1107–1131.
Cheung, S. N. S. (1974). A theory of price control. *Journal of Law and Economics, 17*, 53–62.
Clay, K., & Wright, G. (2005). Order without Law? Property rights during the California Gold Rush. *Explorations in Economic History, 42*, 155–183.
Coase, R. H. (1937). The nature of the firm. *Economica NS4*, 386–405.
Coase, R. H. (1959). The federal communications commission. *Journal of Law & Economics, 2*, 1–40.
Coase, R. H. (1960). The problem of social cost. *Journal of Law and Economics, 3*, 1–44.
de Avila Monteiro, G. F., & Zylbersztajn, D. (2012). A property rights approach to strategy. *Strategic Organization, 10*, 366–383.
de Avila Monteiro, G. F., & Zylbersztajn, D. (2015). Heterogeneity of property rights strategies in a global context: The case of genetically modified soybean seeds. *Global Strategy Journal, 5*(1), 69–83.
Demsetz, H. (1973). Industry structure, market rivalry, and public policy. *The Journal of Law and Economics, 16*, 1–9.
Demsetz, H. (1991). The nature of the firm revisited. In O. E. Williamson & S. G. Winter (Eds.), *The nature of the firm.* Blackwell.
Foss, K., & Foss, N. J. (2000a). Competence and governance perspectives: How much do they differ? And how does it matter? In N. J. Foss & V. Mahnke (Eds.), *Competence, governance, and entrepreneurship.* Oxford University Press.
Foss, K., & Foss, N. J. (2000b). Theoretical isolation in contract economics. *Journal of Economic Methodology, 7*, 313–339.
Foss, K., & Foss, N. J. (2005). Value and transaction costs: How the economics of property rights furthers the RBV. *Strategic Management Journal, 26*, 541–553.

Foss, K., & Foss, N. J. (2008). Understanding opportunity discovery and sustainable advantage: The role of transaction costs and property rights. *Strategic Entrepreneurship Journal, 2*, 191–207.

Foss, N. J. (2003). The strategic management and transaction cost nexus: Past debates, central questions, and future research possibilities. *Strategic Organization, 1*, 139–169.

Foss, N. J., & Hallberg, N. (2014). How symmetrical assumptions facilitate theoretical advance in strategic management: The case of the resource-based view. *Strategic Management Journal, 35*, 903–913.

Foss, N. J., & Klein, P. G. (2016). Reflections on the 2016 Nobel Memorial Prize for contract theory (Oliver Hart and Bengt Holmström). *Erasmus Journal for Philosophy and Economics, 9*, 167–180.

Friedman, M. (1976). *Price theory*. Walter de Gruyter.

Ghemawat, P. (1991). *Commitment*. Free Press.

Giachetti, C., Lampel, J., & Pira, S. (2017). Red Queen competitive imitation in the U.K. mobile phone industry. *Academy of Management Journal, 60*, 1882–1914.

Grossman, S., & Hart, O. (1986). The costs and benefits of ownership: A theory of lateral and vertical integration. *Journal of Political Economy, 94*, 691–719.

Hart, O. (1995). *Firms, contracts, and financial structure*. The Clarendon Press.

Hart, O., & Moore, J. (1990). Property rights and the nature of the firm. *Journal of Political Economy, 98*, 1119–1158.

Hogan, T. (2022, March 31). Will business fight back? *City Journal*. https://bit.ly/39xmiGP

Holmstrom, B. (1979). Moral hazard and observability. *The Bell Journal of Economics, 10*, 74–91.

Hullinger, J. (2015, December 11). *18 secrets of UPS drivers*. Mental Floss. https://www.mentalfloss.com/article/60556/18-secrets-ups-drivers

Khan, L., & Vaheesan, S. (2017). Market power and inequality: The antitrust counterrevolution and its discontents. *Harvard Law and Policy Review, 11*, 235–294.

Kim, J., & Mahoney, J. T. (2002). Resource-based and property rights perspectives on value creation: The case of oil field unitization. *Managerial and Decision Economics, 23*, 225–245.

Kim, J., & Mahoney, J. T. (2005). Property rights theory, transaction costs theory, and agency theory: An organizational economics approach to strategic management. *Managerial and Decision Economics, 26*, 223–242.

Kim, J., & Mahoney, J. T. (2010). A strategic theory of the firm as a nexus of incomplete contracts: A property rights approach. *Journal of Management, 36*(4), 806–836.

Kungl. Vetenskapsakademien. (1991). Press release. https://www.nobelprize.org/prizes/economic-sciences/1991/press-release/

Levinthal, D. A. (2011). A behavioral approach to strategy-what's the alternative? *Strategic Management Journal, 32*(13), 1517–1523.

Lippman, S. A., & Rumelt, R. P. (1982). Uncertain imitability: An analysis of inter-firm efficiency under competition. *Bell Journal of Economics, 13*, 418–438.

Mahoney, J. T., & McGahan, A. (2007). The field of strategic management within the evolving science of strategic organization. *Strategic Organization, 5*, 79–99.

Mahoney, J. T., & Pandian, J. R. (1992). The resource-based view within the conversation of strategic management. *Strategic Management Journal, 13*, 363–380.

McGee, J. S. (1977). Why not "deregulation" for antitrust? *Antitrust Law Journal, 46*, 777–793.

Nelson, R. R., & Winter, S. G. (1982). *An evolutionary theory of economic change*. The Belknap Press.

North, D. C. (1990). *Institutions, institutional change, and economic performance*. Cambridge University Press.

Oi, W. (1983). Heterogeneous firms and the organization of production. *Economic Inquiry, 21*, 147–171.

Oxley, J. (1999). Institutional environment and the mechanisms of governance: The impact of intellectual property protection on the structure of inter-firm alliances. *Journal of Economic Behavior and Organization, 38*, 283–309.

Pejovich, S. (1990). *The economics of property rights: Towards a theory of comparative systems*. Kluwer.

Persson, T., & Tabellini, G. (2000). *Political economics: Explaining economic policy*. MIT Press.

Peteraf, M. A. (1993). The cornerstones of competitive advantage: A resource-based view. *Strategic Management Journal, 14*, 179–191.

Porter, M. E. (1980). *Competitive strategy*. Free Press.

Porter, M. E. (1981). The contributions of industrial organization to strategic management. *Academy of Management Review, 6*, 609–620.

Rumelt, R. P. (2011). *Good strategy, bad strategy: The difference and why it matters*. Currency.

Rumelt, R. P., Schendel, D., & Teece, D. J. (1991). Strategic management and economics. *Strategic Management Journal, 12*, 5–29.

Rumelt, R. P., Schendel, D., & Teece, D. (1994). *Fundamental issues in strategy*. Harvard University Press.

Scherer, F. M., & Ross, D. R. (1990). *Industrial market structure and economic performance*. Houghton-Mifflin.

Schumpeter, J. A. (1911 [1934]). *The theory of economic development: An inquiry into profits, capital, credit, interest, and the business cycle*. Harvard University Press.

Schumpeter, J. A. (1942). *Capitalism, socialism, and democracy*. Harper and Brothers.

Stigler, G. J. (1966). *The theory of price*. Macmillan.

Teece, D. J. (1986). Profiting from technological innovation. *Research Policy, 15*, 285–305.

Teece, D. J. (2007). Explicating dynamic capabilities: The nature and microfoundations of (sustainable) enterprise performance. *Strategic Management Journal, 28*, 1319–1350.

Teece, D. J., Pisano, G., & Shuen, A. (1997). Dynamic capabilities and strategic management. *Strategic Management Journal, 18*, 509–533.

Umbeck, J. (1977a). The California Gold Rush: A study of emerging property rights. *Explorations in Economic History, 14*, 197–226.

Umbeck, J. (1977b). A theory of contract choice and the California Gold Rush. *Journal of Law and Economics, 20*, 421–437.

Wernerfelt, B. (1984). A resource-based theory of the firm. *Strategic Management Journal, 5*, 171–180.

Williamson, O. E. (1975). *Markets and hierarchies: Analysis and antitrust implications*. Free Press.

Williamson, O. E. (1985). *The economic institutions of capitalism*. Free Press.

Williamson, O. E. (1996). *The mechanisms of governance*. Oxford University Press.

Winter, S. G. (2003). Understanding dynamic capabilities. *Strategic Management Journal, 24*, 991–995.

2

Microfoundations for Strategy

One of the more important trends in strategy—and, more generally, macro-management theory—over the last ten to fifteen years has been a concerted push toward building microfoundations for strategy (Felin & Foss, 2005; Felin et al., 2015). To see what this entails and why it is warranted to build microfoundations for strategy, consider some of the perhaps best-known strategy frameworks, namely those that tend to dominate the textbooks, and also shape much research.

Strategy textbooks will typically have an analysis of the environment, perhaps represented through checklist frameworks, such as the PESTEL "framework" (which rounds up the Political, Economic, Social, Technological, Environmental, and Legal forces in the environment of a firm), but also more sophisticated tools, such as the Porter 5-forces framework (Porter, 1980). The textbooks will also feature an analysis of the "resources" (of all kinds) that firms may control, drawing on the resource-based view, and they may add detail on how those resources are actually used by firms, drawing on, for example, Porter's (1985) activity-based view. These generic frameworks are deployed to analyzing firm strategy in various settings, such as emerging markets or declining industries, or

K. Foss and N. J. Foss, *Economic Microfoundations of Strategic Management*, https://doi.org/10.1007/978-3-031-12910-0_2

how strategy is shaped by various new phenomena, such as the emergence of technological platforms, technological convergence, artificial intelligence, big data, and so on.

Such exercises often produce real insight, suggesting that the standard strategy frameworks represent valid and highly useful ideas. However, they leave something fundamental out. Thus, in none of the basic frameworks of strategy textbook is there much mention of *individuals*, notably those individuals who formulate, implement, and execute strategies. Of course, we can see our jobs as strategy scholars, teachers, and advisors/consultants merely as identifying the generic strategy that is best for Company X, the resources Company X should somehow acquire to implement this generic strategy, the organizational structure that may fit a certain strategy and so on. But, there is usually more to the story. For example, whether Company X will actually engage in a certain generic strategy and access a certain resource bundle raises further issues that may depend on the characteristics of the CEO and the top management team. For example, risk-averse CEOs may shy away from a change in something so fundamental as a change in generic strategy. However, suppose that a change is OK'ed by top management. The focus then turns to implementation and execution, which involves accessing resources. Further, some of these resources, namely human resources, need to be motivated before the company can deploy the services of these resources. Again, the focus shifts to individuals. As the saying goes, the devil is (often) in the detail, and in strategy that detail is often the issue of individuals who differ in terms of knowledge, preferences, attitudes to risk, inherent motivation, and so on.

Thus, part of the "microfoundations" perspective has been the critical point that many of our traditional strategy tools have a soft underbelly constituted by individuals who may differ in many ways that are of relevance to strategy (Felin & Hesterly, 2007). Furthermore, this perspective is based on the conjecture that ultimately *all* strategic issues can somehow be reduced to the actions and interactions of individuals. Since our argument in this book is fundamentally microfoundational, we need to take a closer look at what microfoundations entail.

The Structure of Microfoundations

The notion of microfoundations, as laid out by, for example, Felin et al. (2015), is a fairly generic idea. Thus, as Felin et al. (2015) explain microfoundations, they simply mean a quest for reduction in social science/management theory, such that what goes on at a given aggregate or macro or collective level is understood in terms of what goes on at lower levels. "Understood" here means accounting for a mechanism that takes the lower level entities and their behaviors as inputs and turns these inputs into what one seeks to explain at the higher level. Typically, the lower level—and according to the branch of microfoundations known as "methodological individualism" the rock-bottom of explanation—is the level of individuals.

In turn, it is possible to expand this with an explanation of what makes individuals behave, act, and interact in specific ways. This will typically make reference to individual preferences, beliefs, psychological traits, and so on, but it can also make reference to institutions or other phenomena that are "above" individuals. In other words, microfoundations do not rule out making use of macro variables in explanation. What it does rule out, except as parsimonious shorthand, is the use of "aggregate explanation," that is, explain aggregate phenomenon x in terms of aggregate phenomenon y. Thus, strictly speaking we do not want to explain, say, firm profitability in terms of firm capabilities. What we ideally want to do is explain firm profitability in terms of the complex multitude of individuals and their interaction that constitute what we may call "firm capability" (Abell et al., 2008; Vromen, 2010).

There are two fundamental reasons why we "want to" do this. One derives from the basic scientific quest for improving understanding by digging deeper. By uncovering mechanisms at lower levels (e.g., employee motivation and productivity) that generate phenomena at higher levels (e.g., sales and profits), we improve our understanding of the forces that really drive the events we actually observe. The second fundamental reason derives from this and is pragmatic: By digging deeper and thus getting a better understanding of the causal web of influences and effects that drive observed phenomena, we improve the basis for successful management interventions (Coleman, 1990: Chpt. 1).

Consider the central construct of "capability," one of strategy's foundational constructs. Typically, we ascribe capability to a business unit or perhaps to the firm at large. Clearly, capability is a macro or collective-level construct. While managers may seek to "build" or "transform" or "deploy" or "share" such capability, they are also well aware that one cannot manage a capability per se. What can be managed is rather the constituent component of capability, that is, the set of people, processes, assets, etc. that make up a capability.[1] Thus, whether conceived "philosophically" or pragmatically, microfoundations are fundamentally reductionist.

Which Microfoundations for Strategy?

The reductionism of microfoundations and its emphasis on inter-level relations (in particular, aggregation from micro to macro) means that microfoundations do impose an overall structure on explanation in social science, including management theory. However, this does not mean that microfoundations must be of a certain theoretical *kind*, such as being inherently sociological or economics-based or based on psychology. Microfoundations are often associated with rational choice theory, but that association is a historical one, rather than an association of logical necessity. Microfoundations are consistent with many different conceptualizations of action, decision-making, and behavior, ranging from Bayesian expected utility theory over various conceptualizations of bounded rationality and other psychology-based models behavior to completely rule-bound behavior. In other words, microfoundations are consistent with what management scholars typically assume about individuals.

Perhaps because of this inclusiveness the notion of microfoundations has resonated quite remarkably in management theory over the last 10–15 years and much strategy research over the last decade has been

[1] As Chester Barnard (1938), one of the founders of systematic management thinking, reasoned, management always and everywhere begins from individuals.

conducted from explicitly microfoundational premises. These microfoundations have been focused in different ways. Thus, some have developed microfoundations based on the microeconomics of contracts (e.g., Gambardella et al., 2015), while others have started from motivational psychology (e.g., Bridoux & Stoelhorst, 2014) or cognitive psychology (Powell et al., 2011). Still, what is common to such different microfoundations is that they start from the choice or behaviors of individuals.

The emphasis on choice has a long tradition in strategy. Thus, in a seminal essay, Rumelt et al. (1991: 6) explained that firms

> have choices to make if they are to survive. Those which are strategic include: the selection of goals, the choice of products and services to offer; the design and configuration of policies determining how the firm positions itself to compete in product markets (e.g. competitive strategy); the choice of an appropriate level of scope and diversity; and the design of organization structure, administrative systems and policies used to define and coordinate work. It is a basic proposition of the strategy field that these choices have critical influence on the success or failure of the enterprise, and, that they must be integrated. It is the integration (or reinforcing pattern) among these choices that makes the set a strategy.

Similarly, Leiblein et al. (2018: 559) propose "that the field of strategy be defined by and unified around the study of strategic decisions—decisions that are interdependent with other decisions and therefore have the potential to guide other decisions." This of course raises the issue of how "decisions" should be understood. Here, scholars have proposed anything ranging from the rational choice model of mainstream economics and game theory (e.g., Ghemawat, 1991) over models of bounded rationality (e.g., Hambrick & Mason, 1984) to Felin and Zenger's (2017) recent focus on the "theories" that strategists hold, that is, their reasoned instances of strategic "what-if" thinking concerning which combinations of resources and product markets will reach which strategic aims.

In any case, a concern with choice is fundamentally microfoundational as it traces the origin (and implementation and execution) of strategies to individuals, usually top managers (although the role of middle managers in strategy emergence is also recognized; e.g., Burgelman, 1994). Indeed, a key microfoundational issue in a strategy and leadership context is: How much do CEOs matter? An interesting literature in the intersection of finance and strategy examines this (e.g., Bennedsen et al., 2020; Kaplan et al., 2012).

A very different approach focuses on the psychology of decision-making (which is black-boxed in the above CEO research) and places this in a strategic decision-making context. This constitutes an important part of the strategic management research field called "behavioural strategy." This focuses on, for example, biases to decision-making and the role of affect and emotion in decision-making. While most such research focuses on the executive team or the CEO, parts of behavioral strategy also highlight employees. For example, Lindenberg and Foss (2011) consider the "goal frames" of individuals that compel to engage in certain behaviors within organizations, and Foss and Weber (2016) and Weber et al. (2022) discuss how the bounded rationality and opportunism of employees give rise to transaction costs inside firm hierarchies.

Another relatively recent emphasis in strategy (Coff, 1997; Campbell et al., 2017) considers the role of human resources for the creation and appropriation of economic value, drawing on insights from, mainly, human capital theory (Becker, 1962). For example, while employees who contribute much to firm-level creation may seem to be very attractive employees to hire, train, and maintain, this may not necessarily be so. If those employees are also highly mobile, that is, they can easily switch to employment in another firm without reducing their pay, they can leverage considerable bargaining power, in turn appropriating substantial parts of the value they create (with maximum bargaining power, all such value). Similar reasoning applies to any factor of production or "resource," or rather to their owners. However, the critical difference between human capital and other factors of production is that, absent slavery, human capital is tied to the person and can only be owned by the person (of course, a person can teach someone else but that means that the human capital of the person being taught changes). In principle, the owner of human capital can always pull out of a relation. A machine cannot do this, simply because it has no agency that allows it to do this. The owner of the machine can do it, however. But, this possibility can be eliminated if the owner of the machine is willing to transfer title to the machine to other parties in the relation (Hart, 1995). With respect to human capital, title to it cannot be transferred, but firms may seek other ways to limit the mobility of valuable human capital (such as non-compete clauses). In other words, property rights and ownership are at the heart of the understanding of how human capital contributes to firm-level success.

While these are fundamental points that emerged in economics from the early 1960s on (Becker, 1962; Harsanyi, 1982; Grossman & Hart, 1986; Klein et al., 1978), their implications were not systematically explored in strategy until relatively recently. One of the first contributions here was Lippman and Rumelt's (2003) points that there are no "profit" that accrues to the firm, only returns that are fully paid out to individual factors/resources, and no "firm-specific" resources, only co-specialized resources interacting within the legal shell of the firm. An important aspect of such interaction is how resources bargain for what they see as "their" share of created value. The outcomes of such bargaining processes in turn shape the incentives of resources.

Consider an example drawn from such "strategic human capital" reasoning of how microfoundations matter. Laursen and Salter (2020) highlight the role of employees in an "open innovation" context (Chesbrough, 2003). Open innovation is the idea that firms cannot just rely on internal resources for the purposes of innovation; they are heavily dependent on external science, IPR, practical knowledge, etc., much of which is held by users, consumers, suppliers, as well as universities, business schools, etc. In this context, employees are needed to spot potentially useful knowledge in the environment that is external to the firm and bring across firm boundaries so that it can be deployed in the context of innovation. Laursen and Salter call these employees "OI employees." Here is the potential problem they point to: OI employees get exposed to valuable, external knowledge. Even though they share such knowledge internally, they are still likely to have superior knowledge relative to other employees and managers regarding what external knowledge is likely to be "in the money," not just inside the firm, but also potentially to other companies. In fact, as a result of their search efforts, such employees may become more visible to parties external to the firm. This raises their bargaining power, which translates into being able to appropriate more of the value they help to create. While this strengthens their incentives to engage in external knowledge search (and may help create more value overall), their increased bargaining power still means that others in the firm have diminished bargaining power. Thus, their incentives to engage in actions that foster value creation are diminished. Thus, firms may, therefore, seek ways to diminish the bargaining powers of OI employees, taking into account that if they do this too successfully, they will stunt the incentives of these employees. Alternatively, they may give up on trying to reduce their mobility and instead make OI employees explicit residual claimants, that is, give them ownership stakes. Indeed, we would expect particularly successful OI employees to become part owners in the sense of acquiring residual income rights to the firm's profit streams as well as at least some control rights over core corporate assets (e.g., VP positions that relate to R&D). In sum, the dilemma identified by Laursen and Salter can only be understood, and partly resolved, in terms of considering the incentives faced by individual employees, which translates into understanding how property rights are allocated to minimize what economists would call "allocative distortions," that is, losses from incentives not being right.

Conclusions

The microfoundations for strategy that we proffer in this book represent what many would rightly characterize as the economics lens on social phenomena. We thus follow time-honored practice in the strategy field of relying on economic reasoning to generate insight. This is not generally accepted or popular. Economics is seen by many in the strategy community and even (many) more in management research at large as narrow, insular, and "unrealistic."

Partly economists themselves are to blame for such perceptions. Too often economists have extolled the virtues of the supposed "queen of the social sciences" in a way that involved what has often been caricatures of other social sciences. However, it does remain that economics is often misunderstood by its many detractors. For example, what is a fundamentally an empirically useful simplification such as individual wealth maximization is interpreted as an ontological and even sometimes ethical postulate! By broadening the interpretation of preferences and what people are assumed to maximize, including cognitive costs of processing information, modeling ambiguity, and even "unawareness," economics has become increasingly capable of treating many supposedly "soft" phenomena that have traditionally been seen as belonging to the fields and domains of social, motivational, and cognitive psychology, political science, ethics—and management. What characterizes (differentiates) economics is mainly that it is more individualistic and reductionist, so that it seeks to explain social phenomena in terms of choice behavior (in contrast to large swaths of sociology), it thinks systematically about choice under constraints (in contrast to psychology), and that it typically looks for some stable outcome from social interaction (i.e., an equilibrium). Notably, individuals actively bargain with each other, seeking to derive the best possible bargain, and subject to the constraints they face, which may include social norms. Indeed, sometimes it may pay for individuals to violate some such constraints (e.g., engage in "opportunism"; Williamson, 1985). The outcomes of such interaction are the phenomena that we seek to understand and explain in strategy. In the following chapter, we describe these foundations in greater detail.

References

Abell, P., Felin, T., & Foss, N. J. (2008). Building micro-foundations for the routines, capabilities and performance link. *Managerial and Decision Economics, 29*, 489–502.

Barnard, C. I. (1938). *The Functions of the executive by*. Harvard University Press.

Becker, G. (1962). Investment in human capital: A theoretical analysis. *Journal of Political Economy, 70*, 9–49.

Bennedsen, M., Pérez-González, F., & Wolfenzon, D. (2020). Do CEOs matter? Evidence from hospitalization events. *The Journal of Finance, 75*, 1877–1911.

Bridoux, F., & Stoelhorst, J. W. (2014). Microfoundations for stakeholder theory: Managing stakeholders with heterogeneous motives. *Strategic Management Journal, 35*, 107–125.

Burgelman, R. A. (1994). Fading memories: A process theory of strategic business exit in dynamic environments. *Administrative Science Quarterly, 39*, 24–56.

Campbell, B. A., Kryscynski, D., & Olson, D. M. (2017). Bridging strategic human capital and employee entrepreneurship research: A labor market frictions approach. *Strategic Entrepreneurship Journal, 11*, 344–356.

Chesbrough, H. (2003). *Open innovation: The new imperative for creating and profiting from technology*. Harvard Business School Press.

Coff, R. (1997). Human assets and management dilemmas: Coping with hazards on the road to resource-based theory. *Academy of Management Review, 22*, 374–402.

Coleman, J. S. (1990). *Foundations of social theory*. University of Chicago Press.

Felin, T., & Foss, N. J. (2005). Strategic organization: A field in search of micro-foundations. *Strategic Organization, 3*, 441–455.

Felin, T., Foss, N. J., & Ployhart, R. (2015). Microfoundations for management research. *Academy of Management Annals, 9*, 575–632.

Felin, T., & Hesterly, W. (2007). The knowledge-based view, nested heterogeneity, and new value creation: Philosophical considerations on the locus of knowledge. *The Academy of Management Review, 32*, 195–218.

Felin, T., & Zenger, T. (2017). The theory-based view: Economic actors as theorists. *Strategy Science, 2*, 258–271.

Foss, N. J., & Weber, L. (2016). Putting opportunism in the back seat: Bounded rationality, costly conflict and hierarchical forms. *Academy of Management Review, 41*, 41–79.

Gambardella, A., Panico, C., & Valentini, G. (2015). Strategic incentives to human capital. *Strategic Management Journal, 36*, 37–52.

Ghemawat, P. (1991). *Commitment*. Free Press.

Grossman, S., & Hart, O. (1986). The costs and benefits of ownership: A theory of lateral and vertical integration. *Journal of Political Economy, 94*, 691–719.

Hambrick, D. C., & Mason, P. A. (1984). Upper echelons: The organization as a reflection of its top managers. *Academy of Management Review, 9*, 193–206.

Harsanyi, J. C. (1982). *A simplified bargaining model for the n-person cooperative game* (Papers in Game Theory, pp. 44–70). Theory and Decision Library. Springer.

Hart, O. (1995). *Firms, contracts, and financial structure*. The Clarendon Press.
Kaplan, S. N., Klebanov, M. M., & Sørensen, M. (2012). Which CEO characteristics and abilities matter? *Journal of Finance, 67*, 979–107.
Klein, B., Crawford, R. G., & Alchian, A. A. (1978). Vertical integration, appropriable rents, and the competitive contracting process. *Journal of Law and Economics, 21*, 297–326.
Laursen, K., & Salter, A. (2020). Who captures value from open innovation—the firm or its employees? *Strategic Management Review*. https://leeds-faculty.colorado.edu/jere1232/Laursen%20and%20Salter.pdf
Leiblein, M. J., Reuer, J., & Zenger, T. (2018). What makes a decision strategic? *Strategy Science, 3*, 558–573.
Lindenberg, S., & Foss, N. J. (2011). Managing motivation for joint production: The role of goal framing and governance mechanisms. *Academy of Management Review, 36*, 500–525.
Lippman, S. A., & Rumelt, R. P. (2003). A bargaining perspective on resource advantage. *Strategic Management Journal, 24*, 1069–1086.
Porter, M. E. (1980). *Competitive strategy*. Free Press.
Porter, M. E. (1985). *Competitive advantage*. Free Press.
Powell, T. C., Lovallo, D., & Fox, C. (2011). Behavioral strategy. *The Strategic Management Journal, 32*, 1369–1386.
Rumelt, R. P., Schendel, D., & Teece, D. J. (1991). Strategic management and economics. *Strategic Management Journal, 12*, 5–29.
Vromen, J. (2010). Micro-foundations in strategic management: Squaring coleman's diagram. *Erkenntnis, 73*, 365–383.
Weber, L., Foss, N. J., & Lindenberg, S. (2022). The role of cognition and motivation in understanding Internal governance and hierarchical failure: A discriminating alignment analysis. *Academy of Management Review* (in print).
Williamson, O. E. (1985). *The economic institutions of capitalism*. Free Press.

3

Property Rights Economics: An Overview

The Peruvian economist Hernando de Soto (2001) once pointed out that people in developing, poor countries often have access to significant assets and that they have informal ownership to often large parcels of land. De Soto estimated the value of this land at more than 20 times the value of the total all foreign direct investments in all developing countries in the decade before his book was published (*The Economist*, 2020). However, the control over the assets these informal owners own is far from complete, because they cannot prove ownership. First, this means that they cannot use the land they informally own as collateral. The land parcels lack the attribute of being registered in some kind official registrar. Second, others may contest their claims to ownership. Governments may step in and "nationalise" such "unowned" property, or big local land owners may simply take the land through physical force. In other words, many parcels of land are more or less in the public domain, depending on the ability of owners to enforce their informal property rights and the prevalence of local norms that establish some kind rights to the parcels. Because of the informal status of land ownership, other parties may seek to capture the informally held rights to the land. For these reasons, the land parcels, the assets or resources, are worth much

K. Foss and N. J. Foss, *Economic Microfoundations of Strategic Management*, https://doi.org/10.1007/978-3-031-12910-0_3

less than their value if property rights were officially registered and recognized as such, and, moreover, if these property rights could be effectively enforced and traded. The absence of effective delineation of property rights also means less investment in the land parcels.

As *The Economist* (2020) notes "Indonesia, Thailand and Vietnam have pursued vast titling projects, mapping and registering millions of land parcels. India wants to use drones to map its villages. Ethiopia has registered millions of tracts. Rwanda has mapped and titled all its territory for $7 per parcel, thanks to cheap aerial photography. Studies suggest that titling has boosted agricultural productivity, especially in Asia and Latin America. The World Bank wants 70% of people to have secure property rights by 2030." Of course, these countries take such measures in order to improve the value of land and make their nations literally richer by such institutional measures. However, as *The Economist* notes merely mapping and registering private land is not enough: "A legal document is worth little if its owner cannot easily use it. Even in Rwanda, 87% of sales involving parcels of rural land were still done informally five years after the drive to give everyone deeds ended. Other countries have seen similar failures. All too often the institutions needed to enforce property rights smoothly, impartially and transparently are missing" (*The Economist*, 2020).

The example of land ownership—how formalized it is and the ease with which it is registered, enforced, and traded—illustrates that at the most fundamental level, property rights matter to outcomes, such as value creation, because they imply *control*. Control means the de facto ability to do things with an asset that is desirable from the point of view of the controlling individual (i.e., they increase the latter's "utility")—such as growing crops on a parcel of land, or selling it, or just enjoying its natural beauty. More generally, assets may be deployed directly to productive uses (in firms or households), leased to someone else, sold, or even destroyed it if it pleases the controller (e.g., 1960s rock guitarists, such as Pete Townshend of The Who or Jimi Hendrix, probably derived some utility from smashing their guitars on-stage). How control is allocated across members of society determines how conflicts over scarce resources (i.e., competition) are resolved (Alchian, 1965). This matters as different allocations of control imply different outcomes. Control is allocated by contracts and ownership, and by the formal and informal institutions that delineate and enforce control (i.e., property rights) and make it tradeable.

Because control over assets is valued, individuals will seek it out. To a large extent individuals gain control through market exchange: The acquisition of a good or a resource means the acquisition of control over the good or resource such that utility can be derived from it, directly (through consumption) or indirectly (e.g., by deploying it to production). Hence, control is valued, and because of this, individuals will try, either directly or through hired agents, to maintain the control they already hold over assets so as to be able to continue deriving utility from them. In other words, individuals will invest in protecting assets.

Control can be acquired through other means than market exchange (or gifts or bequests). Thus, individuals may assume effective control over assets that no one else makes a claim to (cf. the notion of "finders-keepers" and the idea of homesteading), acquire unowned property by "mixing one's labour with it" (Locke, 1698), or take it from someone else by force or theft or deceit. These latter means all fall under the heading of "capture." The mix of behaviors involving control (i.e., selling or purchasing, capturing, and protecting) that manifest in a social group or society at large depends on the comparative costs and benefits of these behaviors (Barzel, 1997). High costs of protecting property rights translate into low costs of capturing these, as well as into high costs of exchanging them.

An implication of the above remarks is that there will be property rights even in total anarchy (Bush & Mayer, 1974); specifically, it will (likely) be a situation of "might makes (property) right." The case of the California Gold Rush that was used to introduce this book suggests that property rights may emerge from a situation of anarchy (Umbeck, 1981), specifically the absence of a state machinery that uses its monopoly on violence to define and enforce specific ownership and property rights. Of course, the notion of property right as control backed by private power ("might") is somewhat distant from the way we usually talk about "property rights," because in common parlance it usually has the connotation of a *legally sanctioned* right. Indeed, property rights scholars often make a conceptual distinction between "economic rights" and "legal rights" (e.g., Barzel, 1997), pointing out that legal rights, that is, institutionally defined and enforced rights, serve to enforce economic rights. The underlying logic is that legal arrangements will be structured to reflect efficiency considerations, specifically, legal rights serve to improve the delineation and enforcement (and therefore tradeability) of economic rights, that is, control.

In general, the PRE is usually informed by a basic efficiency perspective, such that the definition, exchange, and enforcement of property rights are seen as reflecting economic efficiency. Thus, in Demsetz (1967) account of the emergence of property rights to land among the Montagne native population in Quebec this is linked to the development of the fur trade in terms of attempts to reduce the externalities associated with overly intensive hunting: Defining property rights to land served to (partly) internalize those externalities. Demsetz conjectures that the value of furs to the Indians would increase and the scale of hunting increased. This argument is often generalized in the PRE literature: Observed contracts, organizational forms, and institutions will tend to reflect the maximization of value creation, given the constraints that individuals face.

However, the mechanisms by which this happens are often not explained, and this is one reason why PRE efficiency arguments sometimes smack of Panglossianism ("That which exists must be efficient"). However, first, the efficiency hypothesis is just that—a (default) hypothesis. Second, it is important to recognize a distinction between, say, constitutions and "private orderings" (Williamson, 1996), such as contractual forms and the various ways in which the firm hierarchy may be structured. The latter are more subject to experimentation (because of their smaller scale and the relatively smaller costs of changing them) and to selection by market forces. While constitutions and legislation may also be subject to competitive pressure that limit political discretion in the long run (e.g., Vanberg, 2000), the hand of competition is much less visible than in the case of market competition between different contractual forms. Fundamentally, if the monopoly on violence makes the state a low-cost definer and enforcer of property rights, it may also—under the "right" circumstances—make it a low-cost violator of such rights. For such reasons, while most PRE scholars subscribe to an efficiency explanation of observed contractual institutions, many are skeptical of extending this view to the state (see, e.g., North, 1990; see also Acemoglu and Robinson, 2012).

The above represents, in our view, the basic or core ideas of PRE. In the rest of this chapter, we explain the background to these ideas and elaborate on them in greater detail.

The Evolution of Thinking on Property Rights in Economics[1]

Early Thinking

Ideas on property rights began to emerge as a result of thinking in law, politics, and social science on the role of ownership and as well as the incidence of externalities and what should be done politically to address externalities. Among the important early sources of such thinking is Roman Law (Epstein, 2016), the—very different—contributions of philosophers such as Locke (1698), Hume (1739), and Hegel (1820) to the understanding of property, as well as the early contributions of economists such as Bastiat (1850) and social critics, such as Marx (Pejovich, 1982).[2] However, from an economic perspective, the important period is perhaps rather the interwar period which witnessed a number of fundamental debates that provided impetus to thinking about property rights.

One such debate was the debate on the economics of capitalist versus socialist systems, that is, systems in which the "means of production" are under "public" versus those in which they under "private ownership." In this debate, a key opponent of the economics of socialism, Ludwig von Mises (1920), made the argument for which he is primarily known: that the absence of market prices for capital goods (which follows from the "socialization" of the means of production) means that it becomes impossible to determine the rational uses of such goods. Socialism would

[1] This section may be skipped by those with less of an interest in doctrinal history.

[2] For a historical overview of the evolution of thinking about property, see Garnsey (2009).

descend into calculational chaos and misallocation of resources. But Mises (1936) also pointed out that even if such prices could somehow exist under socialism (as "market socialists" argued), removing the profit motive and residual claimancy (i.e., the (property) right to appropriate economic residuals/profits)—other hallmarks of socialism—would eliminate the incentives of socialist managers to make efficient decisions (for a detailed discussion, see Foss, 1997). Mises specifically pointed to the importance of what would decades later be called the "principal-agent" problem existing in the hierarchical relations between ordinary citizens in a socialist economy, socialist managers, and central planning authorities. He argued that financial markets, board of directors, markets for corporate controls, and other institutions of a capitalist economy would attenuate the principal-agent problem in a way that was not accessible to a socialist economy. In essence, Mises argued that capitalist institutions related to ownership of companies were structured so as to minimize the externalities associated with the agency problem—a classic property rights argument.

Awareness of the importance of principal-agent problems, which are caused by conflicts of interest under asymmetric information also emerged in the context of corporate governance debates, initiated by the publication of Berle and Means (1932) and their revitalization of an insight already pointed to by Adam Smith, namely that acting as the agents of principals-owners, managers couldn't be expected to automatically pursue owner or company interests.

Of course, both principal-agent problems under socialism and under market-based social organization are examples of externality problems, that is, situations when "private" costs or benefits are not aligned with "social" costs and benefits, leading to inefficient over- or under-use of resources. This now-standard terminology was introduced by Pigou (1922), whose work on welfare economics became—albeit indirectly—absolutely central to the evolution of PRE as it provoked an initial brilliant reaction by Knight (1924) and later helped Coase shape the equally brilliant arguments of Coase (1960).

In a famous example, Pigou considers two different roads each connecting the same terminal points, one narrow and short, the other longer and wider. Pigou argues that "too many" drivers will take the short and narrow road, that is, the equilibrium allocation of drivers across the two roads is inefficient. The problem is that they don't take into account the effect of their actions on the costs of others who use the road. However, as Knight (1924) points out, first, access is not restricted to any of the roads (the drivers have a choice between the narrow and the wide road), and, second (but related to the first point), the roads are presumably publically owned and managed, not privately. Knight goes further and argues that if the roads had been private, their services would be priced so that efficiency would obtain (i.e., the price of using the short, but narrow road would be higher than the price of using the wide, but longer road).[3] Thus, Pigou's externality example really indicts public ownership (or non-ownership of resources), not private ownership.

That well-defined privately held ownership titles may solve problems of externality is, of course, an anticipation of ideas contained in Coase's almost four decades later article, "The Problem of Social Cost" (Coase, 1960). Also, Knight's critique of Pigou's argument that the state must intervene to solve externality problems (many of which it has created itself) anticipates Demsetz' (1967) critique of the "Nirvana fallacy" (i.e., comparing real-world outcomes to unrealistic Nirvanas of optimal resource allocation) and his point that the state is not a costless magical wand, but a costly resource allocation mechanism.

These latter contributions emerged in a decade, namely the 1960s, that was extremely fertile with respect to pushing microeconomic thinking beyond the confines of the full information, perfect competition model that had been gradually refined through the contributions of Léon Walras, Knight, Jacob Viner, Joan Robinson, and others, and culminating in the Arrow-Debreu model of the 1950s (Debreu, 1959). Thus, the 1960s witnessed fundamental breakthroughs in the economics of uncertainty and information (Arrow, 1962; Harsanyi, 1967), human capital theory (Becker, 1964), the first stabs at formal agency theory and mechanism design (Wilson, 1968), and many other advances in mathematical economics. There were also fundamental advances in industrial organization economics, public economics, social choice theory, public

[3] Knight's argument presupposes that pricing is not associated with high levels of what would later be called "transaction costs."

choice economics, and much else. All these developments were cross-fertilizing, and to a large extent based on a shared core of understanding of the nature of economics, one that highlighted the centrality of constrained maximization at the level of individuals and equilibrium at the level of interaction.

Where economists may have disagreed would perhaps mainly be with respect to the importance of formalization or mathematization of economics. In the applied price theory tradition flourishing in the 1960s at Chicago and UCLA and represented by, notably, Milton Friedman and Armen Alchian (respectively), formalization wasn't seen as an end in itself and epistemologically speaking at best a way of checking the consistency of reasoning and not an engine of discovering new economic insight. Property rights economists largely followed this methodological posture; most of PRE has been expressed in the verbal model. Another methodological point where economists may have disagreed in the 1960s concerns the applicability of the basic insights of economics. "Imperialists" like Becker insisted on the well-nigh universal applicability of these principles to the understanding of human action and interaction. Becker famously endorsed the "combined assumptions of maximizing behavior, market equilibrium and stable preferences" to be "used relentlessly and unflinchingly." This, he thought (Becker, 1964: 5), formed "the heart of the economic approach as I see it." However, critique against this position was mainly offered by non-mainstream economists (Kirzner, 1962; Winter, 1964).

In any case, the 1960s represented a dramatic expansion of the applicability of economics tools and insights beyond the understanding of the "pure" market institution, either directly or more indirectly (e.g., by refining the understanding of those "market failures" that may create a need for alternative mechanisms of resource allocation). PRE was a main driver in this latter endeavor.[4]

[4] Somewhat parallel developments, but from different disciplinary foundations, took place in the application of psychology, sociology, and political science to organizations (e.g., Cyert & March, 1963; March, 1962; March & Simon, 1958; Selznick, 1957). While these have been important to the evolution of management thought, we will not discuss them here.

The Emergence of Property Rights Economics

PRE ranks as one of the important breakthrough theories of the 1960s. First-generation property rights economists such as Armen Alchian (1914–2013), Ronald Coase (1910–2013), Harold Demsetz (1930–2019), and (Coase student) Steven Cheung (1970) developed a refined and mainly verbal approach to economic explanation that they saw, and advertised, as fundamentally "neoclassical," by which they meant lying in the mainstream of economic thinking. As this basic approach was close to the verbal (Marshallian) price theory tradition of Milton Friedman and the emerging University of Chicago-based "Law and Economics" stream of research (and for a long time informed this stream), and because of the institutional affiliations of the involved scholars, this was sometimes referred to as "Chicago-UCLA price theory." However, they stressed that this new theorizing had much broader explanatory aims. Thus, whereas Coase, Alchian, Demsetz, and Cheung (as well as scholars sympathetic to PRE, such as Henry Manne, William Meckling, Michael Jensen, and others) applied the basic tools of verbal price theory—constrained maximization, supply and demand analysis, Marshallian partial equilibrium and so on—it is important to appreciate that they, in a sense, applied them to an understanding of the nature of the constraints themselves.

Specifically, traditional price theory takes a host of institutions as *given*, such as the (various bodies of) law, property rights, and (therefore) the market institution itself. The important innovation of PRE was to systematically endogenize these institutions, building on the fundamental insight that they exist to resolve conflicts over scarce resources and to reduce the costs associated with such conflicts (Alchian, 1965). While giants of philosophy and social thought like Thomas Hobbes and David Hume had long understood this, the fixation of economists on exchange in the context of given market institutions meant that the issue of the endogeneity of institutions was deemphasized or not addressed at all. Of course, institutional choice was an issue among economists with heavy ideological commitments (such as Marxists) and among applied economists. But, in the "hardening" of the neoclassical research program that began after the First World War, the core of economics became synonymous with allocation of resources by means of the price mechanism. This meant that not only the effects of non-price institutions were seen as lying outside of the orbit of pure economics, but also their inner workings. For example, the influential economist Arthur Pigou explicitly argued that the organization of business firm as well as their marketing activities were out of the explanatory bounds of economics: "… it is not the business of economists to teach woollen manufacturers to make and sell wool, or brewers how to make and sell beer, or any other business men how to do their job. If that was what we were out for, we should, I imagine, immediately quit our desks and get somebody—doubtless at a heavy premium, for we should be thoroughly inefficient—to take us into his woollen mill or his brewery" (Pigou, 1922: 463).

It is perhaps saying something of the status of PRE that one of the earliest and most systematic PRE papers, "Some Economics of Property Rights" by Armen Alchian (1965) was written sometime toward the end of the 1950s, circulated for a few years long time as a RAND Corp memo (Alchian, 1961) before it was finally published until 1965 in an Italian political science journal! Interestingly, as in the case of Coase whose work on the practical problem of allocating use rights to the radio spectrum (Coase, 1959) led to what is now known as the "Coase Theorem" (Coase, 1960), Alchian's work on practical challenges, such as how to make economic sense of the tenure system in academia (Alchian, 1958), seems to have prompted his attempt to codify PRE ideas. Indeed, PRE research has continuously been heavily applied in character, signifying a certain scholarly style where the emphasis is on accounting, usually in verbal, detailed, and empirically informed terms, for the constraints and behaviors that may underlie observed real-world phenomena, the existence of which is puzzling, and where one is skeptical of existing accounts. This is a style of economic explanation that is sometimes called "applied price theory" and which is more or less explicitly contrasted with the solving of puzzles in mathematical economics, seemingly, the critics would argue, for the sake of puzzle-solving alone.

The work of the above scholars served as direct inspiration for the slightly later work of the second-generation PRE theorists such as Louis De Alessi, Yoram Barzel, Eirik Furubotn, (Nobel Prize winner) Douglass North, Steven Pejovich, and John Umbeck, whose work began to emerge in the 1970s. Modern (third-generation) representatives of the PRE are Douglas Allen, Lee Alston, Thrainn Eggertson, Gary Libecap, Dean Lueck, and others. A number of these are still active scholars.

None of the members of the second and third generations fundamentally deviated from the original vision of the first generation of PRE scholars. However, they added several refinements, such as the notion of "attributes" of assets (Barzel, 1997), ideas of rent-seeking and value dissipation (Benson, 1984), and sophisticated equilibrium analysis of the allocation of property rights given costs of protecting and capturing property rights (Umbeck, 1977a, 1977b, 1981).

The above names are just some of the more centrally positioned and prolific PRE scholars. Many less well-known scholars contributed to the perspective. Similarly, many economists and other social scientists have made use of PRE insights without explicitly self-identifying as PRE scholars, such as Nobel laureate Ellinor Ostrom, Richard Posner, Michael Jensen, William Meckling, Jack Hirshleifer, and legal scholars Guido Calabresi and Douglas Melamed,

The Current Status of Property Rights Economics

Since it emerged around 1960, PRE has been directly and strongly influential in the fields of law and economics (Coase, 1960; Posner, 1987), economic history (Alchian & Demsetz, 1973; North, 1990), the economics of the firm (e.g., Alchian & Demsetz, 1972; Jensen & Meckling, 1979), contract economics [e.g., Allen & Lueck, 1995; Cheung, 1970]), early comparative systems research (see Furubotn & Pejovich, 1972), and resource and agricultural economics (e.g., Allen & Lueck, 1998; Cheung, 1969a, 1969b; Libecap, 1989). It has had a large, but less direct, influence on industrial organization, agency theory, and corporate governance.[5]

The current status of PRE is as follows. Most of the pioneers of the approach have passed away, and there is no distinct institutional

[5] The latter includes the "Yugoslav firm" debate (Furubotn & Pejovich, 1972) as well as the debate on "co-determination" (Jensen & Meckling, 1979), debates that revolved around what would today be seen as "stakeholder management" issues.

embodiment (association or similar) for PRE research. Although some PRE research continues to be done and is presented as venues such as the annual meetings of the American Economic Association and the Society for Institutional and Organizational Economics, very few young modern economists probably self-identify as property rights economists. Thus, it may sound as if PRE has experienced the same fate as once-important economic approaches (e.g., early institutional economics or Austrian economics), now living existences outside of the mainstream of economics and having little or no institutional anchoring in more prestigious universities. This, however, isn't the case per se. It is important to remember that PRE is fundamentally a mainstream economics and not a heterodox one. Like many other "schools," "approaches," etc. before it, PRE may have become less visible for the simple reason that many of its key ideas have been incorporated in the standard vocabulary and toolbox of economists. For example, few practicing economists would probably associate, say, the Coase Theorem (Coase, 1960) or ideas on rent dissipation (Anderson & Hill, 1990) with a distinct "property rights economics." These ideas are simply mainstream economics ideas. Moreover, PRE ideas are found in other approaches, past and present. For example, in a number of ways, the PRE is akin in its aims to transaction cost economics. Both acknowledge a fundamental debt to the thinking of Coase (1937, 1960) (Barzel & Kochin, 1992; Williamson, 1996), both place the notion of transaction costs center stage in the explanatory structure of the theory, and there is overlap in terms of what PRE and transaction cost economics seek to explain.[6]

[6] Of course, transaction costs are also central to Williamsonian transaction cost economics, and PRE and TCE share many important features, in particular, a basic contractual and institutional perspective, the rejection of unrealistic standards of comparison and an insistence that feasible alternatives be compared, and an emphasis on studying contracts and institutions as equilibria. However, PRE emerged first; Furubotn and Pejovich's (1972) and Alchian and Demsetz's (1973) stock takings of accomplishments since Coase (1960) were published when Williamsonian TCE was in its infancy (Williamson, 1971). However, the influence of the PRE on Williamson's thinking seems fairly limited. He does not use property-rights terminology, is critical of specific PRE papers (e.g., see the critique of Alchian an Demsetz, 1972, in Williamson, 1985), characterizes the PRE as a distinct approach (e.g., characterizing Barzel's work as the "measurement approach" in Williamson, 1985), and sees property rights lying on a higher analytical level than his own concern with levels of analysis that involve the firm and other private orderings (Williamson, 2000). Moreover, certain distinct features set Williamson's thinking apart from that of most property-rights economists. In particular, Williamson's insistence on bounded

And yet, as often happens when ideas are absorbed into a mainstream, there may be a loss of content. We don't think that all that is interesting, insightful and worthwhile in the PRE has been included into the economic mainstream and is reflected in the leading textbooks and journals. As an example, a different approach, emerging in the mid-1980s (Grossman & Hart, 1986), growing out of formal contract theory as well as key ideas in transaction cost economics, and associated with the work of Oliver Hart and his colleagues and students, is often also referred to as the "property-rights approach" (or sometimes as the "incomplete contracting approach"). This approach, which has become enormously influential in modern economics and made Oliver Hart a Nobel laureate, will be briefly discussed toward the end of the chapter. While it is often lumped together with the "older" PRE approach that is the central source of inspiration for this book, it is in fact quite different in a number of important respects, as we explain in detail in Chapter 4.

Key Tenets of Property Rights Economics

The Forms of Property

Philosophers and social scientists, particularly economists, recognized long before the advent of the PRE that some rights may be held in common, with more or less open access, while other rights are held in private (Knight, 1924). This distinction has of course served to distinguish basic economic systems (Marx, 2000; Mises, 1920). A basic awareness of "property rights regimes"—the different forms of property within or across societies (e.g., Alessi, 1990; Demsetz, 1967)—predates the PRE.[7]

rationality does not resonate with all scholars associated with PRE (e.g., Barzel and Kochin, 1992). On the other hand, key PRE scholar Armen Alchian is one of the originators of the emphasis on the problems caused by asset specificity in the context of incomplete contracting (Klein et al., 1978). The treatment of this problem and its remedies is a key concern in TCE and is not inconsistent with the PRE.

[7] Pejovich (1982: 383) recognizes none other than Karl Marx as, in some key respects, a key precursor of the PRE: "Marx viewed economics as the study of property rights over scarce resources. As man learned to apply human work to the production and use of tools, it became

Thus, at one extreme productive assets may be imagined to exist as completely open access or "placed in the public domain" (Barzel, 1997) or *res nullius* "property." Such assets may or may not be associated with rivalry in use or consumption, but it is non-excludable. Awareness of the "tragedy of the commons" feature associated with non-excludability and the mechanisms that drive the "tragic" outcomes go much beyond PRE. Assets may also be held as public property which is typically managed by some government agency which regulates its consumption and excludability. Property that is excludable and non-rivalrous in consumption is sometimes called "club goods." Private property involves rivalry in consumption as well as excludability. When a group of owners jointly owns property that is rivalrous and these owners make it excludable to non-owners, the phrase "common property" is sometimes used.

Obviously, these different characteristics of property are not something that directly stem from characteristics of the relevant object (although these may influence the form that property takes). For example, a building can in principle be any kind of property. What determines the form that property takes is dependent on specific institutional, contractual, and organizational arrangements. Under an institutional arrangement characterized by universal communism, the building will be open access property (there will only be open access property); in a perfect anarcho-capitalist utopia, it will be private property (there will only be private property).

However, this is a somewhat "macro" way of thinking about property. For example, the distinctions between the different kinds of property above doesn't directly help us to understand the incentives faced by individuals interacting when property takes different forms, the consequences of different forms of property, and why individuals decide that one form of property is preferable to another (e.g., why common property rather than private property?).

While PRE has also contributed to refining the understanding of such more macroscopic "property rights regimes" (Furubotn & Pejovic,

essential to specify the relations among men with respect to the right to use those intermediate goods. And that meant the development and specification of property rights. Thus, Marx deduced the historical necessity of property rights from the initial subordination of man to nature and his survival instincts."

1972), much of the progress in PRE has been driven by a more micro-analytic lens that focuses on unfolding the concept of property rights, rather than forms of property or property rights regimes, and exploring how the property rights to the various "attributes" of assets (i.e., their different uses and functionalities) impact individual incentives (Barzel, 1997). A basic premise is that property rights are fundamentally about who has the (effective) right to make choices over the uses of assets (or, in Barzel: the attributes of those assets), and who should bear the consequences of choices involving the relevant assets. Like the rest of economics, PRE assumes that behaviors vary predictably as a consequence of such incentives.

An Extension of "Standard" Economics

The basic concept and "unit of analysis" highlighted by PRE is, of course, that of "the" property right. The main explanatory aim of the PRE has been to investigate how the delineation, exchange, and enforcement of property rights influence resource allocation, and how this frames an economic approach to institutions and organizations. In all situations where resources are scarce, competition for their use will emerge (i.e., "competition" is not a feature of "capitalism" or "market societies" but a necessary consequence of scarcity), causing conflict (Alchian, 1965). The formal rules regulating such conflict are rules of law, regulating, hierarchical procedures, etc. They delineate and enforce property rights. But property rights may also be rooted in custom (Demsetz, 1967) as well as in the power (Umbeck, 1977a, 1977b).

As already suggested, property rights theorists often portray the PRE as fundamentally an extension of neoclassical or "standard" economics or "price theory," in the sense that.

1. *all* transactions and social interaction in general (including gifts, theft, rent-seeking, etc.) revolve around property rights—a more fine-grained category than goods and services (which in a PRE perspective are bundles of property rights) (Coase, 1960);

2. the utility-maximization hypothesis is applied to *all* choices (Alchian, 1958, 1965; Barzel, 1997);
3. PRE considers *all* of the incentives and constraints implied by the prevailing structure of property rights and transaction costs (e.g., Alessi, 1990; Demsetz, 1964), and
4. PRE explicitly considers *all* relevant contractual, organizational, and institutional implications of (1) and (2). Thus, contracts, etc., are conceptualized as mechanisms for delineating, exchanging, and protecting property rights.

The PRE is predicated on the notion that introduction of the notion of property rights as the central unit of analysis (i.e., point 1) above) is *generative* in the sense that it significantly extends the reach of economics. The main reason for this is that taking the property right as the unit of analysis expands and refines the understanding of individuals' opportunity sets. Thus, although Coase (1960) is usually heralded for its statement of the so-called Coase Theorem, the conceptual innovation of the property right as the unit of analysis and the notion that transactions involve the exchange of property rights (rather than goods and services per se) is at least as important. As Coase explained, property rights to an asset can be partitioned in various ways. Much subsequent work within PRE has consisted of refinements of this insight, applying it to issues like public ownership and the public corporation. Barzel's (1997) work in particular has been taken up with examining the consequences of the multi-attribute nature of most assets. In many of the chapters in this book, we rely on his brand of PRE.

Of course, the four points above were not all present in the earliest PRE writings (e.g., Coase, 1960), but only emerged gradually. The key breakthrough that marks the beginning of a new research program is the introduction of the new unit of analysis, namely the property right. This is done in Coase (1960) in a specific context, namely the analysis of externalities. (1) to (3) only unfold gradually over the following decades. Indeed, many core issues in the PRE are not yet settled. The perhaps prime example is the interpretation of the "Coase Theorem," specifically what are the necessary assumptions for the core idea in Coase (1960) and what are its precise implications. The debate has been so long, convoluted, and complex that Robert Cooter (1982) jokingly referred to it as "the cost of Coase." Thus, since Coase (1960) stated the result—that he didn't refer to as a "theorem" (this was done by Stigler, 1966)—many implications of his core assumption that zero transaction costs were subsequently derived (Demsetz, 1964, 1967), Cheung (1969a, 1969b). Considerable debate has surrounded Coase's result (e.g., from very different perspectives, Cooter, 1982; Barzel, 1985, 1997; Dixit & Olson, 2000; Farrell, 1987; Furubotn, 1991).

The "Coase Theorem"

As indicated already, the first published paper to explicitly put forward the property right as a meaningful unit of analysis is usually taken to be Coase (1960). Coase's introduction of the property right into economic analysis is part of his derivation of the "Coase Theorem," that is, the result that if it is possible to trade externalities and transaction costs are sufficiently low, bargaining between self-interested individuals will lead to a value-maximizing outcome, regardless of the initial allocation of property rights. To reach this result Coase introduces the "corollary" notion of exchange as involving the more or less costly exchange of more or less well-defined property rights. Retrospectively, and in terms of the evolution of the PRE, this is as important an idea as the Coase Theorem itself.

The result is perhaps best illustrated by using the concrete practical example that led Coase to it, namely the regulation of radio frequencies (Coase, 1959). The problem here was if radio stations use the same frequencies, there would be interference. While regulators saw this as calling for an intervention that would allocate frequencies to minimize interference, Coase pointed out that with a market where property rights to frequencies could be traded, stations could bargain between themselves to avoid interference. Furthermore, he pointed out that it did not matter who possessed the initial rights to broadcast on a given frequency as long as that right was tradeable. A station that could use the property right to create more economic value than other stations would probably acquire that right (or simply pay other stations not to interfere). In other words, stations would bargain and trade until a value-maximizing outcome was reached, regardless of who was initially granted the right to broadcast on a given frequency.

While it may sound as if Coase is treating the spectrum of frequencies as factors of production, as in the traditional analysis of externalities in production, Coase (1960: 155) is explicitly critical of such an interpretation. In fact, he argues that "factors of production" should not be seen as physical entities as such but rather as rights to physically perform certain actions. According to Coase (1960: 144), it is often more productive to think of a production factor, not as a physical entity but as a right to perform certain actions: "We may speak of a person owing land and using it as a factor of production but what the land-owner in fact possesses is the right to carry out a circumscribed list of actions." He immediately moves on to noting how such property rights are inherently constrained:

> The rights of a land-owner are not unlimited. It is not even always possible for him to remove the land to another place. For instance, by carrying it. And although it may be possible for him to exclude some people from using "his" land, this may not be true of others. For example, some people may have the right to cross the land. Furthermore, it may or may not be possible to erect certain types of buildings or to grow certain crops or to use particular drainage systems on the land. This does not come about simply because of Government regulation. It would be equally true under the common law. In fact it would be true under any system of law. A system in which the rights of individuals were unlimited would be one in which there were no rights to acquire.

Since property rights are not "unlimited" in this sense, mechanisms for handling their allocation arise. Transactions involve the exchange of property rights (rather than goods and services per se), and property rights to an asset can be partitioned in various ways, such that different individuals may hold (different) property rights to the same asset. Thus, from the point of view of understanding why there is an externality in the use of the radio spectrum and how the situation can be remedied, the important thing is who has the (property) right to do what (when? where? etc.) with the asset, that is, the spectrum of frequencies.

The productivity of the latter is not a "given." On the contrary, the value creation potential of the spectrum depends on how well defined rights to use it are and how well these can be traded (i.e., the extent to which transaction costs constitute impediments to trade). As Coase (1959) explains, when such rights are precisely delineated and can be traded at low or no costs, optimal outcomes will be reached.

The 1960 paper restates the result in the form that when transaction costs are zero and wealth effects are absent, any allocation of property rights results in the same pattern of economic activities under which maximum value is created from the use of resources. This "Coase theorem" or "invariance result" is no doubt one of the most extensively debated pieces of economic thinking (e.g., Cooter, 1982; Usher, 1998). It was quickly applied outside its original context by Coase's student Steven Cheung (1969a, 1969b) who argued that if transaction costs were truly zero, any institutional or contractual form (or what Williamson (1985) would later call "governance structure") would be capable of achieving the same efficient allocation. Demsetz (1964) suggested that under the same conditions, market structure would not matter to allocation, as the same efficient allocation would result under monopoly as under perfect competition.

Coase himself didn't enter most of this debate, because he insisted (Coase, 1988) that his result was simply a benchmark designed to serve as a starting point for analysis involving transaction costs. Thus, he toned down the importance of the Coase Theorem in favor of analysis of the importance of the legal, contractual, and institutional ramifications of transaction costs as these exist in the real world (Coase, 1988). Coase may be right that disproportionate attention has been devoted to analysis of the Coase Theorem. However, it remains an important benchmark, not the least for the remainder of this book, so we offer a few more comments on it.

The Coase Theorem as an Evolving Benchmark

Since Coase's original formulation, the Coase Theorem has morphed somewhat. The context of its emergence, as we have seen, is Coase's discussion of the economic implications of allocating legally delineated rights (liability rights) to a subset of the total uses of an asset, namely those that have external effects on the value of other agents' abilities to exercise their use rights over assets. The benchmark for the discussion is the result that under conditions of zero transaction costs and the absence of wealth effects, how property rights to resource uses are initially assigned does not matter to outcomes. Picked up by Demsetz (1964), it becomes a proposition about the ability of individuals to trade away all inefficiencies (Demsetz, 1964). Cheung (1969a, 1969b) takes it to be a proposition about how any contractual form can realize the efficient outcome. Milgrom and Roberts (1990) explicitly treat the Coase Theorem to be a proposition about value maximization. In the latter interpretation, under the Coase Theorem all resource uses are perfectly identified, enforceable, and tradeable, and because there are no resources used in identifying, etc. these uses, the zero transaction cost condition means that value creation will be at its maximum. Moreover, as long as each individual who participates in a value-creating effort gets at least her opportunity cost, value appropriation will not impact value creation (as long as each resource receives at least its opportunity costs) (Milgrom & Roberts, 1990).

These different interpretations are, of course, all consequences of the same fundamental idea, but the changing emphases reflects a broadening of the interpretations of what the Coase Theorem is fundamentally about, its constituent parts, and its implications for different fields. With respect to the point about implications for different fields, it is intuitive that a notion of the Coase Theorem that stresses maximum value creation is of more immediate relevance for the management field than one that stresses the allocation of liability rights, a fundamentally legal term. One may speculate that the association with the Law and Economics field may have been one of the reasons PRE was not introduced into management research until quite recently.

With respect to the ingredients, the assumptions that motivate the zero transaction cost assumption is that individuals possess perfect information(Barzel, 1985; Coase, 1988) and that legal enforcement is costless. When all conceivable property rights are perfectly identified, delineated, enforced, and protected, by definition there can be no race to define property rights over resources that lie (unowned) in the public domain (Anderson & Hill, 1990; Lueck, 1995) or indeed no inefficiencies ("waste") at all. But, what exactly are meant by "property rights" and "transaction costs?" Consider transaction costs. In Coase (1959, 1960), the emphasis is clearly on the "costs of exchange" (mainly bargaining costs). However, increasingly the PRE literature recognized the costs of defining and enforcing property rights as transaction costs in their own right (Demsetz, 1964, 1967), and the interdependencies of these cost categories (e.g., difficult to enforce or ill-defined property rights may be more costly to exchange) (Barzel, 1997). Various attempts were made to consider the determinants of particular transaction costs. For example, Barzel's 1980s work (Barzel, 1982, 1985) placed the main emphasis on the costs of information about products and services (i.e., determining the level and presence of valued product and service characteristics or "attributes"), what he called "measurement costs." Thinking about transaction costs evolved in tandem with thinking about property rights. We explore this in the following.

Property Rights and Transaction Costs

The understanding of the nature and function of property rights has evolved significantly within the PRE. Coase (1960) was mainly interested in the allocation of use rights to assets. Demsetz (1964) and Alchian (1965) went beyond this, defining property rights as individuals' rights to the use, income, and transferability of assets, a definition corresponding to the partition in Roman law between usus, fructus, and abusus, respectively. Building an economic approach to property rights also involved debating the relation to property law. It became increasingly clear to PRE scholars that property rights can be analyzed conceptually apart from legal considerations, and that property rights may exist in the absence of the state (Bush & Mayer, 1974). Physical force or strong social norms may guarantee de facto control over the uses of and income from a resource, and physical force and social norms may exist in the absence of the state. It also became clear that property rights have an inherently forward-looking dimension and that, therefore, uncertainty is an important aspect of property rights. Finally, it became clear that from an economic perspective property rights can be understood in value terms and that agents seek to maximize the value of the control they hold over assets.

In line with such ideas, Alchian and Allen (1969: 158) offered a highly compact definition of property rights as the "expectations a person has that his decision about the uses of certain resources will be effective" (see also Cheung, 1970). Barzel (1994: 394; emphasis in original) expanded this definition, defining property rights as.

> an individual's net valuation, in expected terms, of the ability to directly consume the services of the asset, or to consume it indirectly through exchange. A key word is *ability*: The definition is concerned not with what people are legally entitled to do but with what they believe they can do.

Essentially, property rights in such definitions refer to an individual's expected opportunity set. This has some perhaps counter-intuitive implications. In contrast to definitions, such as that of Demsetz (1967), which stress that property rights are fundamentally *social* relations and imply that "i]n the world of Robinson Crusoe property rights play no role" (Demsetz, 1967: 347), on the Alchian-Allen-Barzel definition of property rights, Robinson Crusoe does in fact hold property rights. Relatedly, the Alchian-Allen-Barzel definition also completely separates definition of a property right from any legal consideration; to the extent that he holds effective control over an asset, a thief holds property rights to that asset (Barzel, 1997).

Even if we grant the point that conceptually, property rights may exist in the absence of (formal) law, in reality they have legal counterparts and the value of property rights is influenced by legal sanction and enforcement. Not surprisingly, many property rights scholars have strongly stressed the fundamentally social nature of property rights. Thus, Demsetz (1967: 347) argues that.

> Property rights are an instrument of society and derive their significance from the fact that they help a man form those expectations which he can reasonably hold in his dealings with others. These expectations find expression in the laws, customs, and mores of a society. An owner of property rights possesses the consent of fellowmen to allow him to act in particular ways. An owner expects the community to prevent others from interfering with his actions, provided that these actions are not prohibited in the specifications of his rights.

Such definitions direct attention to "macro" determinants of property rights such as norms, customs, and law as the key institutions that define and enforce rights. However, norms and customs defining property rights can exist on lower levels, such as within or between firms. Thus, corporate culture (Jones, 1983) and relational contracting (Williamson, 1996) serve to delineate and enforce property rights. Williamson (1996) even argues that the firm may be seen as constituting its own legal system based on "forbearance." Moreover, property rights are, of course, defined and allocated by means of formal contracts. This suggests that it makes sense to distinguish between the various analytical levels at which property rights can be enforced.[8] Indeed, such a distinction has been made in the PRE literature, notably in the work of Douglass North (1990), whose distinction between organizations and institutions captures the difference between the more micro property rights arrangements in the form of contracts and organizations and the macro property regimes embodied in laws, customs, and the coercive machinery of the state.

By the reasoning of the Coase Theorem, externalities result from the existence of costs of transacting. Transaction costs were introduced by Coase in his 1937 paper on the firm, well before the 1960 paper on social cost (Coase, 1960). Arguably, one reason so little progress was made on the analysis in the first paper is that transaction costs are difficult to define without a clear conception of property rights (Barzel & Kochin, 1992). Indeed, transaction costs are probably most conveniently defined in terms of property rights, and the PRE does exactly this. Thus, transaction costs can be defined as the resources spent on delineating,

[8] Property rights also exist on various levels, e.g., both natural and corporate persons can hold property rights.

protecting, and capturing control over resources in use and in exchange (Barzel, 1997; Eggertson, 1990). A particular case of transaction costs is the measurement costs of inspecting attributes of goods and services elegantly analyzed by Barzel (1982).

However, even Coase (1960) does not systematically *derive* transaction costs from property rights. Instead, Coase defines transaction costs as search costs, communication costs, bargaining costs, contract drafting costs, and costs of monitoring contractual agreements (Coase, 1960: 114). Thus, transaction costs in Coase (1960) are a more elaborate version of the "costs of using the price mechanism" introduced by Coase (1937) (Cheung, 1969a, 1969b). Indeed, the link between property rights and transaction costs that interests Coase (1960) is that when transaction costs exist, property rights are ill-defined. For example, rights to pollute or avoid pollution may not exist. Defining and enforcing such rights are costly activities. Because of these costs markets for these rights do not exist. As a result, they will not be traded, reducing attainable output.

This basic externality argument appears in various manifestations in subsequent thinking on the economic rationale of firms and other contractual institutions (Barzel & Kochin, 1992). Thus, in agency theory the problem is that while rights and duties may be costless to write into contracts, they are costly to enforce, resulting in moral hazard (agents may not deliver the effort they agreed to deliver) that reduces created value [Jensen & Meckling, 1976; Holmström, 1979]). In incomplete contracting theory or "new" property rights economics (Grossman & Hart, 1986; Hart, 1995), important rights and duties in a contractual relation cannot be specified *ex ante*, leading to under-investment in productive assets as the parties fear that the other party may exploit unforeseen events to hold them up (we discuss this theory in the next chapter).

Alchian's (1958) almost simultaneous examination of the absence of private property rights in government links transaction costs and property rights in a different way than in Coase (1960). Alchian develops a general argument that government assets are insufficiently protected and that this leads to a failure of marginal pricing and use of government services. Thus, insecure property rights induce costly racing to capture wealth, an argument later refined in several contributions to the PRE (e.g., Anderson & Hill, 1990; Lueck, 1995). A similar argument emerges in Williamson's (1985, 1996) brand of transaction cost economics which focuses on how ill-defined contractual rights lead contractual incompleteness, in turn giving rise to processes of costly *ex post* haggling between the parties over the "quasi-rents" of the relation. Thus, the causality goes in both directions, that is, transaction costs result in ill-defined property rights, but ill-defined and ill-protected property rights also lead to transaction costs.

. The overall PRE perspective on contracts, organizations, and institutions is that these exist to minimize allocative distortions (Eggertson, 1990; Lueck, 1995).[9] To exemplify, Alchian and Demsetz' (1972) theory of "team production"—production by teams where the productivities of individual resources (but not team output) are costly to observe—posits that team production is a cover for moral hazard: Because individual productivity is costly to observe, self-interested team members will shirk their work duties. They impose the costs of doing this on the rest of the team but gain the benefit from shirking themselves. This externality reduces team output below what is attainable in the absence of moral hazard. Alchian and Demsetz reason that the situation can be remedied by appointing a "monitor" who specializes in observing individual efforts and disciplining shirking team members. This pushes the problem back, as the problem then becomes one of making the monitor supply efficient monitoring. However, this problem can be solved by giving the monitor the rights to residual income from the team's activities (i.e., what is left once team members have been paid). This simple theory elegantly links a particular production technology with rights to lead and monitor and rights to appropriate profits—a basic theory of "the classical capitalist firm."[10]

[9] PRE thus regards property rights as means to further efficiency; they only have normative value in so far as they may improve outcomes. How this utilitarian stance relates to, for example, natural law conceptions of rights is an interesting issue but beyond the scope of this book. Garnsey (2009) reviews much of the normative discussion around property rights in a far-reaching historical perspective.

[10] The theory has several weaknesses, however, such as the assumption that firm organization is always rooted in team production. The obvious counterexample is the conglomerate firm.

Conclusion

This chapter has summarized the key ideas in the PRE as they developed from around the time of Coase's (1960) seminal paper and to a large extent based in the reasoning in this paper. Much of the early PRE focused on identifying differences in outcomes (i.e., allocative efficiency) at aggregate levels of analysis as these outcomes are shaped by alternative systems of property rights (Furubotn & Pejovich, 1972), examining the emergence and transformation of property rights (Demsetz, 1967), the connectedness of property rights in systems (Alchian, 1965), and their connections to law, norms, and customs (Demsetz, 1964).

However, it was increasingly realized that property rights reasoning are fully applicable at lower level of analysis—that is, much closer to the traditional concerns of management scholars—such as the understanding of corporate governance issues (Alchian, 1965; Jensen & Meckling, 1979), contractual forms (Cheung, 1969a, 1969b), and the firm (Alchian & Demsetz, 1972; Jensen & Meckling, 1976). Thus, PRE has influenced management theorizing, sometimes directly (e.g., Foss & Foss, 2005; Jones, 1983; Kim & Mahoney, 2002), sometimes more indirectly, namely through approaches such as contract economics (Hart, 1995) and transaction cost economics (Williamson, 1985, 1996) which are to some extent indebted to core PRE ideas, and important source theories for parts of management theory (Kim & Mahoney, 2005). In the rest of this book, we explore various ways in which the PRE may further inform management thinking.

References

Acemoglu, D., & Robinson, J. A. (2012). *Why nations fail: The origins of power, prosperity and poverty*. Crown.

Alchian, A. A. (1958). Private property and the relative cost of tenure. In P. D. Bradley (Ed.), *The public stake in union power* (pp. 350–371). University of Virginia Press.

Alchian, A. A. (1961). *Some economics of property*. Rand Corporation.

Alchian, A. A. (1965 [1977]). Some economics of property rights. In A. A. Alchian, *Economic forces at work*. Liberty Press.
Alchian, A. A., & Allen, W. R. (1969). *Exchange and production: Theory in use*. Wadsworth.
Alchian, A. A., & Demsetz, H. (1972). Production, information costs, and economic organization. *American Economic Review, 62*, 772–795.
Alchian, A. A., & Demsetz, H. (1973). The property rights paradigm. *Journal of Economic History, 33*(1), 16–27.
Alessi, L. (1990). Development of the property rights approach. *Journal of Institutional and Theoretical Economics, 146*, 6–11.
Allen, D. W., & Lueck, D. (1995). Risk Preferences and the economics of contracts. *American Economic Review, 85 (Papers and Proceedings)*, 447–451.
Allen, D. W., & Lueck, D. (1998). The nature of the farm. *Journal of Law and Economics, 41*, 343–386.
Anderson, T. L., & Hill, P. J. (1990). The race for property rights. *Journal of Law and Economics, 33*, 177–197.
Arrow, K. J. (1962). The economic implications of learning by doing. *The Review of Economic Studies, 29*, 155–173. Oxford Journals.
Barzel, Y. (1982). Measurement costs and the organization of markets. *Journal of Law and Economics, 25*, 27–48.
Barzel, Y. (1985 [2005]). Transaction costs: Are they just costs? Reprinted in C. Mènard (Ed.), *Controversies and challenges in the new institutional economics*. Edward Elgar.
Barzel, Y. (1994). The capture of wealth by monopolists and the protection of property rights. *International Review of Law and Economics, 14*, 393–409.
Barzel, Y. (1997). *Economic analysis of property rights* (2nd ed.). Cambridge University Press.
Barzel, Y., & Kochin, L. (1992). Ronald Coase on the nature of social cost as a key to the problem of the firm. *Scandinavian Journal of Economics, 94*, 19–31.
Bastiat, F. (1850). *The law*. Laissez-Faire Books.
Becker, G. (1964). *Human capital: A theoretical and empirical analysis, with special reference to education*. The University of Chicago Press.
Benson, B. L. (1984). Rent seeking from a property rights perspective. *Southern Economic Journal, 51*, 388–400.
Berle, A. A., & Means, G. C. (1932). *The modern corporation and private property*. Harcourt, Brace and World.
Bush, W., & Mayer, L. (1974). Some implications of anarchy for the distribution of property. *Journal of Economic Theory, 8*, 401–412.

Cheung, S. N. S. (1969a). *A theory of share tenancy*. University of Chicago Press.
Cheung, S. N. S. (1969b). Transaction costs, risk aversion, and the choice of contractual arrangements. *Journal of Law and Economics, 12*, 23–42.
Cheung, S. N. S. (1970). The structure of a contract and the theory of a non-exclusive resource. *Journal of Law and Economics, 13*, 49–70.
Coase, R. H. (1937). The nature of the firm, *Economica NS4*, 386–405.
Coase, R. H. (1959). The federal communications commission. *Journal of Law & Economics, 2*, 1–40.
Coase, R. H. (1960). The problem of social cost. *Journal of Law and Economics, 3*, 1–44.
Coase, R. H. (1988). The nature of the firm: Influence. *Journal of Law, Economics, and Organization, 4*, 33–47.
Cooter, R. (1982). The cost of Coase. *Journal of Legal Studies, 11*, 1–33.
Cyert, R. M., & March, J. G. (1963). *A behavioral theory of the firm*. Prentice Hall/Pearson Education.
De Soto, H. (2001). *The mystery of capital: Why capitalism triumphs in the West and fails everywhere else*. Basic Books.
Debreu, G. (1959). *The Theory of Value*. Wiley.
Demsetz, H. (1964). The exchange and enforcement of property rights. *Journal of Law and Economics, 7*, 11–26.
Demsetz, H. (1967). *Toward a theory of property rights*. Originally published in 1967, reprinted in *Ownership, Control, and the Firm*, idem. 1988. Basil Blackwell.
Dixit, A., & Olson, M. (2000). Does voluntary participation undermine the Coase Theorem? *Journal of Public Economics, 76*, 309–335.
Eggertson, T. (1990). *Economic behavior and institutions*. Cambridge University Press.
Epstein, R. A. (2016). The economic structure of Roman property law. In P. J. Plessis, C. Ando, & K. Tuori (Eds.), *The Oxford handbook of Roman law and society*. Oxford Handbooks Online. https://bit.ly/3yIhhG7
Farrell, J. (1987). Information and the coase theorem. *Journal of Economic Perspectives, 1*, 113–189.
Felin, T., Foss, N. J., & Ployhart, R. (2015). Microfoundations for management research. *Academy of Management Annals, 9*, 575–632.
Foss, N. J. (1997). Economics, institutions, and Ludwig von Mises. *Cultural Dynamics, 9*, 77–96.

Furubotn, E. G. (1991). General equilibrium models, transaction costs and the concept of efficient allocation in a capitalist economy. *Journal of Institutional and Theoretical Economics 147*, 662–686.

Furubotn, E., & Pejovich, S. (1972). Property rights and economic theory: A survey of recent literature. *Journal of Economic Literature, 10*, 1137–1162.

Garnsey, P. (2009). *Thinking about property*. Cambridge University Press.

Grossman, S., & Hart, O. (1986). The costs and benefits of ownership: A theory of lateral and vertical integration. *Journal of Political Economy, 94*, 691–719.

Harsanyi, J. C. (1967). Games with incomplete information played by "Bayesian" players, I-III. part I. *The Basic Model. Management Science, 14*, 159–182.

Hart, O. (1995). *Firms, contracts, and financial structure*. The Clarendon Press.

Hegel, G. W. F. (1820). *Philosophy of right*. Batoche Books.

Holmstrom, B. (1979). Moral hazard and observability. *The Bell Journal of Economics, 10*, 74–91.

Hume, D. (1739). *A treatise of human nature*. Penguin.

Jensen, M., & Meckling, W. (1976). Theory of the firm managerial behavior, agency costs and ownership structure. *Journal of Financial Economics, 3*, 305–360.

Jensen, M. C., & Meckling, W. (1979). Rights and production functions: An application to labor-managed firms and co-determination. *Journal of Business, 52*, 469–506.

Jones, G. R. (1983). Transaction costs, property rights, and organizational culture: An exchange perspective. *Administrative Science Quarterly, 28*, 454–467.

Kim, J., & Mahoney, J. T. (2002). Resource-based and property rights perspectives on value creation: The case of oil field unitization. *Managerial and Decision Economics, 23*, 225–245.

Kim, J., & Mahoney, J. T. (2005). Property rights theory, transaction costs theory, and agency theory: An organizational economics approach to strategic management. *Managerial and Decision Economics, 26*, 223–242.

Kirzner, I. M. (1962). Rational action and economic theory. *Journal of Political Economy, 70*, 380–385.

Klein, B., Crawford, R. G., & Alchian, A. A. (1978). Vertical integration, appropriable rents, and the competitive contracting process. *Journal of Law and Economics, 21*, 297–326.

Knight, F. H. (1924). Some fallacies in the interpretation of social cost. *Quarterly Journal of Economics, 38*(4), 582–606.

Libecap, G. P. (1989). *Contracting for property rights*. Cambridge University Press.

Locke, J. (1698). *Two Treatises of government: In the former the False Principles and Foundation of Sir Robert Filmer and his followers, are detected and overthrown. The latter is an ESSAY CONCERNING the true original extent and end of civil government* (3rd ed.). Awnsham and John Churchill.

Lueck, D. (1995). The rule of first possession and the design of the law. *Journal of Law and Economics, 38*, 393–436.

March, J. G. (1962). The business firm as a political coalition. *Journal of Politics, 24*, 662–685.

March, J. G., & Simon, H. A. (1958). *Organizations*. Wiley.

Marx, K. (2000). *Selected writings*. Oxford University Press.

Milgrom, P., & Roberts, J. (1990). Bargaining costs, influence costs, and the organization of economic activities. In D. M. Kreps (Ed.), *Perspectives on positive political economy*. Cambridge University Press.

Mises, Lv. (1920). Economic calculation in the socialist commonwealth. In F. A. Hayek (Ed.), *Collectivist economic planning* (p. 1935). George Routledge and Sons.

Mises, Lv. (1936). *Socialism*. Liberty Press.

North, D. C. (1990). *Institutions, institutional change, and economic performance*. Cambridge University Press.

Pejovich, S. (1982). Karl Marx, property rights, and the process of social change. *Kyklos, 35*, 383–397.

Pigou, A. C. (1922). Empty economic boxes: A reply. *Economic Journal, 32*, 458–465.

Posner, R. N. (1987). The law and economics movement. *American Economic Review (Papers & Proceedings), 77*, 1–13.

Selznick, P. (1957). *Leadership in administration: A sociological interpretation*. Row, Peterson.

Stigler, G. J. (1966). *The theory of price*. MacMillan.

The Economist. (2020, September 12). Who owns what?

Umbeck, J. (1977a). The California Gold Rush: A study of emerging property rights. *Explorations in Economic History, 14*, 197–226.

Umbeck, J. (1977b). A theory of contract choice and the California Gold Rush. *Journal of Law and Economics, 20*, 421–437.

Umbeck, J. (1981). Might makes rights: A theory of the formation and initial distribution of property rights. *Economic Inquiry, 19*, 38–59.

Usher, D. (1998). The Coase theorem is tautological, incoherent or wrong. *Economics Letters, 61*, 3–11.

Vanberg, V. (2000). Economic constitutions, protectionism, and competition among jurisdictions. In G. Galeotti, P. Salmon, & R. Wintrobe (Eds.), *Competition and structure: The political economy of collective decisions: Essays in honor of Albert Breton*. Cambridge University Press.
Williamson, O. E. (1971). The vertical integration of production: Market failure considerations'. *American Economic Review, 61*, 112–123.
Williamson, O. E. (1985). *The economic institutions of capitalism*. Free Press.
Williamson, O. E. (1996). *The mechanisms of governance*. Oxford University Press.
Williamson, O. E. (2000). The new institutional economics: Taking stock and looking ahead. *Journal of Economic Literature, 38*, 596–613.
Wilson, R. (1968). The theory of syndicates. *Econometrica, 36*, 119–132.
Winter, S. G. (1964). *Economic natural selection and the theory of the firm* (Ph.D. Dissertation). Yale University.

4
Ownership and Property Rights

What is the role of property rights ideas in social science research, including management research, nowadays? It depends. On the one hand, they are very much present in the economics mainstream. As we discussed in the previous chapter, many of the central ideas—notably, the Coase Theorem and its implications (the importance of the definition, enforcement, and tradeability of property rights), competition for property rights and rent dissipation, transaction costs, and much else—have become part of standard economics. And yet, few economists today define themselves as working in the tradition of the property rights economics of the 1960s. In fact, a young modern economist may not associate notion of property rights and ownership with PRE, and he or she may have no knowledge of the contributions of Alchian, Demsetz, Barzel … or even Coase.

Rather, it is likely to be associated with a contemporary approach to the economics of mainly (but not exclusively) the firm that, to confuse matters further, is often called "property rights theory" (Grossman & Hart, 1986; Hart & Moore, 1990; Segal & Whinston, 2012). We call it "Mark II PRE." We do not do this to signal continuity or superiority, but simply to indicate that Mark II PRE is more recent than Mark

K. Foss and N. J. Foss, *Economic Microfoundations of Strategic Management*,
https://doi.org/10.1007/978-3-031-12910-0_4

I PRE. Interestingly, Mark II PRE is more in narrow in its approach than Mark I PRE, as it is mainly taken up with ownership and property rights issues as they pertain to the firm (but for other applications, see Aghion et al., 2016), whereas Mark I PRE had a much broader explanatory scope (cf., e.g., Furubotn & Richter, 2010). Mark II PRE is also a largely formal approach, whereas Mark I PRE was mainly conducted in the verbal mode.

For those who are familiar with the workings of modern economics, it is perhaps not surprising that contributors to the Mark II research stream provide at best sparse reference to the older property rights literature. For example, an authoritative chapter on "property rights" (Segal & Whinston, 2012) which was published in the prestigious *Handbook of Organizational Economics* (Gibbons & Roberts, 2012) only mentions Coase (1960) and Demsetz (1967) in passing, and then concentrate all the attention on the Mark II approach associated with Nobel Prize winner Oliver Hart and his various co-authors. Property rights economists such as Alchian and Demsetz may get an occasional cite for their contributions to the economics of the firm (Alchian & Demsetz, 1972; Klein et al., 1978), but none for their contributions to their other, foundational contributions to PRE.

Such neglect may have partly substantive reasons (and not just be a matter of snobby reluctance to cite "verbal" precursor economists). As we noted in our account of the evolution of PRE in the previous chapter, the very earliest writings on property rights (Knight, 1924; Mises, 1936) focused on differences between property rights systems understood as alternative ownership arrangements, namely collective versus private ownership arrangements. Interestingly, however, the meaning or definition of *what it means to own an asset resource* does not seem to have been pinned down precisely in (Mark I) PRE. However, defining asset ownership unambiguously is central to Mark II PRE, so real differences do exist.

More specifically, Coase defines ownership as the possession of "the right to carry out a circumscribed list of actions" (1960: 144), that is, ownership of an asset is a bundle of rights to use that asset. The vector of rights is circumscribed partly by legal or governmental restrictions, and, as stressed in the works of particularly Umbeck (1981) and Barzel

(1997), partly by the ability of the holder to exclude other agents from the specific uses defined by the rights. Thus, in a Coasian view, ownership does not provide the owner with exclusive rights to assets, only to certain uses of the asset. Indeed, ownership per se is not what primarily interests Coase—his major concern is the allocation of use rights—and his work doesn't offer a crisp definition of ownership.

Indeed, the nature and meaning of ownership is a thorny issue which continues to produce debate among legal scholars as well as economists (Klein & Robinson, 2011). Does the concept of ownership have an essence which holds across time and space (e.g., the right to exclude others from the owned asset)? Or, is it rather simply any bundle of rights that that changing political, legal, and institutional considerations may single out? Is efficient ownership of the firm uniquely associated with a particular category of input owners such as those who supply capital—or, is efficient ownership of the firm also consistent with other categories of input owners (Hansman, 1988)?

In contrast to such ambiguity, management scholars usually take ownership as an unproblematic notion (Foss et al., 2021) and elaborate its role as a vehicle for creating value. For example, the massive literature on mergers and acquisitions in management research often sees ownership as an instrument of control—that which gives the capacity to pull assets out of some uses and deploy it to other, more preferred uses. But ownership has also been taken as fairly unambiguous in parts of economics, particularly financial economics. Agency theory and its applications in corporate governance and corporate finance suggest that granting ownership supplies incentives for effort that mitigate moral hazard. Agency theory—which owes a huge debt to PRE—conceptualizes ownership as residual claimancy; owners are, notably, shareholders (Fama, 1980; Jensen & Meckling, 1979).

Recall that (Mark I) PRE stresses that control is the key aspect of property rights. It is not clear where such control is located in the agency theory conception of ownership; in other words, its notion of ownership seems unrealistically narrow (Bolton & Scharfstein, 1998). However, it is not clear what exactly ownership means in the context of Mark I PRE either. As Demsetz (1988: 12) observed, reflecting on previous

PRE work: "No clear framework for the economics of ownership has emerged."

Given such ambiguity concerning a concept that is very important to decision-makers, and, well, owners, as well as important to a number of academic fields, including management, it is not surprising that the advent of Mark II PRE with the publication of Grossman and Hart (1986) has come to be regarded as a highly important breakthrough in the understanding of what ownership is and what it "does," that is, its economic function (Aghion et al., 2016). In essence, Grossman and Hart proposed to cut the Gordian knot of ownership. They specifically argued that the key feature of ownership is that it confers "residual control rights" over resources, that is, rights to decide resource use in conditions not specified by prior agreement (Hart, 1995). In this chapter, we compare and contrast Mark I PRE and Mark II PRE with respect to its positions on ownership. We will argue that it is less clear than its proponents believe that Mark II PRE represents such an unambiguous advance with respect to our understanding of property rights and ownership.

Ownership in Property Rights Economics (Mark I)

As Demsetz (1988: 12) explains, Coase's seminal 1960 paper, often seen as the foundation of PRE, is in essence a paper about externalities, and a critique of received doctrine about externality—it is not a paper about ownership. The main emphasis of Coase (1960) is on a vector of government-mandated use rights. Perhaps holding a certain minimum bundle of non-trivial use rights makes one the effective owner in this scheme, but Coase basically doesn't touch on this.

Coase's major concern is the allocation of use rights to assets, since externalities can be directly linked to the uses of assets. In the zero transaction cost setting underlying the Coase Theorem, strictly speaking all possible uses (including future ones) of assets are known and can be contracted for (Barzel, 1997; Furubotn, 1991). All rights to "carry out a circumscribed list of actions" (Coase, 1960: 144) will be costlessly delineated and costlessly contracted for. The interest then is in examining the consequences for allocative efficiency of a contractual allocation of use rights without involving the notion of ownership at all. (What is sometimes called "complete contracting" theories, notably agency theory, basically seeks to do the same thing; Holmström, 1979). Conceptually, this allocation can be separated from the ownership, because one can imagine that all possible uses (including future ones) of assets are known and can be contracted for. Under this interpretation, the concept of ownership and the issue of who owns an asset are unimportant—if transaction costs are zero.

Even when Coase relaxes the zero transaction cost assumption, his interest lies more in understanding the allocative consequences of different legal arrangements of use rights than ownership issues. This is line with Coase's statement that the main problem he sought to examine in "The Problem of Social Cost" was the influence of existing, not imagined, legal institutions on resource allocation (Coase, 1988a, 1988b). In any case, a major problem left unaddressed by Coase is how far one needs to "relax" the assumptions underlying the Coase Theorem to produce a role for ownership, if indeed the notion of ownership can be made precise in such a manner. Thus, Demsetz (1988: 19) seems skeptical of such an approach, as he argues that the meaning of ownership is and must remain inherently "vague" because there is no upper bound to the number of attributes, uses, etc. of an asset that can be owned.[1] Perhaps because of the perceived vagueness of the notion of ownership, PRE scholars have been more concerned with the efficiency consequences of property rights allocations across agents when transaction costs are positive than the issue of "who owns an asset."

It seems fair to note that the Mark I PRE literature typically defined ownership opportunistically, that is, depending on the specific explanatory purpose at hand. In their more "aggregate" analyses of property rights systems, PRE scholars often put much emphasis on the rights to exclude non-owners as the key relevant criterion of private ownership in their work on systems of property rights. For example, Umbeck (1981: 39) identifies ownership with the "... abilities of individuals, or groups

[1] However, he does think that "certain rights of action loom more important than others. Exclusivity and alienability are among them" (Demsetz, 1988: 19).

of individuals, to forcefully maintain exclusivity." Owners are those individuals who can successfully exercise these abilities (Alchian, 1965; Demsetz, 1967; Umbeck, 1981). The ability to exclude may depend on what are recognized as legitimate claims and therefore involve historically contingent circumstances relating to the positions of power and the ability to exercise force that define and enforce the rights of the owner.

Interestingly, often these authors change their understanding of ownership when they analyze more "micro" issues related to firm organization and corporate governance, where owners get defined as those individuals possessing "many" use rights (Demsetz, 1967) or residual income rights (Alchian & Demsetz, 1972). The modern finance literature, which to a large extent originates in property rights economics (i.e., Alchian & Demsetz, 1972; Fama & Jensen, 1983; Jensen & Meckling, 1976), has tended to define ownership in terms of residual income rights.

Thus, it seems fair to say that the older property rights literature was vague about the precise role played by other types of economic rights besides the use rights stressed by Coase (1960), such as rights to exclude, alienate, and derive income from assets, in the understanding of ownership. However, for a number of reasons and purposes, it seems problematic to not have a reasonably precise notion of ownership. One such reason is that many people seem to have a reasonably clear, basic understanding of what it means when they own something. For example, I may let you use my car against payment, but we both understand that if you dislike the color of the, you need to get my permission to have it repainted. Regarding purposes, we would like to have a notion of the "boundaries of the firm," that is, where one firm ends and another begins, as it were. Coase (1937) argued that the boundaries of a firm are where the authority of its managers ends, that is, when transactions are no longer managed by these managers, but instead by the managers of another firm. But, surely many will also recognize an ownership dimension that is relevant to understanding the extent of the firm: Some assets are owned by the firm, while other aren't. But, we can only think of firm in terms of asset ownership if we have a good understanding of what we mean by ownership in the first place!

In contrast to the fuzziness of the ownership concept in Mark I PRE, ownership has a concrete meaning in the law: Both actual legislation and jurisprudence distinguish the law relating to contract from the law relating to asset ownership. The law relating to ownership is more than simply part of a low-cost enforcement institution; it provides default rules or a "standard contract" that reduces information and communication costs and has allocative consequences for this reason. Moreover, legal ownership is a low-cost way of allocating hitherto undiscovered uses of assets. For example, giving people legal ownership implies that they hold the legal right to future, as yet undiscovered, attributes of assets, in the sense that courts will not interfere with the use of these assets by the parties identified as the owners. In fact, the overall thrust in economics thinking about property rights has changed from the focus of the Mark I PRE (i.e., the allocation of rights to an asset across multiple agents) to the issue who owns an asset and why this matters, the key concern of Mark II PRE (Grossman & Hart, 1986; Hart, 1995; Hart & Moore, 1990).

The New Property Rights Economics

Whereas the emergence of property rights economics Mark I may conveniently be dated to the publication of Coase (1960), the emergence of the Mark II stream can be similarly dated to the publication of a single paper, namely Grossman and Hart (1986). This paper has come to define how modern economists conceptualize ownership and address its behavioral and allocative consequences. As discussed in Chapter 3, the impetus to Coase (1960) was the question of how to efficiently allocate use rights to assets like the radio spectrum or cornfields across multiple potential users, implying multiple potential rival uses. Mark II property rights economics emerged in the context of a more narrow and specific problem: What explains the vertical boundaries of the firm; in particular, what is the role played by asset ownership in explaining observed patterns of firm boundaries?

Mark II PRE places ownership center stage in the analysis and defines it in a simple direct manner. Mark II PRE is first and foremost a theory of the boundaries of the firm. Until the advent of Grossman and Hart (1986), the dominant theory of firm boundaries—that is, why certain activities or "transactions" are undertaken by a given firm while others are left to "the market" (meaning other firms)—was transaction cost economics (Williamson, 1985, 1996). Building on Coase (1937), transaction cost economics posits that firms "internalize" "transactions" and bring them under the scope of managerial authority to reduce the bargaining costs that may arise in the context of incomplete contracts and assets that are specific to a relation. However, according to critics such as Grossman and Hart, transaction cost economics tends to treat hierarchy as a panacea and does not clarify the role of ownership in shaping the incentives of parties.

Mark II PRE shares the emphasis on incomplete contracts with transaction cost economics. Specifically, the argument is that ownership is only meaningful in a world of incomplete contracts (Hart, 1995). This, of course, is also a world of transaction costs.[2] While Coase had explicitly introduced incomplete contracts in his 1937 paper on "The Nature of the Firm," such contracts don't seem to play a role in the 1960 paper. The key idea in Mark II PRE is that when contracts are incomplete, there will be some asset uses that are not regulated by the contract. In this case, there is a need for an institution that allocates use rights to assets in the face of unforeseen contingencies. This institution is private ownership.

The link between incomplete contracts and ownership is established by means of the distinction between specific rights of control and residual rights of control. The former can be delineated and directly allocated through contract, while the latter are obtained through the legal ownership of assets and imply the "right to decide usages of the asset in uncontracted-for contingencies" (Hart, 1996: 371). Residual control rights encompass not only the rights to use assets, but also the rights to "decide when or even whether to sell the asset" (Hart, 1995: 65). In the new PRE ownership is defined as the legally enforced possession of

[2] We may pause and ask if this is really the case it is more questionable to then infer that there can be no room for the ownership construct in such a world (i.e., that transaction costs have to be present for ownership to be meaningful). For example, wouldn't holding all property rights rights to a given asset qualify one as "the owner," regardless of what is assumed about transaction costs? In any case, such discussions do not explicitly surface in Coase (1960).

an asset. The economic importance of ownership stems from the owner's ability to exercise residual rights of control over the assets. In particular, an owner can issue threats of taking assets out of a relation.

Mark II PRE suggests that joint ownership of nonhuman, alienable assets (machines, buildings, client lists, patents, etc.) is what defines the firm, which means that firm boundaries are delineated by the ownership of such assets. The importance of nonhuman assets derives from their (potential) function as bargaining levers in situations not covered by contract. The allocation of ownership to such levers matters when parties to a relation have to make non-contractible investments in assets that matter to the relation—notably, investments in the parties' own human capital—and these assets are complementary to specific nonhuman assets. The model revolves around the effect of ownership of nonhuman assets on the incentives to invest in human assets. Specifically, bargaining determines the allocation of returns from investments, so that each party gets her opportunity cost plus a share (assumed equal) of the (verifiable) profit stream. Since in this setup individual returns differ from social returns, and agents are sufficiently farsighted to foresee this, investments will be inefficient.

It is possible to influence the investment of one of the parties positively by reallocating ownership rights to nonhuman assets. A reallocation of ownership of physical assets alters the parties' opportunity costs of non-cooperation after specific investments have been made, and thus changes the expected payoffs from the investments. Such a reallocation may increase the total surplus in the relation. However, this only comes about at the cost of reducing one of the parties' investment incentives (excepting the situation in which the parties' marginal costs of investment are equal). This trade-off determines the efficient allocation of ownership and hence the efficient boundaries of the firm. Hence, the central issue become: Who should own the (nonhuman) asset for (second-best) efficiency to obtain? Note that this assumes that it is possible to unambiguously identify *the* owner of an asset.

Comparing Mark I and Mark II Property Rights Economics

Cutting the Gordian Knot?

The inherent vagueness of the notion of ownership in Mark I property rights economics (which these scholars did not necessarily see as a problem; cf. Demsetz, 1988) may seem to be at variance with the rather concrete meaning that ownership has in law. In fact, Hart (1995: 30n) approvingly quotes Oliver Wendell Holmes understanding of ownership in support of his own view: "But what are the rights of ownership? They are substantially the same as those incident to possession. Within the limits prescribed by policy, the owner is allowed to exercise his natural powers over the subject-matter uninterfered with, and is more or less protected in excluding other people from such interference. The owner is allowed to exclude all, and is accountable to no one." (For a broader and more contemporary view, see Honorè, 1961).

In Mark II Pre ownership is defined as the legally enforced possession of an asset. Thus, economic and legal conceptions of ownership are brought together (whereas Mark II property rights theorists increasingly dissociated economic and legal views if rights, as we have seen). Specific rights of control are delineated and directly allocated through contract, while residual rights of control are obtained through the legal ownership of assets and imply the "right to decide usages of the asset in uncontracted-for contingencies" (Hart, 1996: 371), as well as the right to "decide when or even whether to sell the asset" (Hart, 1995: 65).

The Mark II notion that ownership is what allocates residual rights of control would seem to be a conceptual sword cutting through the Gordian knot of the meaning of ownership, one that furthermore is firmly grounded in legal notions of ownership. However, the sword works by means of strong simplifications (Demsetz, 1998; Foss & Foss, 2000), specifically the two closely related implicit assumptions that ownership is (1) perfectly defined and (2) perfectly enforced/non-contestable.

How Well-Defined is Ownership?

In his review of Hart (1995), Demsetz (1998: 449; emphasis in original) points out that "Hart writes as though he thinks that *asset* ownership is an unambiguous concept." Obviously, *assuming* that ownership is unambiguous (because of perfect definition and enforceability of the relevant rights of ownership) is convenient: It allows the equally unambiguous identification of *the* owner of any given (owned) asset. Again, the issue of why and how it matters who owns the asset is the central one in Mark II property rights economics.

However, the logic by which ownership comes to be seen as being an unambiguous construct is not entirely transparent. The other main rival in the literature is the notion of ownership as the possession of residual income rights, typically associated with the corporate finance literature (e.g., La Porta et al., 1999). Hart (1995: 63–66) suggests that the residual income notion is "… not a very robust or interesting theoretical concept" (1995: 64). Residual income rights are not useful as a notion of ownership, since they can easily be divided which residual control rights cannot "in the same way" (1995: 64n). Perhaps Hart means that allocate residual rights of control cannot be allocated *ex ante* between parties. In contrast, residual rights to income can in principle be allocated *ex ante* in any way between the parties.

This is a problematic argument. While it is true that a given residual control right to a specific set of uses of an asset can be difficult to share between parties (Demsetz, 1998), this does not mean that residual control rights to *assets* are necessarily non-shareable between individuals. For example, one can imagine arrangements where an individual effectively controls an asset (e.g., a taxi) on specific weekdays whereas another individual controls it on other weekdays. Hart admits that residual rights of control are in fact divisible in such a way (e.g., he talks about "forms of intermediate ownership" that cover this; Hart, 1995: 61). Of course, while control rights may be divisible someone has to be the "ultimate" owner in the sense that only she can veto the use of an asset. Or, so it would seem. Consider a cooperative or a partnership. In these contractual arrangements, control is exercised by means of majority rule. In effect, decisions on what shall be done with assets in situations that are not covered by contract are decided by any majority that may happen to form. Obviously, such majorities can change over time in terms of their composition. But the example implies that it is not always possible to unambiguously link residual rights of control to any single identifiable individual, and it implies that the whole strategy of assuming that it is possible to unambiguously identify *the* owner of an asset is called into question.

Additionally, Mark II PRE does not address (alienable) assets that are in the "public domain" in the sense that other individuals may spend resources on capturing them without compensating anyone (as in theft, homesteading, etc.) (Barzel, 1997). Thus, Mark II PRE implicitly assumes alienable assets are fully in the private domain in the sense that ownership titles are perfectly defined and perfectly enforced. In contrast, Mark I PRE stressed that all property is potentially and to some extent in the public domain as the definition and enforcement of rights to assets are never perfect (Barzel, 1997; Umbeck, 1981). For this reason, ambiguity concerning who holds effective ownership can easily arise. In fact, Demsetz (1998: 450) declares that the "generally more correct approach is to avoid speaking of asset ownership unless all rights to the asset are owned by one party," which in fact usually will not be the case; hence, Demsetz' position is that ownership is ill-defined in most real-world situations. Relatedly, Barzel (1997) argues that for the purposes of economic analysis, it is more fruitful to focus on property rights to attributes of assets (i.e., as in Coase [1960] their multiple uses) rather than of assets themselves. The reason is that most assets have so many attributes (many may be non-specified or as yet unknown) that the notion of ownership of assets is vague. Similarly, Demsetz argue that "full private ownership" over assets is vague, and "… must always remain so, for there is an infinity of potential rights of actions that can be owned … It is impossible to describe the complete set of rights that are potentially ownable" (Demsetz, 1988: 19).

Asymmetric Treatment of Enforcement A key insight that emerged in the evolution of Mark I PRE is that it is reasonable to draw a distinction between legal and economic rights (Alchian, 1965; Barzel, 1997). Legal rights may not be congruent with economic rights, because the rights can only be enforced and thus exercised at high cost. The shoplifting example in Chapter 1, in which a de facto decriminalization of shoplifting in major US cities over the last few years has predictably caused a surge of shoplifting, illustrates this: Small shop owners found it too costly to enforce their property rights by spending on private security, found the value of their assets (the shop) declining dramatically, and went out of business. Another reason economic rights may not be matched by legal rights is when the costs of capturing rights are small but the costs of securing legal title to those rights are high. Land rights in some developing countries may illustrate: The costs of capturing de facto land rights may be low, but the costs of establishing legal title are very high (The Economist, 2020).

More generally, in the presence of transaction costs, the distinction between legal and economic rights becomes meaningful with respect to potentially *any* asset, whether human capital assets or nonhuman capital assets (Barzel, 1997). However, this point does not seem to be reflected in Mark II PRE. Here, ownership to, and contracts over, physical assets are supposed to be fully and costlessly enforced by the legal system, whereas contracts involving investments in human capital are assumed to be completely unenforceable because the relevant investments are assumed to be non-verifiable.

Do These Distinctions Matter?

A New Lighthouse in Economics?

Coase (1974) argued that economists have too often been prone to offer verdicts on what are optimal ownership or financing patterns based on highly stylized models that are insufficiently grounded in empirical reality. An example may be the use of models of a perfectly competitive economy to argue that issues of allocation and distribution are separable, and efficient outcomes can be realized under "market socialism," a prominent argument in the interwar debate on the economics of socialism (Lange, 1936). However, Coase focuses on a less lofty example, namely how economists have treated the lighthouse as the quintessential public good. Thus, many economists had routinely taken lighthouse services as perfect examples of fully non-excludable and non-rivalrous goods. Looking into the relevant historical records, Coase documented how historically lighthouse services had often been privately supplied, for example, by linking the financing of lighthouse services to harbor fees. Thus, an element of excludability was added by the specific institutional arrangements that were adopted. In contrast, to simply *define* lighthouse services as pure public goods automatically means that the set of institutional alternatives for ownership and financing is not only given but also very small.

The treatment of asset ownership in Mark II PRE is comparable to the traditional treatment of the lighthouse. Thus, economists working within this stream have adopted a highly stylized notion of ownership that while it seems to conform to legal notions of ownership involves the problematic assumptions that ownership is indivisible, perfectly defined, and fully enforceable (just as economists treating the lighthouse as the quintessential public good assumed its services inherently could not be financed by private means). In actuality, it is neither of these. As in the case of the traditional assumptions in the analysis of the lighthouse, this means that the analysis neglects real institutions, legal, and otherwise, and that potentially erroneous explanations are put forward or that there are phenomena that the theory simply cannot address. We offer a few examples in the following.

Consequences and Anomalies

A key difference between Mark I and Mark II PRE is the extent to which the multi-attribute nature of most productive assets is taken into account. Whereas this notion is key in Mark I PRE, it doesn't explicitly play a role Mark II PRE. Ultimately, the multi-attribute nature of assets is the reason why Mark I PRE is reluctant to define asset ownership with much precision (cf. Demsetz, 1988), whereas Mark II proceeds as if such ownership is well defined. Treating ownership as if it is well defined has obvious advantages: Scholars generally welcome reducing ambiguity and adopting clear definitions where none existed previously. However, the neglect in Mark II PRE of the multi-attribute nature of assets and of positive measurement and enforcement costs means that it has difficulties coming to grips with a number of real-world phenomena. Consider the difference between quasi-vertical integration and full integration, a distinction that relates to the understanding of the employment contract.

Quasi-Vertical Integration Quasi-vertical integration is an ownership arrangement where a firm owns a number of the specific assets used by, for example, its supplier. In the US auto industry, this has been a long-standing practice, assemblers owning the special tooling used by suppliers (e.g., Monteverde & Teece, 1982). In contrast, under full vertical integration the manager of a supplier is turned into an employee of the firm and the downstream firm owns all the assets in the relation. However, the economic rationales behind these two clearly discernible arrangements are hard to distinguish in Mark II PRE.

Quasi-vertical integration may be seen as an attempt to protect against holdup on the part of the supplier (Monteverde & Teece, 1982). This is, of course, exactly what vertical integration is supposed to do in the logic of Mark II PRE (as well as transaction cost economics; Williamson, 1996). Moreover, note that on Mark II PRE logic (Hart, 1995, 1996; Hart & Moore, 1990), the manager-owner of the supplier firm in a quasi-vertical integration relation has decreased incentives to invest in his human capital, *exactly* as if he had been turned into an employee of the firm. The reason is that the relative bargaining positions of the parties with respect to sharing the joint surplus from their relation is the same under the two arrangements, as the downstream firm owns the key assets in both cases. In other words: When the assets are owned by the downstream firm, it doesn't matter whether the manager of the supplier firm is an independent operator or whether he is an employee of the downstream firm.

The Employment Contract This indicates that it is may be challenging to explain the employment contract through the lens of Mark II PRE; in fact, the existence of that contract is simply taken for granted. Hart (1995: 71) refers to the idea that a benefit of the employment contract is that carrying out activities within a firm means that information may be exchanged more readily. The reason, Hart speculates, is that the employer's control over assets gives him bargaining power over the employee, which implies that the employee may have an incentive to establish himself as reliable, hence, valuable to the employer and thus possibly increasing his future wage. However, one may counter that quasi-vertical integration may accomplish exactly the same, since ownership of the specific assets of another firm would have the same effect on information revelation. Thus, Mark II PRE may help explain authority, but it does not explain the employment contract.

Mark II PRE has difficulties coming to grips with these distinctions and phenomena because it neglects the multi-attribute nature of assets in a setting with measurement and enforcement cost (where the latter depends on the institutional environment). In such a setting, an agent may engage in capture of unspecified attributes of assets that goes beyond the types of capture investigated Mark II PRE, namely under-investment in human capital or holdup. Making telephone calls to friends in far-away countries, using company cars for holiday trips, withholding effort, inefficiently using or maintaining assets, etc. are all examples of capture that cannot easily be pressed into the Mark II PRE categories of holdup or under-investment in human capital. However, such activities may be essential for discriminating between vertical integration and quasi-vertical integration, that is, explaining the employment contract.

It could be argued that such examples implicitly switch the setting to the asymmetric information setting characteristic of agency theory (in Mark II PRE there is symmetric information between the interacting parties). This need not be the case, however. Even in a symmetrical information setting capture will take place, since even here resources will have to be expended on verifying actions to third parties or estimating consequences of capture. The costs of these actions may depend on whether they take place within an employment contract or within contract between independent parties. The employment contract confers to the employer the right to monitor and sanction the employee in ways that for legal reasons cannot be applied to an independent contractor. This means that the employer is in a better position to choose where and when to monitor the exercise of capture. Thus, the employment contract will be chosen when it minimizes the costs of measuring capture.[3] However, this conclusion can only be reached if explicit allowance is made for that part of the institutional environment that regulates the employment relation.

Costs of measuring are likely to be some positive function of the number of attributes of the relevant assets, given a certain measurement technology. Multi-attribute assets tend to imply the presence of many margins of substitution (Barzel, 1997), some of which may not be specified *ex ante* by the contractors. Demsetz (1988: 18) points out that "[t]he general conclusion is that constraining the ability of persons to exercise specific rights of ownership causes them to rely in greater degree on substitute margins in their attempt to maximize utility." This implies that multi-attribute assets tend to produce a bias toward choosing the employment contract (rather than contracting with an independent supplier) (cf. also Holmström & Milgrom, 1991, 1994). This is due to the adaptability advantage of the employment contract. While an employer's constraining of an employee's abilities to exercise control in some directions likely results in the employee substituting toward hitherto unspecified margins, the employment contract allows for low-cost adaptive handling of such behavior by sanctioning it or reducing it in other ways.

Corporate Governance The understanding of ownership has potentially far-reaching consequences for corporate governance. Thus, drawing on the legal literature, Chassagnon and Hollandts (2014) argue the issue of who owns the firm remains a vexing one. In fact, they conclude that legal scholarship lends support to the notion that no one in particular owns the corporation. Moreover, no one "… owns the firm because beyond the formal aspects of it that are recognized by law, the firm is a social organization that is institutionalized separately from the law" (Chassagnon & Hollandts, 2014: 10). This does not mean that an economic analysis of the corporation is ruled out; on the contrary, the authors recommend

[3] This can be interpreted in an agency theory framework (Holmstrom & Milgrom, 1991, 1994) as a reduction in the error in the signals of effort which agents produce in different tasks due to more effective monitoring in employment relationships.

placing "power" centrally in the analysis of firm boundaries and internal organization. Their notion of power is close to the notion of effective control, highlighted by Mark I property rights theorists as the hallmark of property rights (Barzel, 1997).

Toward a Broader Understanding of Ownership Patterns

In Mark II PRE, ownership is the institutions that confers rights to decide usages of assets in future, uncontracted-for contingencies, and are derived from the legal ownership of assets. The rights of ownership of these assets are assumed to be perfectly enforced. This ties the notion of asset ownership too strongly to an unrealistic institutional setup (i.e., the legal system enforces ownership at zero cost). However, a more realistic setting characterized by less than perfect enforcement, multi-attribute assets, and measurement costs—that is, the settings typically assumed in Mark I PRE—suggests that it is necessary to broaden the notion of residual rights of control.

The basic reason is that in such a setting some attributes of assets will be left undefined and unenforced (cf. Barzel, 1997). Hence, they will be subject to capture attempts, that is, other agents will try to gain control over these attributes or manipulate their services to their own advantages (without compensating others). Such capture takes multiple forms, such as not operating production equipment in the proper way, driving rental cars recklessly, using the office Xerox for private purposes, and so on. Such capture clearly goes beyond the type of capture treated in Mark II PRE where capture only relates to the holdup problem. In a more realistic setting, minimizing the costs due to capture may help determine ownership patterns in a way that differs from Mark II PRE. The reason is that there are other costs of capture than inefficient investments, such as dissipation of wealth (Barzel, 1997). In the following example, these costs are also included and help determine ownership patterns.

An Example

Jones is a mechanic who is considering whether to make a specific and non-contractible investment in his human capital (repair skills) that makes his costs of repairing three specific but identical cars lower than the prevailing market price of car repair.[4] There are three potential drivers, A, B, and C of the cars who also invest in their human capital (augment their skills of driving the cars). Jones' investment is complementary to the human capital investments undertaken by A, B, and C such that Jones prefers to have the investing drivers as customers, and the investing drivers prefer to have Jones repairing the cars.[5] Thus, there are potential gains from trade. We also assume that Jones's marginal investment costs are much greater than the costs of A, B, and C.

This example stays close to the basic Mark II PRE setup. According to the logic of Mark II PRE, efficiency dictates that Jones assumes ownership of the cars. Otherwise, he will be held up by the owner(s) of the cars in the sense that they will share the rents on Jones's investments in accordance with the Nash bargaining solution. However, we shall argue that a different ownership pattern may result if provision is made for the possibility that A, B, and C can capture unspecified valued attributes of the cars when Jones cannot perfectly verify such capture.

The efficient use of durable assets, such as the three cars, requires not only that they are paid their marginal products, but also that they are paid for use-induced depreciation. Use-induced depreciation may take place with respect to a number of attributes of the car. N has two options of recovering use-induced depreciation, namely (1) to charge an *ex ante* price that is independent of the actual (*ex post*) depreciation or (2) to negotiate *ex post* a charge reflecting the depreciation. The problem with the first option is that of moral hazard, while the problem with the

[4] For example, Jones specializes in repairing racing cars. However, he still preserves outside options, since he can continue to repair ordinary cars, although his productivity in these options is not improved. Thus, his threat points are unchanged by his human capital investment.

[5] A, B, and C still preserve the option of driving non-specific cars or have their specific cars repaired by another mechanic than Jones, but their utility from these outside options is not improved by their human capital investments. Thus, their threat points are unchanged by their human capital investments. To simplify the example, we also assume that A, B, and C's marginal benefits of investing in their human capital are equal.

second option is one of strategic behavior under bargaining. Remedying both problems requires costly verification of the actual depreciation. Assume, realistically, that it is costly to verify the depreciation of cars after they have been used. This implies that an owner who rents out the cars will confront costs that can be avoided by the owner/driver. Because of his opportunity costs of time, an owner who rents out cars will rationally choose not to verify the depreciation of some attributes. Hence, he will not price these. Assume also that it is less costly to carelessly drive than to carefully drive the car, because careless driving reduces driving time. This means that while an owner/driver must trade-off time against depreciation and safety, the renter/driver must only trade-off time against safety.

Consider the situation where Jones owns the cars and A, B, and C are renters/drivers. Is this an efficient ownership pattern? Fig. 4.1 depicts the different opportunity cost schedules of careful driving of the three drivers. Driver A has the highest opportunity costs of careful driving, while driver C has the lowest opportunity costs of careful driving. Also shown in the figure are three cost lines. The hh line corresponds to the cost schedule confronted by a hypothetical owner/driver if Jones has not

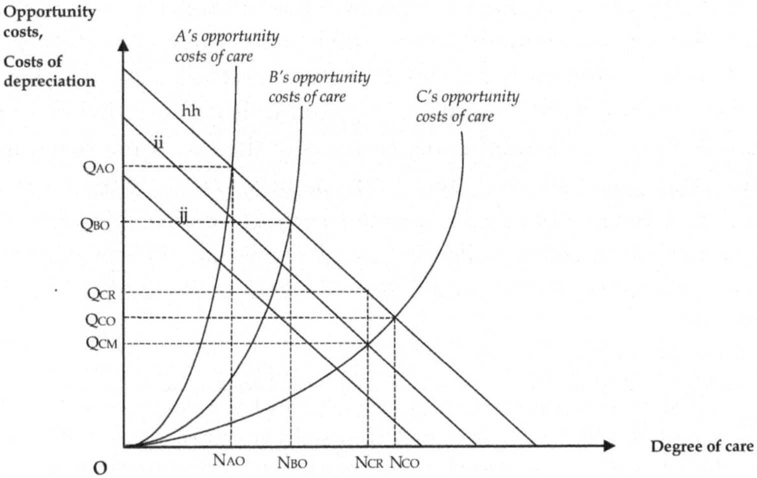

Fig. 4.1 Efficient asset ownership

invested in his human capital or if the owner/driver drives a non-specific car. This schedule reflects the market price for repair services for different degrees of care. For example, if driver A exercises the degree of care corresponding to N_{AO}, he will impose a depreciation on the car that can be measured by the costs of remedying that depreciation through repairing the car by others than N (i.e., Q_{AO}). The opportunity cost schedules of A, B, and C as owner/drivers cross this schedule at the points (Q_{AO}, N_{AO}), (Q_{BO}, N_{BO}), and (Q_{CO}, N_{CO}). These points represent A, B, and C's optimal trade-offs between the degree of care they exercise and the costs of depreciation.

The cost line, jj corresponds to the cost schedule of repairing specific cars that Jones confronts after having made a specific investment in his human capital and with A, B, and C as customers. It is closer to the origin than the hh line, because the investment reduces Jones' cost of repairing the specific cars. For a given degree of care, the vertical distance between the hh line and the jj line represents the rents from Jones' human capital investment if Jones were an owner and if there were no costs of verifying depreciation. This mirrors the basic setup in Mark II PRE (e.g., Hart, 1995). However, when Jones rents out the cars, he will not perfectly verify depreciation, and this decreases the rents he can appropriate. This is different than the basic Mark II setup.

The cost line, ii represents the market price of repairing the depreciation Jones chooses to detect. For high degrees of care, he will choose to verify most of the depreciation. The vertical distance between the ii and the hh line indicates (for any degree of care) the amount of rent from Jones' human capital investment that the driver/renter captures. The driver/renter can capture this rent because N chooses not to verify the depreciation of certain attributes.[6] The vertical distance between the ii and jj lines indicates (for any degree of care) the rent on Jones' own human capital investment that he can capture as an owner when renting

[6] We simplify by assuming that the distance between hh and ii is the same for any degree of care (and therefore for both drivers/renters). A possible interpretation is that certain attributes are inherently more difficult to verify than others and therefore will be left unverified for any degree of care (and type of driver/renter). A possible (self-experienced) example concerns minor scratches on rental cars in Palermo, Sicily, where rental firms apparently expect any car to be harmed in this way, making verifiability particularly costly. One is thus not charged for minor scratches.

out the cars. We make the strong assumption that this line also shows the division of rents between Jones and A, B, and C, respectively, if they are owners of the specific cars. That is, it shows A, B, and C's abilities to hold up Jones for half of the rents on specific investment (for each repair service). This also corresponds to the basic Mark II PRE setup. Given this setup, what is the optimal ownership pattern? In particular, will Jones rationally choose to own all specific cars. Again note that according to the logic of Mark II PRE, he should own them all.

Consider Fig. 4.1 again. Jones wishes to extract the maximum rents from his investment. His incentives to invest are influenced by how much rent he can extract (as in Mark II PRE). This means that he wishes the rental price of cars to reflect to the largest possible extent the costs of depreciation. The price cannot exceed the opportunity cost to an owner/driver of owning a non-specific car, that is, Q_{AO}, Q_{BO}, and Q_{CO} in Fig. 4.1 (where A, B, and C are indifferent between owning a non-specific car and renting a specific car). However, Jones cannot reach these three points because of the costs of verifying depreciation and will accordingly charge for the depreciation at points that lie below these points.

To find out what are the consequences of his inability to perfectly measure depreciation, consider driver/renter C in Fig. 4.1. In a first-best world of zero costs of verification, total rents accruing to Jones would be equal to the vertical distance between hh and ii, measured at N_{CO} that is, the difference between the market cost of repair and Jones's cost of repair. However, given non-zero costs of verification, N will charge C a rental price that reflects the market price of repairing the *verified* depreciation (Q_{CM}). Given this, C will adjust his exercise of care accordingly (i.e., choose N_{CR}). This set of choices will induce a sharing of rents equal to that obtaining if C owns the specific car. Quite similar operations may be performed with respect to drivers A and C.

Recall from Fig. 4.1 that Q_{CO} is the charge that leaves C indifferent between being an owner and being a renter, when he is paying the full marginal costs for the depreciation he imposes on the car. Thus, if C is a renter, Jones can at most choose a markup on the rental services amounting to Q_{CO}–Q_{CM}. This markup may reflect both measurement costs and Jones' attempt to extract more rents of the drivers/renters.

As the opportunity cost schedules of the drives are drawn, Jones can impose a higher markup on B and an even higher one on A, leaving them indifferent between being an owner of a non-specific car and being a renter of a specific car. Jones's optimization problem is to choose the markup that maximizes the rent he extracts from all drivers. If Jones chooses a too high a mark-up, he will induce one or more of the drivers to switch to non-specific cars, making him loose rents on repair services. Therefore, it will be efficient for Jones to let these drivers own a specific car, continue to repair their cars, and allow them to extract half of the rents on his investment. An equilibrium may then exist in which A and B are renters/drivers and C is an owner/driver. This is because A and B's gains from not being fully marginally charged for the depreciation they impose on the car they drive are not overwhelmed by the markup.

Implications

The above example has shown that capture, costly measurement (verification), and different types of individuals (A, B, and C) help explain who owns an asset. Moreover, although the example stays very close to the basic Mark II PRE setup, it tells a story that contradicts the prediction of this theory that an individual who undertakes a human asset investment that is specific to some physical assets should also be the owner of those assets. In the example, ownership may thus fall in the hands of C rather than Jones, not in order to create threat points under *ex post* bargaining and avoid inefficient (i.e., third-best) investments, but in order to avoid a markup. Ultimately, the markup arises as a consequence of the driver/renters' capture of unspecified use rights over the car. This leads to depreciation of the cars, costly attempts to verify this depreciation on the part of Jones and a markup that is uniform over the drivers/renters because of Jones's costs of verifying depreciation.

Note that in the example there is a link between the economic function of ownership and the legal system. This link is established through the notion of costly verification, although in a way that differs from Mark II PRE. Costly verification influences who owns an asset, not because it creates a holdup problem (as in the Mark II PRE), but because it makes it costly to charge a correct marginal price of rental services.

Although ownership is structured to minimize capture, the example thus suggests that this structuring can take place in ways that differ from the Mark II PRE model. In turn this suggests that the Mark II PRE model is a special case of a more encompassing model of ownership in which the notion of capture of unspecified attributes also include those that are left unspecified due to measurement costs. To illustrate the partial nature of the basic Mark II PRE setup, conclusions in conformity with Mark II PRE may be derived from the above example. Recall that Mark II PRE reasoning would lead to the conclusion that N should own all cars. In the context of the example, this requires that an incentive contract is made between the owner and the renters of the cars. The contract makes the charge contingent on the verified depreciation. Moreover, the verification of all attributes has to be sufficiently precisely so that an agent has a sufficient belief that he will be charged a correct rent. Otherwise, some of the renter/drivers may still prefer to be owners.[7]

Conclusion

The publication of Grossman and Hart (1986) fundamentally changed discourse on property rights in economics. At first glance, the notion of ownership as residual rights of control appears to be a conceptual sword cutting through the Gordian knot of the meaning of ownership in the older property rights literature. However, it does so by means of some drastic simplifications (Foss & Foss, 2000), notably by making the asymmetrical assumption that ownership to, and contracting over, physical

[7] In their multi-task agency models, Holmström and Milgrom (1991, 1994) arrive at conclusions that are somewhat related to the ones above. What they call "multi-tasking" is thus one representation of the multi-attribute nature of many assets. Relatedly, they also stress measurement costs. However, in contrast to this paper, they assume risk aversion on the part of agents and asymmetric information. We only assume risk-neutrality and a certain degree of non-verifiability. Most importantly, however, in the Holmström and Milgrom models, capture is seen as function of measurement errors on signals on effort whereas in our example, capture is a function of purposefully leaving certain attributes unspecified. This means that in our example an incentive contract will not diminish the amount of capture.

assets is fully and costlessly enforced by the legal system, while contracts involving investments in human capital are completely unenforceable because of non-verifiability.

In Mark I PRE, ownership was never pinned down with much precision, and interpretations of what exactly ownership entails fluctuated somewhat over the course of development of the older approach. Most understandings highlighted exclusivity and alienability of property rights as central to the definition of ownership. This makes effective ownership dependent on private and legal enforcement of claims to ownership, establishing a broader link to institutions. Mark I property rights economics also stressed how assets have multiple attributes to which rights may be held by many different individuals (Alchian, 1965; Barzel, 1997). Some of these rights may be contested and captured. Individuals may rationally decide not to protect certain rights. This all makes ownership a more contingent phenomenon, depending on the social institutions, private enforcement, and public policy existing at any given point of time. This was, however, never seen as a problem by Mark I property rights economists. On the contrary, the complex and contingent nature of real ownership arrangements points to the many margins on which individual can exercise capture of rights, how they seek to protect their rights, the resources consumed in this process, and the role of institutions in facilitating and constraining such processes (cf. Alessi, 1990). This institutional research program, outlined in its essence by Coase (1960), is considerably richer than the one implied by Mark II property rights economics.

To a large extent Mark II PRE has superseded Mark I PRE in the discourse of modern economists, in spite of its more narrow scope and its constraining assumptions. There may be a broader lesson here. Stigler (1983) argued that on efficient research markets, the true theoretical value of older contributions to economics will be internalized in contemporary contributions in more rigorous and pure form. Thus, with such markets, economic science grows with perfect recall, as it were. However, the economics profession is forgetful. A simple reason why ideas may be forgotten is when the discoverer of those ideas dies and becomes interested in other subjects, etc. in other words, when the relevant ideas are no longer promoted (Anderson & Tollison, 1986). Moreover, even in spite of promotion efforts by the inventor of ideas, the profession may remain ignorant of the relevant, important ideas if insufficient alertness (Kirzner, 1973) is exercised by its members. The spread of ideas needs promoters *and* discoverers; both of these may be lacking to some extent. Such informational inefficiencies provide some economic content to the Kuhnian idea of "loss of content" (Kuhn, 1970). Perhaps the change from Mark I to Mark II PRE is such an instance of a Kuhnian loss of content. Seemingly, Mark II property rights economics was able to resolve a number of unresolved problems in the older approach, such as the central issue of what it means to own an asset. The notion of residual rights of control seems to offer a clean answer to this. However, it is an answer that comes at the expense of making strong assumptions concerning the enforceability of titles to ownership and the divisibility of residual rights of control. When such assumptions are relaxed, ownership becomes a much more blurry concept. Although one can still meaningfully talk about who owns specific rights to use or income, it may often not be unambiguous who owns an asset or indeed the corporation. However, this direct attention to the many ways through which individuals in actuality regulate the uses of assets and how individuals protection as well as capture of rights are enabled and constrained by real institutions, including legal and political institutions. Examining the multi-faceted nature and many different manifestations of ownership, and how these can be analyzed as the outcomes of constrained maximization within an institutional and political matrix, was a central explanatory task of Mark I PRE. In essence, this program was laid down in Coase (1960). Compared to this rich and ambitious program, the change from Mark I to Mark II PRE has resulted in a considerably more narrow analytical scope and more strongly simplified assumptions—in short there has arguably been a Kuhnian loss of content.

In contrast, in Mark I PRE, ownership was never pinned down with much precision, and interpretations of what exactly ownership entails fluctuated somewhat over the course of development of the older approach. Most understandings highlighted exclusivity and alienability of property rights as central to the definition of ownership. This makes effective ownership dependent on private and legal enforcement of claims to ownership, establishing a broader link to institutions. Mark I property rights economics also stressed how assets have multiple attributes to which rights may be held by many different individuals (Alchian, 1965; Barzel, 1997). Some of these rights may be contested and captured. Individuals may rationally decide not to protect certain rights. This all makes ownership an ambiguous and fleeting phenomenon, depending on the social institutions, private enforcement, and public policy existing at any given point of time. This was, however, never seen as a problem by Mark I property rights economists. On the contrary, the complex and contingent nature of real ownership arrangements points to the many margins on which individual can exercise capture of rights, how they seek to protect their rights, the resources consumed in this process, and the role of institutions in facilitating and constraining such processes (cf. Alessi, 1990). This institutional research program, outlined in its essence by Coase (1960), is considerably richer than the one implied by Mark II PRE. In the following, we continue to explore its implications for strategy (and revert to talking generally about "PRE").

References

Aghion, P., Dewatripont, M., Legros, P., & Zingales, L. (2016). *The impact of incomplete contracts on economics*. Oxford University Press.

Alchian, A. A. (1965 [1977]). Some economics of property rights. In A. A. Alchian, *Economic forces at work*. Liberty Press.

Alchian, A. A., & Demsetz, H. (1972). Production, information costs, and economic organization. *American Economic Review, 62*, 772–795.

Alessi, L. (1990). Development of the property rights approach. *Journal of Institutional and Theoretical Economics, 146*, 6–11.

Anderson, G. M., & Tollison, R. D. (1986). Dead men tell no tales. *Journal of the History of Economic Thought, 8*, 59–68.

Barzel, Y. (1997). *Economic analysis of property rights* (2nd ed.). Cambridge University Press.

Bolton, P., & Scharfstein, D. S. (1998). Corporate finance, the theory of the firm, and organizations. *Journal of Economic Perspectives, 12*, 95–114.

Chassagnon, V., & Hollandts, X. (2014). "Who are the owners of the firm: Shareholders, employees or no one?" Post-Print halshs-01372370, HAL.
Coase, R. H. (1937). The nature of the firm. *Economica NS4*, 386–405.
Coase, R. H. (1960). The problem of social cost. *Journal of Law and Economics, 3*, 1–44.
Coase, R. H. (1974). The lighthouse in economics. *The Journal of Law and Economics, 17*, 357–374.
Coase, R. H. (1988a). *Notes on the problem of social cost, in the firm, the market, and the law*. University of Chicago Press.
Coase, R. H. (1988b). The nature of the firm: Influence. *Journal of Law, Economics, and Organization, 4*, 33–47.
Demsetz, H. (1967). *Toward a theory of property rights*. Originally published in 1967, reprinted in *Ownership, Control, and the Firm*, idem. 1988. Basil Blackwell.
Demsetz, H. (1988). A framework for the study of ownership. In H. Demsetz, *Ownership, control, and the firm*. Basil Blackwell.
Demsetz, H. (1998). Review of Oliver Hart, "Firms, contracts, and financial structure: Clarendon lectures in economics". *Journal of Political Economy, 106*, 446–451.
Fama, E. (1980). Agency problems and the theory of the firm. *The Journal of Political Economy, 88*, 28–49.
Fama, E. F., & Jensen, M. C. (1983). Agency problems and residual claims. *Journal of Law and Economics, 26*, 327–349.
Foss, K., & Foss, N. J. (2000). Competence and governance perspectives: How much do they differ? And how does it matter? In N. J. Foss & V. Mahnke (Eds.), *Competence, governance, and entrepreneurship*. Oxford University Press.
Foss, N. J., Klein, P. G., Lien, L., Zellweger, T., & Zenger, T. (2021). Ownership competence. *Strategic Management Journal, 42*, 392–328.
Furubotn, E. G. (1991). General equilibrium models, transaction costs and the concept of efficient allocation in a capitalist economy. *Journal of Institutional and Theoretical Economics, 147*, 662–686.
Furubotn, E., & Richter, R. (2010). *Institutions and economic theory: The contributions of the new institutional economics*. University of Michigan Press.
Gibbons, R. S., & Roberts, J. (Eds.). (2012). *The handbook of organizational economics*. Princeton University Press.
Grossman, S., & Hart, O. (1986). The costs and benefits of ownership: A theory of lateral and vertical integration. *Journal of Political Economy, 94*, 691–719.

Hansmann, H. (1988). Ownership of the firm. *The Journal of Law, Economics, and Organization, 4*, 267–304.
Hart, O. (1995). *Firms, contracts, and financial structure*. The Clarendon Press.
Hart, O. (1996). An economist's view of authority. *Rationality and Society, 8*, 371–386.
Hart, O., & Moore, J. (1990). Property rights and the nature of the firm. *Journal of Political Economy, 98*, 1119–1158.
Holmstrom, B. (1979). Moral hazard and observability. *The Bell Journal of Economics, 10*, 74–91.
Holmström, B., & Milgrom, P. (1991). Multitask principal-agent analyses: Incentive contracts, asset ownership, and job design. *Journal of Law, Economics, and Organization, 7*, 24–52.
Holmström, B., & Milgrom, P. (1994). The firm as an incentive system. *American Economic Review, 84*, 972–991.
Honorè, A. M. (1961 [2013]). Ownership. *Journal of Institutional Economics, 9*, 223–255.
Jensen, M., & Meckling, W. (1976). Theory of the firm managerial behavior, agency costs and ownership structure. *Journal of Financial Economics, 3*, 305–360.
Jensen, M. C., & Meckling, W. (1979). Rights and production functions: An application to labor-managed firms and co-determination. *Journal of Business, 52*, 469–506.
Kirzner, I. M. (1973). *Competition and entrepreneurship*. University of Chicago Press.
Klein, B., Crawford, R. G., & Alchian, A. A. (1978). Vertical integration, appropriable rents, and the competitive contracting process. *Journal of Law and Economics, 21*, 297–326.
Klein, D. B., & Robinson. (2011). Property: A bundle of rights? Prologue to the property symposium. *Econ Journal Watch, 8*, 193–203.
Knight, F. H. (1924). Some fallacies in the interpretation of social cost. *Quarterly Journal of Economics, 38*(4), 582–606.
Kuhn, T. S. (1970). *The structure of scientific revolutions*. University of Chicago Press.
Lange, O. (1936). On the economic theory of socialism I. *The Review of Economic Studies, 4*(1), 53–71.
LaPorta, R., Lopez-de-Silanes, F., & Shleifer, A. (1999). Corporate ownership around the world. *Journal of Finance, 54*, 47.
Mises, Lv. (1936). *Socialism*. Liberty Press.

Monteverde, K., & Teece, D. J. (1982). Appropriable rents and quasi-vertical integration. *Journal of Law and Economics, 25*, 321–333.

Segal, I., & Whinston, M. (2012). Property rights. In R. S. Gibbons & J. Roberts (Eds.), *The handbook of organizational economics*. Princeton University Press.

Stigler, G. (1983). Nobel lecture: The process and progress of economics. *Journal of Political Economy, 91*, 529–545.

The Economist. (2020, September 12). Who owns what?

Umbeck, J. (1981). Might makes rights: A theory of the formation and initial distribution of property rights. *Economic Inquiry, 19*, 38–59.

Williamson, O. E. (1985). *The economic institutions of capitalism*. Free Press.

Williamson, O. E. (1996). *The mechanisms of governance*. Oxford University Press.

5

Resources and Value Creation

In his Nobel Prize speech, Coase (1992: 716) noted that "[b]usinessmen in deciding on their ways of doing business and on what to produce have to take into account transaction costs … In fact, a large part of what we think of as economic activity is designed to accomplish what high transaction costs would otherwise prevent." For example, consider the DeBeers diamond cartel and the practice they have adopted for organizing sales. A customer informs DeBeers of her wishes for a specific number and quality of stones. DeBeers then offers the customer a packet of stones—a "sight"—that roughly corresponds to the customer's wishes. The sight is offered on a "take-it-or-leave-us" basis, where refusal to take the sight means that DeBeers refuses to deal with the customer anymore. The price is calculated based on the overall characteristics of the stones and no negotiation over the price is allowed.

Does this strategy reflect raw market power on the part of a player that controls 80% of the world market for raw diamonds? Property rights economists have argued that it does not (Barzel, 1982; Kenney & Klein, 1983). Rather, this is a practice that maximizes created value in firm-customer relations by reducing the costs customers otherwise would

K. Foss and N. J. Foss, *Economic Microfoundations of Strategic Management*, https://doi.org/10.1007/978-3-031-12910-0_5

have expended on sorting[1] and negotiating, and it arguably exists for this reason (it would be superfluous in a zero transaction cost world). DeBeers sorts the product, but only in a coarse manner. The "take-it-or-leave-us" practice and the non-negotiable price mean that all negotiation costs are effectively eliminated. As only minimum resources (i.e., transaction costs) are spent on sorting and negotiating, DeBeers' practice maximizes the total created value that the parties to the transaction can split. Similar practices can be observed in many other industries, such as the prepackaging of fruit and vegetables in grocery stores, or block booking in the movie industry (Barzel, 1982, 1997; Kenney & Klein, 1983).

Strategic management research has paid little attention to transaction cost-reducing practices. However, their theoretical explanation has important implications for strategic management and, in particular, the resource-based view (the "RBV") that we briefly discussed in Chapter 2 (Barney, 1991; Peteraf, 1993). Including transaction cost in the RBV adds to view's understanding of value creation as well as value appropriation.

First, transaction costs and value creation are linked. In terms of the above examples, sorting costs, which are part of transaction costs, reduce created value in an exchange (Barzel, 1982). However, certain sales practices may reduce transaction costs, increasing created value. In other words, they "accomplish what high transaction costs would otherwise prevent." Second, transaction costs and value appropriation are also linked. Suppose DeBeers posts prices that reflect the mean quality of the diamonds in a given sight. If DeBeers then allows customers to sort between the diamonds in a sight, customers will only pick high-quality stones. DeBeers' sales practice strongly raises customers' (transaction) costs of sorting, allowing DeBeers to maximize the share of created value that it can appropriate from its resources.[2]

---

[1] Specifically, customers' sorting costs are reduced because they do not have to spend resources to be among the first to sort among the diamonds.

[2] In fact, the sales practice may itself be a valuable resource for DeBeers.

In this chapter, we further explore the relations between transaction costs, and the core strategy questions of value creation and appropriation, specifically relating the discussion to the RBV. The key idea is that property rights, as understood through the lens of what was called Mark I PRE in the previous chapter, are important to strategy because a resource owner's ability to create, appropriate and sustain value from resources partly depends on the property rights that he holds and how well they are protected. In turn, transaction costs—the costs of exchanging, protecting and capturing property rights—are important to strategy because they influence the value that a resource owner can appropriate. This conceptualization unifies the theoretical constructs of resources, property rights, transaction costs, value creation, and appropriation.

Our contribution to clarifying the micro-foundations of the RBV is related to Lippman and Rumelt's (2003a, 2003b) recent attempt to construct a cooperative game theory foundation for the RBV. They point out that prices and, therefore, the share of created value that is appropriated by a particular resource owner are bargaining outcomes, and they perceive value creation as mainly driven by search for new uses of resources. We broadly agree with this view. However, unlike Lippman and Rumelt we stress the crucial importance of transaction costs for value creation and appropriation. Our explicit focus on transaction costs helps explain how value can be created by reducing transaction costs and brings attention to ways of appropriating created value beyond bargaining. The sales strategy of DeBeers illustrates a means of increasing the value appropriated from customers. DeBeers raises the value it can impute to its bundle of resources solely by reducing overall transaction costs—without altering its bargaining power.

Refining Resource Analysis: Property Rights and Resource Value

The PRE stresses that transactions involve the exchange of property rights rather than the exchange of goods per se (Coase, 1960). Hence, the unit of analysis is the individual property right. Although the units of analysis of PRE and the RBV differ, the PRE view agrees with the

RBV position that resources matter for the analysis of value creation and appropriation, and ultimately for sustained competitive advantage. However, the PRE *refines* the RBV understanding of resources, and how they create and appropriate value.

Different definitions of "resources" are provided in the RBV literature (see Wernerfelt, 1984; Barney, 1991; Grant, 1991). However, they all tend to see resources as "elementary particles"—irreducible units. Resources are often better thought of as "molecules" that are composed of bundles of rights to attributes. "Attributes" consist of the different functionalities and services (Penrose, 1959) that assets can supply. Property rights are held to such attributes (Barzel, 1997) and consist of the right to use/consume, obtain income from, and alienate these attributes (Alchian, 1965). For example, a Hi-Fi system can play different kinds of music, with different levels of bass or treble at different volumes. All of these functionalities are attributes over which the owner holds property rights. However, the Hi-Fi's ability to play extremely loud music may not be realized if the law or neighborhood norms prevent this service. The relevant use rights are then constrained. Strategic assets, such as brand names, may also have multiple attributes, some of which may be similarly constrained. An owner of a brand name can decide in which contexts he wishes to deploy the brand name. However, her use rights may still be constrained, for example, if he is prohibited from using the brand name as a domain name on the Internet. How property rights are constrained by the law, agreements or norms influences how much value a resource owner can create and appropriate from the resource.[3]

Resources as Bundles of Property Rights

These examples suggest that it is useful to think of resources as *bundles of property rights to attributes*. This is related to Coase's critique of the

[3] This adds a property rights dimension to Penrose's (1959) distinction between resources and the services they yield. The services that a firm can derive from its resources (i.e., the fungibility of the resources) are not only constrained by path-dependencies, the functionalities of the resource, and managerial imagination (Penrose, 1959), but also by the transaction costs of realizing the economic potential of the property rights and by the way in which those property rights are constrained.

Pigovian tradition in welfare economic. Coase (1960: 155) notes that a reason for its failure to come fully to grips with externality issues lies in its "faulty concept of a factor of production." Coase is essentially making the point we are making here (albeit in a different context), namely that resources/factors of production are better seen as bundles of rights. The resource remains an important aggregation of the unit of analysis (the individual property right), because resources are traded or accumulated more often than individual property rights over attributes. The way in which attributes are bundled in goods often reflects production costs and technical constraints. However, transaction costs also play an important role.[4] Attributes are usually traded in bundles to economize the costs of specifying and trading individual resource attributes. Firms often acquire the entire bundle of property rights to a resource, such as a production facility, to avoid the costs of specifying and trading only those attributes that are of economic interest to the firm. However, such transaction costs hinder the resource owner in realizing the full potential value of the resource, because some attributes that are not used by the current owner are not traded (e.g., production time may be costly to trade). If the relevant transaction costs are somehow reduced so that such attributes can be specified and traded, the resource owner may appropriate more value from the resource.

Thinking of resources in terms of property rights to valued attributes implies that resources are not given, but may rather be seen as the *outcomes* of processes of economizing with transaction costs. Obvious examples are those resources that only exist because of transaction costs, such as contracts, and the DeBeers sales practice.[5] An interesting implication of thinking of resources as endogenous to transaction costs is that seemingly identical (e.g., physically identical) resources may be economically different when they are controlled by firms that are not equally capable of protecting the relevant resource attributes. For example, the

[4] Relevant transaction costs are costs of drafting contracts (i.e., contracts become incomplete), costs of monitoring (which make moral hazard viable), measuring attributes (which induces adverse selection), and costs of protecting against entry and imitation (which reduce property rights to income streams from controlling certain market shares and resources).

[5] For example, whether goods such as copying machines and servicing agreements are sold as a combined good (i.e., a "tying arrangement") depends on the costs to the seller or lessor of monitoring the impact of non-standard servicing on the machine (Elzinga & Mills, 2001).

"same" kind of employees, employed in different firms with different incentive systems, will engage in different morally hazardous activities. From an economic standpoint, they are different resources and will be paid differently.

Resource Value and Transaction Costs

Another implication of the property rights view of resources is that transaction costs influence the value that a resource owner can create and appropriate. The resource value that an owner can create depends on the bundle of property rights that he holds to the attributes of the resource, the constraints imposed on these property rights, *and* the costs of trading them. The value that a resource owner can appropriate also depends on transaction costs. Value appropriation presupposes that the owner can exclude non-owners from using or destroying attributes to which he holds property rights. While the resource owner has the legal right to exclude non-owners from using and obtaining value from his resources, he may still find it too costly to exclude non-owners from all possible uses of the resource. In effect, he cedes the relevant rights (Barzel, 1997). Similarly, given costs of protecting property rights over attributes, owners often choose to control the relevant property rights to varying degrees, an aspect reflected in the value that a resource owner can appropriate. For example, in a franchise chain the value of a brand name to the franchisor will be eroded (Dierickx & Cool, 1989) when it is too costly to the franchisor to exclude franchisees from using the name to sell low quality products.

To sum up: When resources are conceived of as bundles of property rights, the potential value that a resource owner can create and appropriate does not only depend on supply and demand conditions for the entire bundle of property rights, but also on how this bundle is constrained, the transaction costs involved in realizing the value of individual property rights, and the transaction costs of controlling the property rights to the attributes that constitute the resource. Attempts to maximize resource value must take such transaction costs into account.

Controlling Property Rights: The Capture and Protection of Property Rights

An important part of transaction costs are the costs of using legal and/or private means of protection. Positive transaction costs imply that most property rights are not fully protected and can be subject to capture efforts (henceforth, "capture"). By "capture" we mean resource-consuming activities to appropriate value from other strategizers *without compensating them.*[6] Moral hazard, adverse selection and holdup are familiar examples of capture. While capture is different from exchange, it may take place in exchange relations. For example, two parties to a transaction agree on a price for a resource with certain attributes, (such as a certain quality level); however, the supplier may deliver a resource of poorer quality. Such moral hazard on the part of the supplier amounts to capturing (some) valued resource attributes from the buyer (Chi, 1994).[7]

Given this definition of capture, "protection efforts" (henceforth, "protection") can be defined as the resource-consuming activities that strategizers undertake to reduce others strategizers' incentives to capture property rights. Since capture takes many forms, the notion of protection in PRE goes significantly beyond how strategy has traditionally talked about protection, namely making and keeping resources costly to imitate or substitute (Barney, 1991; Teece, 1986). In addition to such protection strategies, property rights may be protected by choosing governance structures in order to reduce capture in the form of moral hazard or holdup (Chi, 1994; Hart, 1995; Mahoney, 1992; Williamson, 1996), using the legal system, establishing private orderings (Williamson, 1996), deterring entry (Tirole, 1988), writing contracts, and adopting sales strategies to hinder adverse sorting (as in the DeBeers example) (Barzel, 1982; Kenney & Klein, 1983). The RBV mainly considers a subset of these protection activities, namely protecting against imitation, but stands to gain from considering a broader set than it presently does.

[6] Thus, capture creates what economists call "externalities."

[7] There is also a dimension of capture to competition. Competitive imitation and substitution, as well as competition in terms of quality, technology and price, may be seen as capture because these competitive activities reduce the value that a resource owner can appropriate without compensating the owner of that resource (Barzel, 1994; Foss, 2003).

To illustrate, consider an insurance company that is the first to market a particular kind of accident insurance concept, which in turn comes heavily into demand. The product can be fully protected from imitation using legal means. Moreover, assume that suppliers and customers can only bargain for a small part of the value created by the new concept. Given all this, the insurance company would seem to implement "... a value creating strategy not simultaneously being implemented by any current or potential competitors and ... these other firms are unable to duplicate the benefits of this strategy" (Barney, 1991: 102). In other words, the company seems to have realized a sustained competitive advantage. However, this may not be the case. The price of insurance contracts cannot perfectly reflect the true accident risks of each individual who takes out insurance due to transaction costs. Given variation in risks, some customers, namely those with high accident risks, capture value in excess of what they pay for (i.e., "adverse selection," Akerlof, 1970). At the limit, all of the rents from the new strategy will be eroded through the value capture/adverse selection of customers.

This example implies that protection of resource value goes beyond keeping resources non-imitable. Resources are not fully protected from value erosion unless they are protected from *all* kinds of capture. In the example, the proper way to protect value would be to segment the customer base. The example further indicates that PRE has implications for value creation, appropriation, and sustained competitive advantage, implications which add to the RBV. In order to explore these implications, we first examine value creation and appropriation in a setting where transaction costs are zero, which is the setting underlying the Coase Theorem (Coase, 1960, 1988). The zero transaction cost setting serves as a useful benchmark, because it represents a state in which maximum value is created. We then explicitly consider transaction costs, and examine their implications for value creation and appropriation relative to the benchmark situation.

Relating Transaction Costs to Value Creation and Appropriation

The Coase Theorem

As noted in Chapter 3, the Coase Theorem implies that all value that can be created from the exchange and use of an economy's available goods will, in fact, be created when transaction costs are absent. The underlying assumptions are that in such a surplus-maximizing equilibrium, strategizers have full information,[8] there are no costs of defining and protecting property rights to (all attributes of) all resources and there are no bargaining costs.

As the costs of exchanging property rights are zero, all property rights to all attributes can be exchanged and are optimally bundled into resources.[9] In this situation, there will still be constraints on the use rights over resources, but these constraints will be defined in a value maximizing manner. In other words, externalities cause no avoidable loss of value. Given the optimal constraints and costless exchange, resources will be put to their best possible uses. In this benchmark situation, the maximum value that resources can create will be realized.

Another way of stating that the cost of exchanging property rights is zero is that the prices for all those resource uses that are realized in the value-maximizing equilibrium emerge immediately from costless bargaining processes. For example, consider a parking area that is located adjacent to a supermarket. Since information and bargaining costs are zero, the supermarket owner will bargain with all users of the parking area so that all property rights to the various attributes of the parking area will be priced. Relevant attributes may be the time, date, and proximity to the supermarket entrance. Different prices for different bundles of property rights for these attributes will likely emerge. Since prices are perfect signals of scarcities, all attributes will be perfectly rationed, so that no queues emerge and re-allocating the use rights for the parking spaces

[8] This is a strong version of the Coase Theorem (as in Coase, 1988; Barzel, 1997).

[9] However, the very notion of a "resource" becomes somewhat redundant in this extreme, as many exchanges will involve property rights over attributes rather than resources per se.

cannot increase created value. However, while the zero transaction cost condition implies that total resource value will be at its maximum, the issue of value appropriation is not directly addressed. For this, further theoretical apparatus, namely bargaining theory (Lippman & Rumelt, 2003a), is required.

As bargaining is costless, the value created by the use of resources is always independent of the value that each individual resource owner appropriates. One may think of parties to transactions (i.e., resource owners) as first agreeing to maximize the value that can be created from their resources, and then splitting this value through bargaining to define each party's share of the created value (Milgrom & Roberts, 1992). Since all promises are enforceable, resource owners will always receive at least their opportunity costs and resource investments will always be covered (Hart, 1995). In other words, value creation is independent of value appropriation when transaction costs are zero.

The zero transaction cost setting does not imply long-run, perfect competition, and is therefore compatible with resource owners earning rents. As Coase (1960) notes, rents may be earned when the supply of input resources is not perfectly elastic, independent of whether transaction costs exist or not. As property rights are perfectly protected, these rents are sustainable. However, since bargaining (and forming coalitions) is costless, the owner of a scarce resource is unlikely to appropriate all rents.

While the rudiments of the resource-based view of sustainable competitive advantage (Barney, 1991; Peteraf, 1993) are thus far consistent with the zero transaction cost assumption, this assumption only leaves limited room for understanding the links between resources and sustained competitive advantage. In order to explore more such links, the assumption that transaction costs are zero must be abandoned.

The introduction of transaction costs brings both bad and good news to strategizers. The bad news is that in a positive transaction cost world, realizing the full potential of all resources is impossible with respect to value creation. Moreover, resource value can be eroded in numerous ways by the creative attempts of other strategizers to capture value. The good news is that the presence of transaction costs generates sources of value creation and appropriation (i.e., strategic opportunities) that would not exist if the transaction costs were zero.

Value Dissipation and Value Erosion: Bad News for Strategizers

In a positive transaction cost world, some *value dissipation* is strictly unavoidable. Dissipation results because protecting property rights is costly and because a lack of protection induces strategizers to expend resources on costly capture. If a strategizer increases the protection of her property rights in order to reduce others' capture, he may reduce one kind of value dissipation while increasing another one. Similarly, reducing protection in order to save on protection costs increases others' capture efforts. Therefore, for a given strategizer there is an optimal amount of dissipation, namely the amount that maximizes appropriated value.[10] Given such an optimum, changes in the costs of protection and capture change the amount of dissipation. For example, a strategizer's cost of protection may decrease because he adopts or creates new sales practices (as in the DeBeers example), contractual forms, or sorting or monitoring technologies. Capture and protection efforts will be different in the new equilibrium.

Direct and indirect dissipation Two kinds of dissipation exist. Protection and capture *directly* reduce realized value compared to the zero transaction cost situation because the efforts themselves are costly and therefore consume value. Protection efforts, such as attribute measurement and exclusion of non-owners, are examples of direct dissipation. An example of capture that directly dissipates value is customers who sort between unsorted goods of varying qualities in order to select only those that have a higher value than the posted price.

[10] Value creation therefore requires that resource owners consider not only their own costs of protection, but also the costs to other strategizers of engaging in capture (Skaperdas, 1994).

Protection may also lead to *indirect dissipation* to the extent that the value-creating exchange of property rights is hindered, as when knowledge is kept in-house in order to protect against imitation (cf. Reed & DeFilippi, 1990). While this is typically seen as something positive in strategy thinking, the other side of the coin is that the knowledge that is kept in-house does not become an object of know-how exchange within a network of reciprocating firms (von Hippel, 1988). Losses in the form of unrealized gains from knowledge exchange constitute one form of indirect dissipation, while capture may be another. For example, if many customers sort, there will be a waste of value compared to the situation where the goods are sorted only once (e.g., by the first customer). Moreover, customers may engage in costly competition, such as spending time in a queue, over unprotected property rights (Barzel, 1997). If capture is sufficiently intensive, indirect dissipation emerges in the form of reduced transaction volume in the market. Other sources of indirect dissipation arise from morally hazardous behavior that induces sub-optimal levels of production, and from hold up and imitative efforts that diminish investments.

Value erosion The RBV notion of value erosion (Dierickx & Cool, 1989)—value dissipation as seen from the perspective of a resource owner—is easily aligned with the PRE notion of dissipation. Specifically, value erosion refers to the reduction in a resource's value that is induced by a reduction in other strategizers' capture costs or by an increase in the resource owner's own protection costs. Value erosion thus measures the change in a resource owner's appropriated value due to changes in the equilibrium amount of capture efforts and protection costs. For example, producers of digital products experience value erosion due to the declining cost of copies for private users. Value erosion is caused by both direct dissipation (i.e. users' capture costs and producers' protection costs) and indirect dissipation (i.e., investments in intellectual assets decline).

Unowned resources and value erosion Supporters of the RBV sometimes argue that unique locations are sources of rents (see Lippman &

Rumelt, 2003b). For example, a unique, non-imitable riverside location for a production site would seem to have the potential of creating sustained competitive advantage due to the low transportation costs it provides to the firm. However, the interdependence between the resource (the site) and the public good (the river) creates a problem of sustaining rents that has not been considered in the RBV literature. While the location may stay inimitable, *ex post* competition may develop for use of the river as other firms located further inland develop less expensive means to bring goods to the river (i.e., the equilibrium is disturbed by a technological innovation). These other firms will also use the river for transportation. If congestion occurs, the actual cost to the firm of transportation is high although the monetary price it pays is low. In the extreme, the firm's locational rents may be completely eroded by queuing costs.

This example illustrates a situation in which a firm can fully protect its own property rights to resource attributes, with the exception of its income rights related to the location of the land. Rents are initially earned because of complementary relations between resources. However, only one resource is under the control of the firm, which makes it harder for the firm to limit indirect dissipation. Even if all resources were owned by the firm, efficiently rationing the use of resources (such as pricing the use of the river) may be costly, and some property rights over attributes may be left uncontrolled with respect to the use internally in the firm. In those instances, resources are not necessarily sources of sustained rents (even if they fulfill the requirements of being non-imitable, etc.), since increases in the demand of some attributes may result in value erosion of other resources. In sum, the PRE adds to analysis of value erosion in the RBV (Dierickx & Cool, 1989: 1108).

Sources of Value Creation: Good News for Strategizers

The above reasoning points to two main (related) sources of value creation that emerge with the introduction of transaction costs. The first is to reduce protection costs so that *direct* value dissipation diminishes.

The second is to reduce *indirect* dissipation. The following example illustrates how the reduction of direct and indirect dissipation translates into value creation.

Consider a uniquely located (hence, inimitable) parking area that is adjacent to and owned by a supermarket.[11] In this case, customers value the combined good, namely the combination of what the supermarket offers and the parking spaces. This will be reflected in both the demand the supermarket faces and the prices it can charge. The supermarket will earn a profit from being located next to the parking space. The source of this profit is the positive externality in consumption. Thus, use rights to the parking space are unprotected in the sense that non-owners can use this attribute without directly compensating the owner. However, the owner will still make the parking space available to non-owners when he can appropriate its value through its complementarity to the supermarket's offerings.

Assume now that the supermarket's pricing decisions can be represented in terms of the monopoly diagram familiar from economics textbooks (see Fig. 5.1).

In the diagram, D_1 is the demand curve that the supermarket would face in the absence of the parking space. Created value is represented by the area IJHC. However, if the supermarket constructs a parking space and does not restrict its use, D_2 is the combined demand curve for the goods offered by the supermarket *and* the free services of the parking space. The price is lower in the absence of the parking space (p_1), because consumers value having access to a parking space. Total created value increases by BFHC to IJFB. The supermarket can appropriate EFHG (= BFHC) by charging the higher price (p_2) for its goods. However, when a limited number of parking spaces are offered for free, customers queue for those spaces. This results in direct dissipation of value in the form of waiting time and indirect dissipation in the form of a smaller

[11] If instead the supermarket did not own the parking space, it would be more costly for it to take measures to control dissipation of the value created by the parking space: Patrons of other shops would compete with the supermarket's customers for the parking space, and such competition would gradually erode the rents earned by the supermarket on its location. This is the same situation as in the above example of the riverside location.

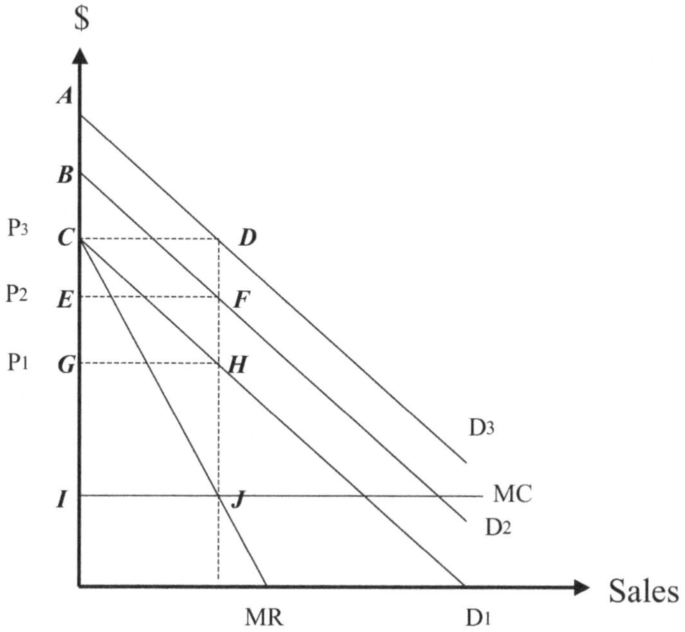

Fig. 5.1 Value-creating price rationing

transaction volume than would have obtained if queuing costs were zero (in Fig. 4.1 it is assumed that not all value is dissipated in this way).

Value dissipation can be reduced if the supermarket extends the number of parking spaces, or if it protects its property rights and charges patrons for parking. The demand curve will shift outward because customers have to expend fewer resources on queuing. Total created value increases by ADFB to IJDA. If the supermarket charges the equilibrium price that fully rations parking space (i.e., $p_3 - p_1$), and prices supermarket goods at p_1, it can appropriate the extra value (CDFE) generated by pricing the parking space.[12] The cost of pricing the parking space has to

[12] Here, we have assumed that extending the parking lot is more costly than pricing parking services. Although customers are never worse off in the example, the monopolist supermarket captures all created value from the parking space and from pricing parking spaces. In other words, customers have no bargaining power. Also, we have assumed that customers have similar queuing costs and valuations of parking spaces. Relaxing these assumptions does not compromise the overall conclusion.

be subtracted from CFDE, so as long as this cost is less than CFDE, the supermarket gains value by pricing the parking services.

Thus far we have assumed that the value of each parking space to customers is independent of location and time. However, in reality customers value parking spaces next to the entrance higher than other spaces, and they value parking at peak shopping hours more than at other hours. A single price will therefore not perfectly ration the use of parking spaces. If the supermarket can devise means of reducing the cost of pricing and enforcing property rights to these attributes, it will appropriate an even greater portion of the resource's value. In the case of a parking space, this may require investments in resources such as ticket and control systems. The ability to reduce indirect dissipation and capture a greater share of the value of attributes provides incentives to invest in such transaction cost-reducing technology.[13]

Pricing the parking spaces is not the only means by which the supermarket can limit indirect dissipation. Alternatively, the supermarket can limit the time cars are allowed to park or it can limit access to the entire parking area.

However, the only way to *fully* limit indirect dissipation is to price each parking space according to its attractiveness to costumers. This may suggest that resource attributes should always be priced to fully realize their value-creating potential. This intuition is incorrect, as pricing is costly in the presence of transaction costs (Coase, 1960, 1988).[14] Resource attributes are not priced when it is prohibitively costly to exclude non-owners from capturing property rights to the attributes,

13 Will the supermarket earn rent on the parking lot? The answer to this question depends on: (1) its ability to keep the transaction cost-reducing resources inimitable, (2) the costs of acquiring these resources, and (3) its bargaining with landowners and construction companies as well as other strategizers who are interested in acquiring the land for resale to the supermarket. It may be common knowledge that parking spaces adjacent to supermarkets create value for the supermarket although the supermarket is unable to price each parking space. Rents may then be captured by suppliers, or by strategizers who acquire the land for resale to the supermarket. The amount of rent captured by third parties depends on the specificities of the bargaining situation.

14 Cf. Lippman and Rumelt's (2003a: 1085) observation that "... intuition suggests that a resource bundle will be more valuable if it can be accurately priced." Transaction costs determine whether resources "can be accurately priced."

when attributes are costly to define and measure in ways that are verifiable to the parties to a potential transaction and/or a third party, and when resource attributes are not in demand. More generally, some attributes and entire resources are more costly to accurately price than others, making it more costly to constrain dissipation for these resources. However, by restricting access to such resources, firms can limit dissipation and maximize value they can appropriate from them. This type of restriction arises when resources are kept in-house, a key theme in the RBV (Dierickx & Cool, 1989; Reed & DeFilippi, 1990).[15]

Transaction Costs and Sustained Competitive Advantage

The PRE is not a strategic perspective per se and does not directly address the issues of why some firms are persistently more successful than others. Thus, the issues of why firms are heterogeneous and pursue different strategies are not directly addressed by PRE.[16] In contrast, firm heterogeneity is central to the RBV and much research has been directed toward

[15] Resources may also not be priced because they are extremely firm-specific (Lippman & Rumelt, 1982). Such resources are best used in-house. The fact that there are no prices on such resources does not imply a potential for value creation. However, we doubt that such resources are common.

[16] However, in a remarkable analysis of the link between profitability and industry concentration, PRE theorist Harold Demsetz (1973: 2) observes that "It may well be that superior competitive performance is unique to the firm team, and unobtainable to others except by purchasing the firm itself. … Here, although the industry structure may change because the superior firm grows, the resulting increase in profit cannot easily serve to guide to similar success. The firm may have established a reputation that is difficult to separate from the firm itself and which should be carried at higher value on its books. Or it may be that the members of the employee team derive their higher productivity from the knowledge they possess about each other in the environment of the particular firm in which they work, a source of productivity that may be difficult to transfer piecemeal. It should be remembered that we are discussing complex, large enterprises, many larger (and more productive) than entire nations. One such enterprise happens to 'click' for some time while others do not. It may be very difficult for these firms to understand the reasons for this difference in performance or to know to which inputs to attribute the performance of the successful firm. It is not easy to ascertain just why G.M. and I.B.M. perform better competitors. The complexity of these organizations defies easy analysis, so that the inputs responsible for success may be undervalued by the market for some time." Clearly, Demsetz is here anticipating the core ideas of the RBV, as later codified in, e.g., Barney (1986, 1991) and Peteraf (1993).

establishing the circumstances under which firms earn sustainable rents from superior resources. Unlike the RBV, the PRE does not distinguish between the resources that give rise to sustained rent and those that do not. Nevertheless, the PRE can contribute directly to strategic analysis.

PRE's contribution to the analysis of sustained competitive advantage starts with the central point of the preceding discussion. The value that strategizers will realize and appropriate from resources depends on transaction costs. Thus, the rent differentials that resources create are partly a function of the differential costs of protecting resource attributes from capture. If a resource owner is able to create and appropriate more value from her bundle of resources compared to the competition, he has the potential of enjoying a sustained competitive advantage. In other words, sustained competitive advantage depends on transaction costs.

Determining the conditions under which firms enjoy a sustained competitive advantage is one of the main issues in the RBV. Barriers to competition are particularly important here (e.g., in the notions of ex ante and ex post limits to competition, Peteraf, 1993), and much effort has been put into the identification of factors (such as the nature of the resource or the resource accumulation process) that create such barriers. Competition is also important in the PRE (Alchian, 1965), but the main focus is on competition for less than perfectly protected property rights (Barzel, 1997; Hirshleifer, 2001). As has been argued, such competition is important in determining the value that a resource can create and the value that the owner of the resource can appropriate. Analysis of how transaction costs influence competition over less than perfectly protected property rights, therefore, provides important contributions to the RBV with respect to understanding the conditions for sustained competitive advantage.

Peteraf (1993) has elegantly summarized much of the RBV into "four cornerstones of competitive advantage" that represent necessary conditions for sustained competitive advantage. In the following, these cornerstones serve as a means of more precisely identifying the contribution of PRE to furthering the RBV analysis of sustained competitive advantage.

Heterogeneity The RBV analysis of heterogeneity stresses inherent efficiencies of resources (Peteraf, 1993) and differences in resource complementarities (Denrell et al., 2003; Dierickx & Cool, 1989) as sources of firm heterogeneity. The PRE contributes a further dimension to the understanding of resource and firm heterogeneity by stressing that resources are composed of property rights to attributes. Property rights are typically bundled in resources due to the cost of exchanging individual property rights and the cost of protecting these rights. Resources are therefore outcomes of processes of economizing with transaction costs, and they vary in their efficiencies and potential for being combined in a complementary manner because they encompass different attributes.

By implication, resource heterogeneity fluctuates with innovations in sales practices, contracting practices, and other transaction cost-reducing technologies as well as with changes in legislation and norms. Firms thus have heterogeneous resources not just because of different initial resource endowments and subsequent learning effects, but also because they are subject to different regulations (i.e., constraints on use rights), and face different costs of protecting and utilizing resource attributes in production or exchange. When resources change with changes in transaction costs and legislation, so do the values they can create and that the firm can appropriate.

Barriers to ex ante competition The RBV stresses informational barriers to *ex ante* competition as a necessary condition for rents (Barney, 1986; Makadok & Barney, 2001). The PRE adds a different mechanism by which discrepancies between value and price may be established on strategic factor markets.

In the PRE, resource heterogeneity is caused by variations in the types and levels of valued attributes that resources embody. Such variation requires costly measurement (Barzel, 1997). Costly measurement implies that not all attributes are priced and that some strategizers may be able to capture value from non-priced attributes (Barzel, 1982). Strategizers on strategic factor markets that have low costs of capture because of superior efficiencies in searching and/or low opportunity costs for searches will be able to purchase resources—bundles of property rights over attributes, including the highly valued one—at prices below their value to the seller. This indicates that rent capture is connected to transaction costs (in this case, measurement costs), and that variation in the attributes of resources is a dimension that is important for understanding rent capture.

Barriers to ex post competition The general lesson from both the RBV and the PRE is that barriers to *ex post* competition are a necessary condition for the sustainability of competitive advantage. However, *ex post* competition may be conceptualized more broadly in the PRE than in the RBV. In the RBV, *ex post* competition is mainly a matter of competitive imitation and resource substitution (Barney, 1991).

The PRE adds that this by pointing to *ex post* capture in many other forms, such as moral hazard, adverse selection and hold up, and to other as elements of competition over less than perfectly protected attributes (see further Barzel, 1997). All of these capture activities can be subsumed under *ex post* competition for unprotected property rights over resource attributes. The value that the focal firm can appropriate from its resources is determined by the capture activities of other firms, the firm's bargaining power *vis-à-vis* suppliers, buyers and employees, and the capture of employees. If capture activities are fully foreseen before the resource is acquired, their impact on value creation and appropriation will be taken into account in the reservation price of buyers (or sellers). However, if estimating capture creates transaction costs and if there is unforeseen changes in transaction costs, value erosion will occur. Thus, when forming expectations about future resource values (Makadok & Barney, 2001), managers should also assess the capture potential that is associated with these resources.

The PRE can expand the avenue of research pursued in the RBV with respect to identifying resource characteristics that may limit *ex post* competition and contribute to sustained competitive advantage. In the RBV, causal ambiguity is often seen as a characteristic that supports sustainability (Lippman & Rumelt, 1982). However, from an PRE perspective, causal ambiguity may also make it costly to write contracts and enforce performance norms. Causal ambiguity may therefore reduce value creation and appropriation. This creates a tradeoff between protecting against imitation and protecting against other forms of capture.

Immobility While the RBV suggest that resource immobility is preferable from the firm's point of view, transaction costs may imply that immobility leads to under-investment. Granting resources outside options, such as giving patent rights to research scientists, may increase their bargaining power (make them more "mobile") *and* improve their investment incentives (Hart, 1995). This points to a tradeoff in certain situations between immobility and value creation, and therefore refines the analysis of immobility as a condition of sustained competitive advantage.

Conclusions

Coase's (1992: 716) insight that "… a large part of what we think of as economic activity is designed to accomplish what high transaction costs would otherwise prevent" has important implications for the RBV of strategic management. Incorporating transaction costs more fully into the RBV introduces new sources of value dissipation and erosion, and therefore a better understanding of the value creation potential of resources. As suggested by the Coase quotation, strategizers will actively seek to reduce the value dissipation and erosion caused by transaction costs. In essence, strategic opportunities arise from reducing transaction costs.

The purpose of this chapter has been to clarify how transaction costs create opportunities for value creation and appropriation. The argument used the PRE lens to develop a more refined understanding of the notion of a resource and of the determinants of resource value. Resources can usefully be conceptualized as bundles of property rights to resource attributes, where the relevant property rights are subject to potential capture and therefore need protection. Capture and protection are costly activities that directly and indirectly diminish created value relative to the maximum value attainable if transaction costs are zero. Thus, transaction costs, along with conditions of scarcity, demand, imitability, and sustainability, influence resource value. Strategizers have incentives to create value by reducing dissipation, taking into account that such reduction is also costly and provided they can appropriate a sufficient part of the created value. The reduction of dissipation takes various forms, including the pricing and protecting of resource attributes. These insights refine the RBV analysis of sustained competitive advantage by adding new dimensions to notions of resource heterogeneity, *ex post* and *ex ante* competition, and immobility (Peteraf, 1993).

Taken together, all this indicates that the PRE can significantly contribute to the RBV analysis of strategic opportunities. According to Lippman and Rumelt (2003a: 1080), the RBV predicts that firms will focus their energies on developing "… complex 'homegrown' resources … Yet a glance at corporate reality reveals that much more effort is devoted to combinations, deals, mergers, acquisition, joint venture and the like." They therefore suggest that more attention be devoted to such resource assembly, particularly under conditions of super-modularity. We concur, but argue that created value is not only constrained by knowledge of resource complementarities, but also by the transaction costs that attend the exchange aspects of "combinations, deals, mergers, acquisition, joint venture and the like." Even more generally, the PRE indicates that resource value is significantly influenced by transaction costs, and that strategic opportunities arise when the transaction costs of defining, protecting, capturing, and exchanging property rights change.

In this chapter, we have primarily examined how notions of transaction costs and property rights refine the understanding of resources and value creation and appropriation. Further theoretical development may proceed along at least three paths. The first begins with the observations that resource value is threatened by all sorts of capture efforts, and that competitive activities may be understood in terms of the capture and protection of property rights (Barzel, 1994). PRE may help to integrate the RBV with strategic theory that is more concerned with the external environment (Porter, 1980). A second path of development is to address those resources that create value because they economize with transaction costs, such as specific ways of sorting goods (e.g., in the retail and in such markets as fruit and vegetables; Foss, 1996), sorting customers (e.g., credit classes in banking), contracting, and the use of private orderings (Barzel, 1997; Williamson, 1996). While such resources have been neglected in the RBV (but see Chi, 1994; Mahoney, 1992), they are important sources of value creation. A third path is to connect with the significant amount of the literature on technological spillovers (externalities) (Shy, 2001). This literature highlights the central tradeoff between limiting spillovers to other firms (i.e., protect property rights to knowledge resources) *versus* sharing with these firms (and under what circumstances), and the links this tradeoff has to R&D investment incentives. While PRE can frame the central ideas of the spillover literature, the latter adds an emphasis on competitive dynamics that is not included in this paper's approach.

Formal modeling of RBV-PRE models The development of mathematical RBV models has recently begun (e.g., Makadok, 2003). The PRE draws attention to many variables, margins, and tradeoffs (Foss and Foss, 2001). Formal modeling is necessary to fully clarify the potentials and limits of this approach with respect to furthering the RBV. One attractive line of research is to apply and develop formal game theory models on contests over insecure (i.e., costly to protect) property rights, and how such contests dissipate value (e.g., Hirshleifer, 2001; Skaperdas, 1994). In these treatments, strategizers are explicitly modeled as having (in our terminology) capture and protection functions, and differential endowments of resources to spend on these activities. Predictions as to which player will win in contests over insecure property rights, how much value will be dissipated, and how alternative kinds of social organization may reduce such dissipation can therefore be made. The relevance of this formal, game theoretical approach to the non-formal approach developed in the present paper is that the formal apparatus can give precise meanings to such key PRE concepts such as capture, protection, and dissipation. The formal approach can also model the interaction between strategizers that have differential resource endowments and differential capture and protection efficiencies (i.e., differential capabilities in these activities).

Empirical research One avenue of empirical research in the RBV has been to pursue the implications for performance of different resource types. For example, Miller and Shamsie (1996) discuss the sources and sustainability of competitive advantage in the Hollywood film studios in terms of "property" and "knowledge-based" resources. Empirical RBV work can accommodate the unique insights that PRE brings to the RBV by incorporating in such exercises the "transaction cost resources" mentioned above—forms of contracting, sorting systems, credit rationing systems, and other practices that firms adopt to protect resource value. While there is reason to suspect that such resources are very important in a number of industries, extremely little is empirically known about their contribution to sustained competitive advantage. Work on this issue may utilize operationalizations and measures that have been developed in the empirical literature on transaction cost economics (David & Han, 2004).

References

Akerlof, G. (1970). The market for lemons: Quality uncertainty and the market mechanism. *Quarterly Journal of Economics, 84*, 488–500.

Alchian, A. A. (1965 [1977]). Some economics of property rights. In A. A. Alchian (Ed.), *Economic forces at work*. Liberty Press.

Barney, J. B. (1986). Strategic factor markets. *Management Science, 32*, 1231–1241.

Barney, J. B. (1991). Firm resources and sustained competitive advantage. *Journal of Management, 17*, 99–120.

Barzel, Y. (1982). Measurement costs and the organization of markets. *Journal of Law and Economics, 25*, 27–48.

Barzel, Y. (1994). The capture of wealth by monopolists and the protection of property rights. *International Review of Law and Economics, 14*, 393–409.

Barzel, Y. (1997). *Economic analysis of property rights* (2nd ed.). Cambridge University Press.

Chi, T. (1994). Trading in strategic resources: Necessary conditions, transaction cost problems, and choice of governance structures. *Strategic Management Journal, 15*, 271–290.

Coase, R. (1992). The institutional structure of production. *American Economic Review, 82*, 713–719.

Coase, R. H. (1960). The problem of social cost. *Journal of Law and Economics, 3*, 1–44.

Coase, R. H. (1988). *Notes on the problem of social cost, in the firm, the market, and the law*. University of Chicago Press.

David, R. J., & Han, S. (2004). A systematic assessment of the empirical support for transaction cost economics. *Strategic Management Journal, 25*, 39–58.

Demsetz, H. (1973). Industry structure, market rivalry, and public policy. *The Journal of Law and Economics, 16*, 1–9.

Denrell, J., Fang, C., & Winter, S. G. (2003). The economics of strategic opportunity. *Strategic Management Journal, 24*, 977–990.

Dierickx, I., & Cool, K. (1989). Asset stock accumulation and the sustainability of competitive advantage. *Management Science, 35*, 1504–1511.

Elzinga, K., & Mills, D. (2001). Independent service organizations and economic efficiency. *Economic Inquiry, 39*, 549–560.

Foss, K. (1996). Transaction costs and technological development: The case of the Danish fruit and vegetable industry. *Research Policy, 25*, 531–547.

Foss, N. J. (2003). The strategic management and transaction cost nexus: Past debates, central questions, and future research possibilities. *Strategic Organization, 1*, 139–169.

Grant, R. (1991). The resource-based theory of competitive advantage: Implications for strategy formulation. *California Management Review, 33*, 114–136.

Hart, O. (1995). *Firms, contracts, and financial structure*. The Clarendon Press.

Hirshleifer, J. (2001). *The dark side of the force: Economic foundations of conflict theory*. Cambridge University Press.

Kenney, R. W., & Klein, B. (1983). The economics of block booking. *Journal of Law and Economics, 26*, 497–540.

Lippman, S. A., & Rumelt, R. P. (1982). Uncertain imitability: An analysis of inter-firm efficiency under competition. *Bell Journal of Economics, 13*, 418–438.

Lippman, S. A., & Rumelt, R. P. (2003a). A bargaining perspective on resource advantage. *Strategic Management Journal, 24*, 1069–1086.

Lippman, S. A., & Rumelt, R. P. (2003b). The payments perspective: Microfoundations of resource analysis. *Strategic Management Journal, 24*, 903–927.

Mahoney, J. T. (1992). Organizational economics within the conversation of strategic management. *Advances in Strategic Management, 8*, 103–155.

Makadok, R. (2003). Doing the right thing and knowing the right thing to do: Why the whole is greater than the sum of the parts. *Strategic Management Journal, 24*, 1043–1055.

Makadok, R., & Barney, J. B. (2001). Strategic factor market intelligence: An application of information economics to strategy formulation and competitor intelligence. *Management Science, 47*, 1621–1638.

Milgrom, P., & Roberts, J. (1992). *Economics, organization, and management*. Prentice-Hall.

Miller, D., & Shamsie, J. (1996). The resource-based view of the firm in two environments: The Hollywood Film Studios from 1936 to 1965. *Academy of Management Journal, 39*, 519–543.

Penrose, E. T. (1959). *The theory of the growth of the firm*. Oxford University Press.

Peteraf, M. A. (1993). The cornerstones of competitive advantage: A resource-based view. *Strategic Management Journal, 14*, 179–191.

Porter, M. E. (1980). *Competitive strategy*. Free Press.

Reed, R., & DeFilippi, R. (1990). Causal ambiguity, barriers to imitation and sustainable competitive advantage. *Academy of Management Review, 15*, 88–102.

Shy, O. (2001). *The economics of network industries*. Cambridge University Press.

Skaperdas, S. (1994). Contest success functions. *Journal of Economic Theory, 7*, 283–290.

Teece, D. J. (1986). Profiting from technological innovation. *Research Policy, 15*, 285–305.

Tirole, J. (1988). *The theory of industrial organization*. MIT Press.

Von Hippel, E. (1988). *The sources of innovation*. Cambridge University Press.

Wernerfelt, B. (1984). A resource-based theory of the firm. *Strategic Management Journal, 5*, 171–180.

Williamson, O. E. (1996). *The mechanisms of governance*. Oxford University Press.

6
Strategizing and Positioning

Concepts of property rights and transaction costs have been central to the development of strategic management theory for more than two decades (Foss & Foss, 2005; Kim & Mahoney, 2005; Mahoney & Pandian, 1992; Peteraf, 1993; Rumelt et al., 1991). Theorizing about property rights and transaction costs has generated key insights into organizational form and firm boundaries (Williamson, 1985) and the acquisition, building, and organization of resource bundles (Barney, 1986; Dierickx & Cool, 1989; Williamson, 1996). Such theorizing has also recently been brought to bear on organizational heterogeneity (Argyres et al., 2012), which has traditionally been explained by knowledge-based and capability theories (but see already Oi, 1983). Argyres and Zenger (2012), for example, argue that differential firm capabilities result from deploying specific investments that are optimally organized by the hierarchical governance structures prescribed by transaction cost economics.

However, one central area of strategic management theory has remained largely immune to property rights and transaction cost reasoning, namely the part of competitive strategy that focuses on defending positioning by creating barriers to entry and mobility and by engaging in pricing tactics that allow for "monopoly" profits (Porter,

K. Foss and N. J. Foss, *Economic Microfoundations of Strategic Management*,
https://doi.org/10.1007/978-3-031-12910-0_6

1980, 1981). Traditionally, the analysis of this aspect of competitive strategy has been founded on the "market power" framework of industrial organization economics (Porter, 1981). However, the effectiveness of strategies based on market power depends on characteristics of property rights and transaction costs. Like Argyres and Zenger (2012), we show that novel insight derives from applying such theorizing to a new and unusual field of application. We specifically argue that (a) competitive strategy research already implicitly relies on property rights and transaction cost notions; (b) making these notions explicit generates novel theoretical insight; and (c) important links between the efficiency and the market power branches of competitive strategy theory, traditionally seen as very different (Williamson, 1991), can be illuminated by focusing on property rights and transaction costs.

Our starting point is Coase's (1960) discussion of property-rights solutions to externality problems, which was discussed in Chapter 3. Coase defined transaction costs as the costs of finding trading partners, writing contracts, and enforcing agreements and argued that in the absence of these costs, all gains from trade will be exploited (i.e., the Coase Theorem). These kinds of transaction costs are implicit in the notion of competitive imperfections or "frictions" that are highlighted in competitive strategy (Barney, 1986; Porter, 1980), such as barriers to entry and exit between industries or strategic groups (intra-industry clusters of similar firms).

Such imperfections imply unexploited gains from trade (Demsetz, 1964) and generate what inefficiencies. PRE argues that all such inefficiencies are the result of transaction costs that prevent individuals from reaching agreements for mutual gain. Coase (1960) famously illustrated this argument with examples of property disputes (e.g., a rancher's cattle straying onto a farmer's land, damaging the crops, and asking why the farmer and rancher could not come to a mutual agreement to assign the land to its highest valued use, splitting the joint gains). However, Coase's model and the broader PRE insight that all inefficiencies are rooted in transaction costs apply to *any* situation over which individuals can bargain—including the situations treated in competitive strategy research.

A starting point for much research on competitive strategy is the monopoly model of economics textbooks (Porter, 1981): A producer, facing an inelastic demand curve above the "competitive" equilibrium price, raises the price above this competitive level, increasing its own profit while reducing "consumer surplus" (typically by more than its own profits increase, leading to a "deadweight loss"). Research based on this reasoning (e.g., Porter, 1980) advises firms to seek out markets in which they can create and exercise such monopoly power. Of course, positioning theory assumes a large set of buyers, each of whom is too small, independently, to bargain with the seller, and not a single large buyer (like Walmart); in Porter's (1980) terminology, buyer power must be low. However, even if there are many small buyers, the ability to maintain prices above marginal costs, generating deadweight losses, assumes a kind of bargaining failure. If the loss of consumer surplus from monopoly pricing is really greater than the monopoly gains, then consumers can jointly offer the monopolist a payment that is equal to or greater than the monopoly profit, but less than the value of the lost consumer surplus—a win-win situation. Or, they can stall monopolization attempts by refusing to contract with a would-be monopolize and instead contract with other incumbent managers and potential entrants.

This reasoning generalizes: If the transaction costs of entering into and enforcing contracts are sufficiently low, any party that is harmed by monopolization (consumers, suppliers, rivals, complementors) can form coalitions that mobilize what Galbraith (1952) called "countervailing power" against a would-be monopolizing firm. In fact, if transaction costs are zero, then entry barriers or possession of unique resources are not enough to generate and sustain monopoly profits if they generate deadweight losses, because deadweight losses can always be bargained away. When transaction costs are positive—that is, in the real world—the kind of coalitions described above are less likely, to the benefit of the focal firm. Some of these transaction costs may be exogenous from the point of view of the focal firm; however, other transaction costs are partly endogenous: Strategizing managers may seek to increase transaction costs while trading partners, actual and potential rivals, and other market participants may seek to reduce them or try to contract around them. However, a central contribution of our paper is that countervailing power is present only when consumers and other parties that are harmed by monopolization face transaction costs that are sufficiently low. In other words, effective competitive strategy requires managers to identify, interpret, and influence the transaction costs that affect their ability to capture value by building, protecting, and exercising market-power.

Building from the PRE foundations outlined in Chapter 3 (Alchian, 1965; Barzel, 1994, 1997; Coase, 1960; Demsetz, 1967), in this chapter we systematically unfold the argument that transaction costs are among the determinants of the focal firm's opportunities for building, protecting, and exercising market power and show how it leads to new thinking on strategic positioning. Thus, whereas the emphasis in the previous chapter was on the resource side of strategy, in this chapter we focus on market positioning. Extant research has identified factors like information costs, scale advantages, concentration, and sources of entry and mobility barriers such as irreversible investments (e.g., Caves & Porter, 1977; Porter, 1980; Scherer, 1980; Tirole, 1988), and competitive strategy research has built on these and other deviations from the model of perfectly competitive markets in making sense of market power and profits (Rumelt et al., 1991). We add the important, but in key respects overlooked, variable of transaction costs to extant theory and explore its implications.

Theoretical Foundations

Property Rights and Transaction Costs

Ideas about property rights and transaction costs have been important in the development of competitive strategy research. In particular, Williamson's brand of transaction cost economics has been highly influential, leading to insight in the transaction costs of organizing and governing the resource combinations that form the foundation of strategies, or sourcing services that are necessary for those strategies (Argyres & Zenger, 2012; Chi, 1994; Ghosh & John, 1999; Nickerson, 2003; Nickerson et al., 2001). Property rights have been treated as antecedents of firms' boundary choices (e.g., Oxley, 1999; Teece, 1986) and of firm-level value creation (Foss & Foss, 2005) and appropriation (Kim & Mahoney, 2005).

Here, we focus on a new area of application for transaction costs and property rights notions, namely how they influence strategy choices in *product markets.* Our arguments build directly on PRE, which suggests that economic activity revolves around the definition, protection, capture, and exchange of property rights (Alchian, 1965; Barzel, 1997; Umbeck, 1981). We define property rights as the de facto rights to exercise choices over productive resources and to keep the income derived from their use (Alchian, 1965). As explained in Chapter 3, at the heart of the (economic) notion of property right is effective *control*, defined as "an individual's net valuation, in expected terms, of the ability to directly consume the services of the asset, or to consume it indirectly through exchange" (Barzel, 1994: 394). Note that this approach defines property rights in terms of the income that owners can actually appropriate, not the income to which they are legally entitled; a reduction in asset value caused by actions of competitors is a reduction of de facto property rights, but of course not a violation of the owner's legal rights.

Transaction costs, in this conception, are not simply the "frictions" associated with trading—finding trading partners, writing contracts, hiring lawyers—but are more generally the resources spent on delineating, protecting, and capturing de facto property rights (Barzel, 1997; Eggertson, 1990), whether they are being traded or not. Allen (2000) usefully distinguishes between a narrow, trade-based notion of transaction costs, which he calls the "neoclassical approach," and a broader, property-rights view (see also Benham & Benham, 2010). In the neoclassical view, transaction costs are analogous to search costs or transportation costs, and can be analyzed as any other cost of doing business. They are important for strategy only in the sense that they are costs like any other cost of engaging in trade, the size of which could give one or another firm a competitive advantage.

The property rights conception of transaction costs has far more important implications for strategic management, however. In particular, property rights understood as de facto control over resources have direct links to value creation and capture. For a firm to execute a competitive strategy, it must hold use rights that allow it to exercise choices over goods and services (i.e., resources and the services that they yield). For a firm to benefit from the strategy, it must have rights to a specific and/or residual amount of the value created from its strategy (Alchian & Demsetz, 1972). These income rights are not legally enforced but depend on the firm's ability to deter others from capturing a share of the value created from the assets it owns (e.g., by establishing barriers to entry and exit). Defining and enforcing property rights is in this sense a critical element of strategy. Transaction costs shape how property rights are delineated, the extent to which they can be captured, and how effectively they are enforced (Coase, 1960); as such, transaction costs and property rights are "two sides of the same coin" (Allen, 2000: 897; see also Cheung, 1969: 16), Transaction costs, in turn, influence the value that firms can create and appropriate. Unfortunately, transaction costs and property rights are ignored in large parts of competitive strategy research.

Implicit Property Rights and Transaction Costs in Competitive Strategy Research

At the core of research in the positioning branch of competitive strategy (Porter, 1980) is building, exercising, and protecting market power (Hoskisson et al., 1999; Makadok, 2011; McGee & Howard Thomas, 1986; McWilliams & Smart, 1993; Porter, 1981; Williamson, 1991). This conceptualization is directly based on industrial economics (Ghemawat, 1997; Porter, 1981; Shapiro, 1989). The basic thrust of decades of industrial economics research may be viewed in terms of the familiar Structure-Conduct-Performance causal sequence, with the addition of a feedback loop from conduct to structure which captures strategic entry barriers built through signals of commitment (Ghemawat, 1991; Sutton, 1991; Tirole, 1988). Although industrial economics research and its strategic management applications usually make no reference to property rights and transaction costs, the basic model include numerous implicit assumptions about property rights and transaction costs that drive the conclusions about how managers can build and sustain profitable positions against the forces that determine industry competition.

Market structure is conventionally defined as the number of producers in an industry, the market share of the largest producers, the nature of cost, the extent of product differentiation, and so on. For example, if the production technology in an industry is characterized by significant economies of scale, we expect only a few large firms with high market shares. Influenced by industrial organization economics (e.g., Scherer, 1980), virtually all empirical studies of firm performance in the strategic management literature include some measures of market structure as explanatory or control variables (firm size, market share, market growth, industry concentration ratios or Herfindahl indexes; important examples include Christensen & Montgomery, 1981; Cool & Dierickx, 1993; Hansen & Wernerfelt, 1989).

Of course, this is a static, not dynamic argument, and market structure is less important in models of "Austrian" or Schumpeterian competition (High, 1984; Sidak & Teece, 2009; Young et al., 1996). Even in the static case, however, this argument implicitly relies on transaction costs. Arguments about scale are based on indivisibilities of assets like factories and machines. As these fixed assets are used more intensively, unit production costs fall. However, if producers can costlessly rent out their excess capacity, then firm size and market share are indeterminate. As Teece (1980, 1982) points out, firm size is determined by the cost of transacting over asset use, not the technical production costs. Thus, important elements of market structure (firm size, market shares, entry barriers based in cost advantages), even absent dynamic considerations, are only fully determinate in the presence of transaction costs.

The *conduct* part of the causal sequence concerns (incumbent) firms' behaviors aimed at protecting rent streams *vis-à-vis* other incumbents as well as entrants. Conduct is assumed to be influenced by market structure. Specifically, the less concentrated the structure, the more intense the rivalry. In property rights terms, each firm's costs of protecting its residual income rights rise as the number of other firms in the industry increases. However, industrial organization scholars have long argued that firms' conduct (e.g., their protective actions) may decisively influence structure (Scherer, 1980). For example, firms can make sunk cost investments in R&D and advertising to protect their market positions and thereby their income rights by means of entry deterrence (Cowling & Mueller, 1978; Sutton, 1991).

In the market power approach, *performance* is said to follow from structure and conduct (cf. Scherer, 1980; Vickers, 1995). Thus, highly concentrated market structures allow for a kind of conduct (i.e., setting price substantially above cost, leading to deadweight losses) that causes inefficient outcomes. Moreover, further inefficiency is caused by managers' (allegedly) unproductive investments as they scramble for profitable positions that they cannot all occupy (Cowling & Mueller, 1978; Littlechild, 1981; Posner, 1975). This argument, too, implicitly relies on transaction costs. Thus, if transaction costs are zero all inefficiencies will immediately be traded away (Barzel, 1997; Coase, 1960). The mechanism is that buyers will gain from trading with those firms seeking to exercise market power, persuading them to expand their production in return for a share of the created value, generating mutual gains (Demsetz, 1964). As before, the costs of bargaining, negotiating agreements, and enforcing those agreements lurk in the background of familiar arguments about market behavior.

The above suggests that positioning strategies based on building, exercising, and protecting market power (i.e., strategies associated with unexploited potential gains from trade) cannot exist without positive transaction costs. The other side of the coin is that the scope for positioning that involves the exercise of market power is limited by transaction costs, and that making sense of strategies based on market power entails taking transaction costs into account. This strongly suggest making those transaction costs explicit and factoring them into analysis of competitive strategy.

Enter Transaction Costs

The zero transaction cost setting that underlies many economics models implies—unrealistically—that individuals have full information, and that the delineation, exchange, and enforcement of property rights is costless (Barzel, 1997; Coase, 1988). In this setting, firms can perfectly appropriate value streams, as the zero transaction cost assumption means that value streams are contractually guaranteed and perfectly enforced. Thus, there is no value capture in the form of resource-consuming attempts to take effective control over value without compensating those who stand to lose from such attempts. Thus, the very notion of rivalry that results in one firm acquiring market share at the expense of competitors is strictly limited in this world.

However, when transaction costs are positive, some income streams are imperfectly protected, and control over these streams emerges endogenously as managers attempt to capture value by, for example, competitively lowering prices (Tirole, 1988), introducing new types of products and services (D'Aveni, 1994; Salop & Scheffman, 1983), or lobbying in favor of their own product standards (Capron & Chatain, 2008). In turn, managers respond to capture attempts by lobbying for legal or administrative trade and entry barriers (Capron & Chatain, 2008), deploying secrecy strategies (Teece, 1986), engaging in entry deterrence (Salop, 1979; Sutton, 1991), and so on. Consider Napster and similar peer-to-peer sharing programs which seriously began to threaten the recording industry about a decade ago. Prior to the emergence of these, the recording industry did not engage in litigation to protect copyrighted songs because they (rightly) expected that other players did not have the technology and resources to contest their rights (i.e., capture their created value) on a large scale. The advent of sharing technologies reduced consumers' costs of capturing control over songs dramatically, which made it worthwhile for the recording industry to begin defending its residual income from copyrighted songs, both through the courts (to protect their *de jure* rights) and by investing in copy protection technology.

How much parties will invest in protecting these rights depends on the size of the contested created value (Skaperdas, 1992), the effort and other resources that managers are willing to spend on capturing and protecting value (Skaperdas, 1992; Skaperdas & Syropoulos, 1995), the capture and protection capabilities of firms (Hirshleifer, 1989), and managers' expectations regarding these. The resulting equilibrium may be upset, for example, by changing capture capabilities. In the case of the recording industry, the existing equilibrium was upset by consumers' use of peer-to-peer sharing programs. As an example of a protection capability, Apple has enjoyed particular advantages with respect to collaboration with the "big four" music companies (Universal, Sony BMG, Warner and EMI) because of the superior digital rights management system (FairPlay) that it uses on its online iTunes store. Indeed, many of the dynamics in the software and music industries revolve around competitive investments in such protection capabilities (Penenberg, 2005).

Given the transaction costs of protecting property rights, managers will only protect those rights they deem worthy of protection (i.e., the most valuable ones, net of protection costs), leaving others imperfectly protected and making them available to those who spend resources on their capture. Firms adjust their protection efforts to the capture attempts they expect from non-owners, and vice versa. As initially pointed out by Demsetz (1967), rights to residual income streams emerge endogenously, depending on marginal benefits and costs, as a result of the strategizing actions of the relevant parties. The question then is how this overall property rights insight unfolds in the more specific context of competitive positioning. The fundamental idea that we elaborate in the following is that property rights and transaction cost refine the understanding of the constraints and the opportunities that strategizing firms face with respect to building, exercising, and protecting market power.

Property Rights and Transaction Cost Conditions of Successful Strategizing

Extended Rivalry and Countervailing Power

Strategic management theory and the industrial economics it partly builds on have a tendency to focus on major oligopolistic firms that possess significant bargaining and market power (Williamson, 1991). Thus, theory often focuses on the strategizing actions of such firms *vis-á-vis* rival incumbents. It is recognized that firms also engage in strategic activities relative to buyers, suppliers, and partners—what Porter (1980: 6) calls "extended rivalry"—but these are often treated as passive victims of the exercise of power (Barzel, 1994) and the main action lies with the horizontal interaction between incumbents and entrants.

However, often "victims" are far from passive, and can actively seek protection against firms that seek to exercise their market or bargaining power. Galbraith (1952: 119) formulated the notion of "countervailing power" to capture this phenomenon:

> The fact that a monopolist enjoys a measure of monopoly, and is reaping a mea-sure of monopoly return as a result, means that there is an inducement to those firms from whom he buys or those to whom he sells to develop the power with which they can defend themselves against exploitation. It means also that there is a reward for them, in the form of a share of the gains of their opponents' market power, if they are able to do so. In this way the existence of market power creates an incentive to the organization of another position of power that neutralizes it.

Galbraith (1952) had in mind formal organizations such as labor unions, chain stores, and buyers' cooperatives which, he argued, emerged in response to increasing concentration among large manufacturers. Critics pointed out that Galbraith did not specify carefully the conditions under which such countervailing institutions would emerge (Stigler, 1954; Whitney, 1953). In particular, for our purposes, he ignored the transaction costs of coalition formation. Moreover, he did not discuss many of the mechanisms by which potential targets of monopolization (or, more generally, the exercise of market power of a dominant firm) can resist such monopolization.

Our perspective suggests that whether parties that potentially are harmed by market power can defend themselves against attempts to capture their income streams is fundamentally a transaction cost issue. Specifically, we argue that transaction costs influence whether potential targets can successfully engage in *contracting* that protects them against the building, exploitation, and protection of market power. The other side of the coin is that strategies of building, exercising, and protecting market power require the presence of transaction costs that hinder "protective action," for example, by making it too costly to form coalitions among potential targets of the exercise of market power. This suggests an important point: For the purpose of understanding whether or not specific positioning strategies will be successful, it is necessary to examine the transaction costs faced by the relevant firms and individuals, alone or in groups.

While this overall idea is new to positioning research (and strategic management in general), the idea that contracting defines property rights and as such influence the actions of individuals is a familiar and important idea in new institutional economics. For example, similar ideas are emphasized in transaction cost economics, and its familiar notion that individuals seek to avoid "hold up" by building safeguards into contracts, making contracts more complete, etc.—all depending on the transaction costs of such actions (Williamson, 1996). Likewise, the idea that small buyers facing a monopoly seller, or small sellers facing a monopsony buyer, can organize themselves into a bargaining cooperative, is familiar to agricultural economists (Cook, 1993; Hueth & Marcoul, 2003; Ladd, 1974), However, the new institutional economics and agricultural cooperatives literatures apply this idea primarily to vertical relations and not to the competitive interaction at the core of strategy research.

To lend structure to the understanding of how property rights and transaction costs are relevant in the context of understanding positioning strategies and moves, we treat the building, protection, and exploitation of market power as three distinct phases of strategizing in a context of extended rivalry and building on the above property rights model. In actuality, these are often more or less simultaneous processes—for example, a firm that builds market power may have to simultaneously protect its efforts by fending off rivals—but a sequential representation eases the discussion.

Building Market Power

A long tradition in industrial economics has routinely interpreted the arrangements and behaviors of firms, particularly large firms, as means to build market power. Many of these arguments have been discredited (often by bringing in transaction cost considerations); for example, the view that vertical integration is an instrument to build market power has little credibility in modern research (Williamson, 1985). Also, horizontal mergers may often be justified on grounds of realizing economies of scale (Farrell & Shapiro, 1990). However, competitive actions such as engaging in price wars and "predating" on rivals or even investing in R&D or advertising in order to "raise rivals' costs" (Salop & Scheffman, 1983) are often seen as instruments to build market power. Yet, such arguments neglect transaction costs.

Consider so-called predatory pricing (Joskow & Klevorick, 1979), a particularly dramatic approach to creating (or expanding) market power by changing the structure of an industry (cf. Demsetz, 1982; Snyder, 1996; Weigelt & Camerer, 1988). A predating firm eliminates competitors ("preys," in the terminology of this literature) by setting prices below its marginal costs (which are at least as low as those of the preys), raising industry concentration. It then raises prices toward the monopoly level after the elimination has been completed. In terms of property rights theory, this particular competitive strategy aims at, first, capturing incumbent firms' property rights to the value that they create, and, second, capturing a larger share of buyers' property rights to the value that is created in transactions with the predator. Thus, the predating firm seeks to redefine the delineation of property rights in its own favor at the expense of competitors, buyers, and suppliers.

The success of predatory pricing, as a lasting way of building market power, requires that the predator is able to avoid new entry into the industry once it raises prices to monopoly level. In other words, it must be able to protect the property rights it captures. A long, protracted debate in industrial economics led to the conclusion that, unless the predator is protected by natural entry barriers, there must be sufficient uncertainty among industry incumbent and other potential entrants about whether the predator is one who benefits from giving way to re-entrance or from engaging in retaliation. Industry incumbents will rationally choose not to re-capture market shares from predator if they have sufficiently strong expectations that entry is deterred. The predating firm must establish a reputation for retaliation against entry, which it can do by fiercely protecting its property rights in the early stages after successful predation—even though it is in its short run interest to share markets with an entrant (Kreps & Wilson, 1982). In later stages potential entrants, who are unsure of the actual pay-off to the predator, takes the initial protective action as an indication that the predator benefits by defending its property rights even in the long run, and that it therefore does not pay to attempt entering the industry.

This analysis overlooks, however, that those who are harmed by the actions of the predator also include buyers and suppliers, who suffer when the predating monopolist reduces production levels and raises prices after having driven out rivals. Thus, forward-looking buyers who anticipate the exercise of market power by the predator may seek to protect their property rights to created value. For example, if the transaction costs of coordinating a coalition among buyers and negotiating and enforcing a contract with incumbent firms are low, a sufficiently large number of buyers may strike a long-term supply contract with incumbents who would otherwise be subject to predation. Such a contract, that stipulates the prevailing price as the one under which future transactions will take place, protect the incumbent from suffering losses as the predator reduce prices in order to increase its market share (Barzel, 1994).

This argument is sensitive to whether buyers understand the true type of the predator (e.g., do they see it as a would-be predator or as a firm that can drastically lower prices because of cost advantages?). However, given that a sufficient number of buyers hold the correct understanding of the predator's type the argument stands that with transaction costs contracting can stall attempts at building market power through predatory pricing. In fact, it generalizes beyond the context of predatory pricing. For example, if transaction costs are sufficiently low and buyers correctly expect a would-be monopolizer to invest in R&D and advertising in order to raise rivals' costs, drive them out of the industry, and then take advantage of its market power, buyers can thwart attempts at monopolizing by contracting or simply refuse to deal with the would-be monopolizer. More generally, attempts to build market power by raising rivals' costs can succeed only under particular configurations of transaction costs. Consider, for example, a firm that signs exclusive-dealing contracts with low-cost suppliers, forcing its rivals to buy from less efficient, higher-cost suppliers (Salop & Scheffman, 1983; Scheffman & Higgins, 2003). To increase the focal firm's profits, the increase in rivals' production costs must exceed not only the surplus the firm transfers to its exclusive suppliers, but also the transaction costs of negotiating and enforcing the exclusive-dealing contract.

Our reasoning suggests the following proposition:

Proposition 1 *Competitive strategies aimed at building market power through predatory pricing, horizontal merger, or raising rivals' costs are feasible only if transaction costs are high enough to prevent buyers, suppliers, rivals, and customers from exercising countervailing power by bargaining.*

Protecting Market Power

Firms seek to protect their market power so as to keep earning rents from monopolistic positions. The protection of market power is traditionally seen as a matter of maintaining entry and exit barriers (Conner, 1999; Porter, 1980, 1981; Shapiro, 1989). A general implication of the vast literature on strategic entry barriers (Salop, 1979; Salop & Scheffman, 1983; Tirole, 1988) is that sunk cost investments (i.e., exit barriers) are necessary to sustain entry barriers in equilibrium (Porter, 1980). The paradigmatic case is excess capacity, which simultaneously represents sunk costs and signals a credible threat (Tirole, 1988). In the absence of sunk costs, markets are said to be "perfectly contestable" (Baumol et al., 1982). In competitive strategy research, this line of thinking is reflected in work on "commitment strategies" (e.g., Ghemawat, 1991, 1997) which stresses that advantages may stem from inflexibility: threats to deter entry become more credible when the firm issuing the threat has visibly reduced its flexibility, notably by undertaking sunk cost investments.

In antitrust cases, contestability has been one of the favorite defenses of incumbent dominant firms. Microsoft argued that its dominance of the market for PC operating systems did not translate into market power in that market because of the presence of potential competition (United States v. Microsoft, Civil Case 98-1232, 1998). Because such arguments involve unobserved, latent actions and because most dominant firms have sunk substantial costs in their markets, they may be easy to dismiss.

However, our property rights approach suggests that the presence of sunk costs is not sufficient for protecting market power. Specifically, transaction costs are low, then potential entrants can offer long-term contracts to buyers before actually entering the market, the length of the contract being equal to the economic life of the sunk investment. This makes the industry contestable, as the contracts protect entrants from post-entry competition, at least until their sunk costs are recovered (cf. Innes & Sexton, 1994), and they will therefore enter the industry. In fact, the mere threat of such contracts offers can be sufficient to discipline incumbents (Stefanadis, 2003). Potential entrants may also offer contingent contracts, similar to the airline industry practice in which the major producers sign buyers on a contingent basis before actually committing to produce a new aircraft (Spulber, 2004: 326). From the entrants' perspective, the attraction of this strategy is that it reduces the risk associated with sunk cost investments. Entrants have an incentive to engage in this practice when the transaction costs of negotiating with customers and policing and enforcing agreements with them are low relative to the costs of entry.

In short, a firm's ability to protect its market power is limited by the costs of entering into and enforcing contracts between potential entrants, buyers and/or suppliers that cover sunk cost investments. Thus, if transaction costs are low, markets are contestable, even in the presence of sunk costs. This suggests the following proposition:

Proposition 2 *Competitive strategies aimed at protecting market power through sunk cost investments are feasible only if transaction costs are high enough to prevent potential entrants from exercising countervailing power by contracting with buyers.*

Exercising Market Power

Conventionally, a firm is said to exercise market power when it can limit industry output and raise prices, giving rise to a profit/monopoly rent (Scherer, 1980). The firm directly captures value from buyers, and because output is lowered, the firm also demands fewer inputs, imposing a loss on suppliers. Industrial organization economists have long realized that a small number of incumbent firms in an industry is not, in itself, sufficient for these firms to be able to exercise market power. For example, in a homogenous good duopoly, Bertrand (price) competition results in the equilibrium price established at the competitive level, leaving the entire surplus to the buyer. Specifically, those consumers or buyers who value the product or service higher than the price stand to gain. Under competitive conditions, they effectively hold secure income rights to such surpluses.

However, incumbents may engage in coordinated actions related to such factors as pricing or territorial restrictions, or they can merge, thereby capturing parts of the buyers' surplus by restricting supply (Farrell & Shapiro, 1990). We have already discussed the transaction cost conditions under which such actions are feasible. However, even if transaction costs are such that a collusive arrangement or a merger can be established, the would-be monopolizers may still not be capable of *exercising* market power.

Consider the case of a perfectly price-discriminating monopolist. Such a firm can charge each buyer the maximum price she is willing to pay. Economic reasoning shows that this leads to same level of production as under fully competitive conditions (Varian, 1989), but, in offering these differentiated prices, the price-discriminating monopolist captures all the "consumer surplus" (i.e., the value each buyer gets beyond the price she pays for a product or service). Usually, the analysis stops at this stage. However, if the transaction costs of creating secondary markets are sufficiently low, consumers can arbitrage (among themselves) and bargain (with the would-be discriminating monopolist) to protect property rights to "their" surplus (Varian, 1989).

Proposition 3 *Competitive strategies aimed at exercising market power through pricing above cost are feasible only if transaction costs are high enough to prevent buyers from exercise countervailing power by trading among themselves and bargaining with the seller.*

Summary

As the above examples show, the success of standard competitive strategies aimed at building and protecting positions depends on a host of assumptions—typically hidden—about the transaction costs of building, protecting, and exercising market power. When these transaction costs are low, the usual market power arguments do not hold, and attempts to achieve superior financial returns through this kind of positioning will be unsuccessful. Our arguments so far are summarized in the two first columns of Table 6.1, while the following section elaborates on the third column, that is, more specific implications for competitive strategy.

Table 6.1 Transaction costs and their implications for competitive strategy

Type of transaction cost	Actions affected by transaction costs	Implication for competitive strategy
Costs of delineating property rights *Definition*: Costs of establishing effective control over the use of resources, including the ability to control income streams (Coase, 1960; Demsetz, 1967)	• Buyers forming a cooperative or other contractual coalition to bargain with monopolist (or sellers and monopsonist) • Sellers forming bargaining coalitions (e.g., advertising and other attempts to recruit potential users [e.g., Linux])	• If these transaction costs are high and exogenous (e.g., because of low population density, inefficient communication technology, poorly functioning court system), then don't worry about countervailing actions, and pursue monopolization aggressively
Costs of exchanging property rights *Definition*: Costs of establishing and executing agreements for exchanging rights to control resources and income streams, including costs of bargaining and measuring (Cheung, 1969; Coase, 1937)	• Buyers offering side payments to incumbent monopolist to expand output and reduce price (same with sellers and a monopsonist) • Buyers or suppliers bargaining with one or more incumbent to avoid harm from entry barriers, predatory pricing, etc.	• Implement resale price maintenance, exclusive-dealing contracts [e.g., DeBeers], customer, and territorial restrictions (e.g., slotting contracts) to prevent agreements between consumers and rival firms

(continued)

Table 6.1 (continued)

Type of transaction cost	Actions affected by transaction costs	Implication for competitive strategy
Costs of protecting or capturing property rights *Definition:* Costs of taking control over resources and/or income streams without compensating trading partners (e.g., opportunistic holdup; Williamson, 1985); the costs of protecting against such capture (Barzel, 1997)	• Sellers preventing copying or theft through legal action or technological innovation (e.g., record industry's response to file sharing) • Potential entrants in markets with sunk costs offering long-term contracts to buyers which allow them to recover their own sunk investments	• When countervailing power is possible, – try to increase transaction costs of coalition formation – Offer price concessions to certain buyers to prevent them from forming coalitions; bundling and loyalty discounts – Offer non-transferrable warrantees to discourage resale among buyers • Lobby for certification and quality standards that cannot be provided in secondary markets • Signal willingness and ability to engage in product differentiation • Offer frequent product updates • Produce "vaporware"

Note that even if transaction costs are low enough to allow countervailing power can be exercised, there is no guarantee that the countervailing power will succeed in stymying attempts to build, protect, or exercise market power. Strategizing firms can often resist countervailing power. One example is the case of Webhouse Club (a licensee of Priceline.com) that aimed at being a power broker for individual consumers *vis-a-vis* major consumer companies, in effect, building countervailing power on behalf of consumers Webhouse Club failed, because P&G, Kimberly-Clark, etc., did not want to play Webhouse's game, that is, they refused to offer major discounts and no major consumer company was willing to "undercut" its rivals (InternetNews.com, 2000)

Differentiating Transaction Costs: Implications for Strategic Positioning

So far we have treated transaction costs generically, as the costs of delineating (Barzel, 1997; Demsetz, 1967), exchanging (Alchian, 1965; Coase, 1960), capturing and enforcing (Barzel, 1997) property rights. But we can add additional insight by distinguishing more specifically among these and other categories of transaction costs. For example, a particular type of transaction cost may be central to delineating property rights, but less important for exchanging these rights. Some transaction costs are, from the perspective of the strategizing firm, exogenous—for example, costs of recording property titles, costs related to the efficacy of the legal system, costs of negotiation that are determined by characteristics of consumers, and so on. Other transaction costs can be increased or decreased by the strategizing firm and are endogenous to value creation and capture. This section of the paper explores some of these distinctions in greater detail, focusing as before on the effect of transaction costs on competitive strategies based on market power.

Transaction Costs of Delineating, Exchanging, and Protecting Property Rights

As noted above, transaction costs can be defined as the costs of delineating, exchanging, and protecting (or capturing) property rights. Each aspect of dealing with property rights involves its own set of transaction costs. Consider each in turn.

Delineating property rights Economics and strategy research often begins with the analysis of exchange—as Williamson (1975: 20) famously put it, "in the beginning, there were markets"—but exchange presupposes clearly delineated property rights. If the transaction costs of defining property rights are sufficiently high, then no trade can take place.

Delineation requires systems of measuring, parceling, recording, and certifying (Benham & Benham, 2010; Wallis & North, 1986). For many commercial transactions, these transaction costs are trivial. In other cases, however, the costs of delineation may be prohibitive. A well-studied example is the lack of well-developed markets for water rights in places like the American West (Libecap, 2005). Despite substantial potential gains from trade by moving water from places where water is plentiful (typically agricultural areas) to urban and suburban areas (where water is more scarce), such transfers rarely take place because water rights are difficult to define, and hence not easily exchanged. In contrast, mineral rights are more easily defined—minerals, unlike groundwater, stay in one place stationary—and markets for mineral rights function smoothly (Libecap, 1978, 1989). Another example concerns rights to radio spectrum, a problem analyzed by Coase (1959) in the study that inspired his later article on property rights (Coase, 1960), as we saw in Chapter 3. Spectrum is easy to define, and spectrum rights have been recorded by regulatory agencies since the advent of commercial radio in the 1920s, and frequently exchanged among providers. In the 1990s, as the value of spectrum rose dramatically following the development of digital wireless telephony, large blocks of spectrum were auctioned by US and European regulators to wireless providers, generating hundreds of millions of dollars in revenues (Cramton, 2002). The feasibility of such auctions, and the gains from trade from spectrum transactions among firms, depends on the costs of defining and exchanging legal titles to spectrum. Fortunately for the industry, and for wireless consumers, these transaction costs are typically low.

Exchanging property rights Even when property rights are clearly delineated, they may be costly to trade. The costs of exchanging well-defined property rights—the "neoclassical" approach transaction costs described above—are familiar to researchers in economics and in strategy. These are the costs emphasized in Coase's "Nature of the Firm" (1937)—the costs of locating trading partners, discovering the relevant prices, and writing contracts. As Coase famously argued, when these costs are low, any configuration of products and services can be produced by networks of independent contractors, without any need for hierarchical firms. In strategizing terms, attempts to build, protect, and exercise market power assume that customers or suppliers who are harmed by such strategies cannot organize their own, alternative production structures as networks of independent contractors. Indeed, firm-specific advantages from unique capabilities can only exist when these advantages cannot be duplicated by independent agents contracting in the market.

The software industry provides a useful illustration. Software production involves large fixed costs and low incremental costs, a cost structure typically identified with substantial entry barriers, thus generating substantial profits for incumbent producers. Microsoft, for example, enjoyed a near-monopoly on desktop operating systems throughout the 1980s and the web browser in the 1990s. But the rise of free, open-source products like Linux and Mozilla Firefox has introduced significant competition in these markets (Lerner & Schankerman, 2010). These products come from diffused networks of independent producers (programmers) collaborating to produce a rival product to the dominant firm's product. In our terminology, the transaction costs of exchanging property rights—to computer code, labor, reputations—were sufficiently low to allow the dominant firm's customers to collaborate to produce a competing product. Open-source code can be exchanged freely via the web and email, programming labor is easily traded, and reputations for programming skill (which typically translate into higher long-term wages) can be communicated at low-cost (Lerner & Tirole, 2002). Hence Microsoft's attempt to exercise market power by offering a unique, differentiated product was partially thwarted by the low transaction costs of collaboration among buyers.

Of course, Microsoft's Windows is still the dominant platform in desktop operating systems (though its market share in "personal computing devices" is shrinking rapidly, if one includes smartphones, tablets, gaming consoles, and the like). But Microsoft's Internet Explorer has lost much of its market share to Mozilla Firefox and Google's Chrome browser. Had Microsoft been more aware of the potential competition from open-source projects, it might have done more to improve the early versions of Internet Explorer.

Protecting property rights Another set of transaction costs revolves around the protection, enforcement, and capture of property rights.

These include the costs of taking control over resources or income streams without compensating trading partners, as in the costs of "holdup" associated with transaction cost economics (TCE) (Williamson, 1985). The costs of hierarchical governance, in the TCE sense, can be interpreted as the parallel costs of preventing holdup—i.e., the costs of protecting the property rights to relationship-specific investments against opportunistic behavior by others. More generally, resources devoted to policing—monitoring, inspecting, enforcing—emphasized by Barzel (1997) can be interpreted as the transaction costs of protecting property rights.

The Transaction Cost Environment and Transaction Cost Arrangements

Just as the literature on the new institutional economics literature (Klein, 2000; Williamson, 2000) distinguishes between the "institutional environment" (rules of the game such as property and contract law, political institutions, norms, and culture that are beyond the decision-maker's immediate control) and "institutional arrangements" (contracts and firms that are established by decision-makers to achieve particular goals), it is useful here to distinguish between the firm's *transaction cost environment* and its *transaction cost arrangements*. The transaction cost environment, analogous to the institutional environment as that term is used in the new institutional economics, embodies transaction costs that are outside the firm's control. These are determined by the legal system and property-rights regime, which affect the cost of forming coalitions and contracting around a particular entry barrier; information technology, density, and other factors affecting communications cost; and social norms and other attitudes toward cooperation or collective action. To the extent that these are specific to particular industries or markets—relating to the information structure of the market, asymmetries among buyers or suppliers, and the like—managers wishing to build and sustain market power will tend to seek these industries or markets, other things equal.

In some markets, managers may be able to affect transaction costs through transaction cost–increasing arrangements, as in the examples in the previous section. The ability of crafting such arrangements is an important firm-level capability, and variation in this capability may help explain within-industry differences in firm performance. Like other capabilities, it is tacit, may be manifest in routines, and is likely subject to learning. Just as contracting is a learned capability (Argyres & Mayer, 2007; Mayer & Argyres, 2004), making it more difficult for others to contract has the same characteristics. More generally, strategizing firms must carefully consider the means available to buyers and suppliers wishing to undermine incumbents' attempts to build and leverage market power, such as what Williamson (1996) calls "farsighted contracting," coalition formation, subsidizing alternative suppliers, and engaging in political action (Capron & Chatain, 2008). In other words, the impact of market power on a strategizing firm's residual income depends on the firm's transaction cost environment and its ability to craft effective transaction cost arrangements.

Hence managers that better understand, and know how to react to, their transaction cost environment will capture more value than managers that do not take the transaction cost environment into account when formulating strategy. In terms of competitive advantage, this suggests that firm performance depends not only on the usual competitive conditions, but also on the firm's transaction cost environment, and its ability to design transaction cost arrangements that prevent other firms from contracting around competitive imperfections. In other words, an important source of competitive advantage is the ability to characterize the transaction cost environment and to create appropriate transaction cost arrangements.

Exogenous transaction costs: the transaction cost environment First, consider cases such in which transaction costs affecting buyers, suppliers, rivals, and perhaps regulators can be taken as exogenous. In this situation, if the firm's strategy is based on exercising market power, it will seek market settings (industries, partnerships, geographically distinct markets or market segments, etc.) in which transaction costs are sufficiently high to prevent other parties from contracting around the inefficiency leading to market power. An example is markets in which the parties that are harmed by market power are independent, anonymous, geographically dispersed consumers, for whom organization into coalitions is impractical. The available communications technology, as well as the ability of courts or private arbitrators to enforce contracts and adjudicate disputes in the focal industry, are also relevant.

Proposition 4 *If transaction costs are perceived to be exogenous, firms will seek industries in which the transaction costs of organizing production are perceived to be low, and the transaction costs of exercising countervailing power are perceived to be high.*

Note here the role of perception; transaction cost conditions are difficult to measure and, like production costs (Buchanan, 1969), production plans (Kirzner, 1966; Zander, 2007), and resource attributes (Foss et al., 2007), subjectively perceived and interpreted. The ability to perceive transaction cost conditions—both levels and stickiness—should vary by firm and by industry and may be interpreted as a firm capability, like the ability to craft transaction cost arrangements discussed above. Where the transaction costs of organizing production are perceived to be low, while the transaction cost of exercising countervailing power are perceived to be high, firms will try to exploit competitive frictions, as in the usual strategic positioning approach, while remaining cognizant of opportunities for buyers, suppliers, and rivals to contract around the relevant frictions, comparing the resulting benefits to the transaction costs of exploiting such opportunities. If the costs of organizing countervailing power are perceived to be low, then firms will tend to avoid the pursuit of profit by building, protecting, and exploiting market power.

Proposition 5 *If the transaction costs of exercising countervailing power in a particular industry are perceived to be high, then firms will attempt to build, protect, and exercise market power.*

These arguments assume that strategizing managers have some way of measuring the characteristics of the transaction cost environment facing the firm. Transaction cost conditions cannot, unfortunately, be captured by simple metrics like concentration ratios, Herfindahl indexes, industry Betas, and the like. Indeed, as noted above, perceptions and interpretations of transaction cost conditions may be subjective and tacit. Moreover, managers will tend not to attach a number to the magnitude of transaction costs in one industry or another, but to compare (perceived) transaction costs across market settings, and choose those settings where the transaction costs of production are relatively low, and the transaction costs of exercising countervailing power are relatively high.

However, we know a great deal about the costs of organizing more generally, from the new institutional economics literature on the institutional environment (Brousseau & Glachant, 2008; Ménard & Shirley, 2005) and the large collective action literature stemming from Olson (1965), Libecap (1989), Ostrom (1990), and other sources. To some degree, the transaction cost environment may be rooted in economy wide, institutional factors such as the characteristics of the legal system, the degree to which the political environment protects property rights, social norms about contracting, and the like. Within countries, industry-level factors such as concentration; the size of the expected gains from establishing, exercising, and sustaining market power; the distribution of the expected gains from contracting around inefficiencies; the heterogeneity within potential coalitions; the information structure of the market; and network density among buyers, suppliers, and rivals. Ultimately, identifying and measuring transaction costs is a matter of entrepreneurial judgment.

Endogenous transaction costs: transaction cost arrangements The more interesting cases are those in which market participants can shape the transaction costs of particular markets. In particular, the costs to buyers, suppliers, and entrants of engaging in countervailing actions are not necessarily exogenous. Both the strategizing firm and its potential prey can take actions to influence transaction costs. For example, in the software industry firms may engage in frequent product updates, and they may offer complementary services, in part, because such services make it costly for users to switch to other standards. Specifically, long-term contracting may be rendered unattractive under these circumstances because (1) there is no guarantee that incumbent competitors or potential entrants can match the upgrading efforts of the would-be monopolizer, and (2) even if they can, renegotiating contracts is costly. Therefore, frequent product upgrades may not only serve to preserve market power by means of "non-price predation" (i.e., raising rivals' costs, cf. Salop & Scheffman, 1983), but also by making it more costly for prey to enter into contracts that may counteract the exercise of market power. "Vaporware"—announcing an upcoming product, whether it exists or not, which effectively freezes competitors' sales, can also be interpreted as an example of strategizing aimed at blockading contracting between buyers and competitors (Shapiro & Varian, 1999: 275). Other tactics may also be applied, such as signaling the ability to engage in product differentiation and price discrimination, because these factors make it more costly for users to organize and protect against the would-be monopolizer's capture.

Various forms of downstream vertical restraints such as resale price maintenance, exclusive-dealing contracts, territorial and customer restrictions, and the like can be interpreted as attempts to make it more difficult for downstream partners to transact with the strategizing firm's rivals. Consider the slotting or "shelf-space" contracts analyzed by Klein (2003) and Klein and Wright (2007). Slotting contracts are payments from manufacturers to retailers for promotional retail shelf space, including product displays and in-store advertisements, designed to highlight the manufacturer's product over that of competing products. Such arrangements have often been subject to antitrust scrutiny—indeed, Microsoft's contracts with computer manufacturers to control what icons appear on the Windows desktop, a major issue in the US case against Microsoft in the 1990s, can be interpreted as a kind of slotting contract, one that was largely successful before being restricted by law. In the case of grocery retailing, however, where slotting contracts are most prominent, retailers have responded by continuing to stock the products of the most popular manufacturers, who do not pay for shelf space, charging higher slotting fees, and increasing the total amount of shelf space (Klein & Wright, 2007). In this industry, while some manufacturers benefit from paying for shelf space, it has not been an effective way of preventing retailers from stocking their preferred portfolio of products.

Firms may also attempt to raise transaction costs in secondary markets by restricting the value of product guarantees, so that they apply only if original components are used or if products are bought in approved stores. Lobbying for certification and quality standards, and making the provision of complementary services or insurance dependent on such standards, is another means of using transaction costs to raise the costs of establishing secondary markets. Innes and Sexton (1993) model the "divide and conquer" pricing strategies that monopolists can use to raise costs for buyers forming coalitions. A basic assumption is that there are economies of size in coalition building. (Although Innes and Sexton do not include transaction cost considerations, such economies may derive from initial fixed transaction costs being spread out over a larger set of coalition participants). Price-discriminating monopolists can exploit this feature by offering some buyers price concessions sufficient to deter them from joining large coalitions. The remaining buyers cannot then achieve a coalition size that is sufficient to make the rejection of the monopolist's price attractive.

As these examples show, when transaction costs are low, strategizing firms will try to make them higher, to prevent buyers, suppliers, and rivals from forming coalitions to contract around the relevant frictions. This might involve reducing the benefits to buyers or suppliers of contracting around the friction (for instance, by offering frequent updates, as discussed earlier). Another approach is to try to facilitate price discrimination by increasing the cost of organizing resale markets (e.g., by imposing warrantee restrictions on resold products). This reasoning leads to the following proposition:

Proposition 6 *If the transaction costs of exercising countervailing power in a particular industry are perceived to be low, firms will attempt to make these transaction costs higher or exit the industry.*

Edlin and Farrell's (2011) notion of "improving coalitions" can be helpful here. Focusing on antitrust policy, they define the competitive process as one of "buyers and sellers exercising [the freedom to trade] and forming improving coalitions (i.e., new configurations of trading partners). In a highly competitive market a seller who does not give its customers good deals will find that rivals offer better deals to attract these customers. The process of firms fighting over customers and offering them better and better deals raises consumers' utility skyward." They argue that antitrust authorities should intervene to stop firms' attempts to limit the formation of such coalitions. But this is exactly what, in the property rights perspective, strategizing firms attempt to do, namely to keep buyers, suppliers, or rivals interacting with the focal firm under its preferred terms (i.e., in the original coalition). Firms may attempt to do this via bundling, loyalty pricing, and vertical restraints. Edlin and Farrell (2011) recognize that such practices can sometimes increase efficiency (as emphasized by Williamson, 1975, 1985), even while increasing the focal firm's share of any joint surplus. The implication for strategizers is to consider all possible improving coalitions and take actions to reduce the chances of them being formed.

More generally, our argument is that a manager evaluates the transaction cost environment and makes decisions about transaction cost arrangements, other things equal. The exact tradeoffs between investments in increasing transaction costs relative to other investments, along with the number of potential countervailing actions that can be thwarted, the number of coalitions that must be considered, and so on, depend on firm and industry characteristics.

The De Beers diamond company provides an intriguing example (Lenk & Ghemawat, 1990). In the 1930s, De Beers executive Ernest Oppenheimer established the De Beers Central Selling Organization (CSO) to coordinate world production, distribution, and marketing of rough and cut diamonds. The CSO sorts and grades diamonds, coordinates prices through explicit agreements and stockpiling, supervises physical product flows, monitors wholesale and retail activity, coordinates marketing, and more. To maintain the viability of the CSO, De Beers works hard to prevent producers and resellers from forming their own coalitions that would disintermediate the CSO, by signing long-term, exclusive-dealing contracts with producers; punishing defectors with unfavorable terms; and using its geopolitical influence, particularly in Africa, to maintain producers' dependence on the CSO. In short, De

Beers takes advantage of transaction costs that hinder independent coordination among its suppliers, buyers, and rivals, and uses its political influence (and the information gathered from its extensive intelligence-gathering operations) to keep these transaction costs high. Assembling and announcing alliances, as when Sun gathered allies in support of Java and took out full-page advertisements listing the companies behind the Java coalition, may a such purposes. In consumer markets, several studies have illustrated that consumer groups, such as the National Consumer League and the Public Citizen in the United States, can wield power against dominant firms or would-be dominant firms. For example, Shaffer and Ostas (2001) and Castellblanch (2003) found that consumer groups were able to thwart lobbying efforts of larger firms by establishing coalitions with smaller ones. In other examples, the specific actions considered, coalitions deterred, and so on will be different.

Even if transaction costs for entering contracts or establishing coalitions are very high, the gains from countervailing actions may be so large that they offset the transaction costs. The larger the potential inefficiencies from output restrictions, the greater the potential gain from countervailing actions. Therefore, a second piece of advice for firms that wish to build market power is to consider the losses arising from inefficiencies that are imposed on other parties, and the possibility that avoiding these losses may outweigh the costs of organizing countervailing actions.

Moderating effects The transaction cost environment and transaction cost arrangements are not independent. Unlike the case with other aspects of the institutional environment such as administrative law, regulation, bureaucratic rules, and the like, there is little firms can do, in the short run, to influence the transaction cost environment of a particular industry or market setting. So the transaction cost environment is reasonably treated as exogenous. But it can also have a moderating effect on the firm's ability to craft transaction cost arrangements, conditioning the degree to which attempts to capture value by creating and exercising market power increase the focal firm's performance.

Concluding Discussion

Contribution to Theory

Our primary purpose has been to establish that property rights and transaction costs ideas can inform the foundations of competitive strategy by showing how value capture by means of building, protecting, and exercising market power is limited by transaction costs, and that this fundamental idea leads to new insight thus, in the absence of transaction costs, many phenomena of central interest to competitive strategy simply evaporate, because there is no scope for strategies based on market power under these conditions. While differential rents may exist even when transaction costs are zero (as resources may still differ in terms of efficiency) and strategizers may have different bargaining powers (i.e., value appropriation may differ across strategizers), competitive strategy understood as building, protecting, and exercising market power does not apply. The presence of transaction costs is, therefore, a necessary condition for market power-based competitive strategies.

The transaction costs that are first and foremost the costs of organizing coalitions among the potential or actual targets of the exercise of market power and the costs of contracting (including the enforcement of such contracts) with alternative suppliers. When such costs are low, sufficient countervailing power may be mobilized to stall attempts at building, exercising, and protecting market power. Therefore, strategies of building market power through, for example, mergers and predatory pricing, exercising market power through price discrimination, and protecting market power by means of entry deterrence are all infused with the hidden assumption that transaction costs are sufficiently high to prevent the mobilization of countervailing power.

Our arguments also suggest that property rights are endogenous. In particular, de facto control of income streams emerges from competitive interaction and bargaining in processes of extended rivalry and dependent on the matrix of transaction costs that players face. In contrast, strategic management theory typically focuses on situations in which property rights to an advantage and, perhaps, the rent stream it may yield, are effectively already held (cf. Lippman & Rumelt,

2003a, 2003b). Thus, the resource-based view (Barney, 1991) focuses on strategic resources (i.e., those that are valuable, rare, and difficult to imitate and substitute). It therefore takes the process of delineating and protecting property rights to these resources for granted. Property rights to economic rents may sometimes be owned to begin with (e.g., particular human skills), but advantages and market power usually need to be established. In other words, the relevant property rights need to be delineated. Strategy researchers seldom examine such processes, perhaps because of the equilibrium assumptions that dominate economics-based competitive strategy research. In contrast, our approach directs attention to these processes.

Strategizing and Economizing

The distinction between "strategizing" and "economizing" approaches to strategy was introduced by Williamson (1991). By "strategizing," Williamson means theory that emphasizes market power as a key construct and is fundamentally rooted in industrial economics (Bain, 1956; Tirole, 1988). By "economizing," Williamson means those approaches—such as the resource-based view (Barney, 1991), the dynamic capabilities approach (Teece et al., 1997), and transaction cost economics (Williamson, 1985)—that stress efficiency rather than market power as the main source of competitive advantage. Williamson claims that "between economizing and strategizing, economizing is much the more fundamental" (Williamson, 1991: 75). This is so, because strategizing is "relevant principally to firms that possess market power—which are a small fraction of the total," whereas economizing is universally relevant, and strategizing will not succeed if it is "seriously flawed in first-order economizing respects" (idem.).

Strategizing theories have predominantly conceptualized strategic actions as aimed at increasing profits by restricting supply (Porter, 1981). Conversely, most economizing theories have not considered market power. However, we suggest that key insights in the strategizing approach related to building, exercising, and protecting market power make strong implicit assumptions about property rights and transaction costs—constructs that are usually associated with the economizing perspective. Our claim is not that efficiency-based explanations for superior returns are identical to explanations based on market power, as the key theoretical mechanisms are different (Demsetz, 1982; Makadok, 2011; Williamson, 1991). We do not argue that earning superior returns from serving consumers in a superior way or having lower (production, transport, and transaction) costs is *reducible* to earning superior returns from being able to restrict supply, or vice versa. However, there is a fundamental transaction cost dimension to strategizing. Specifically, transaction costs limit the opportunities for building, exercising, and protecting market power in an industry. In this sense, then, "strategizing" is based on "economizing."

A few contributions have combined ideas from these two branches of strategy theory (notably, Nickerson & van den Bergh, 1999; Nickerson et al., 2001; Nickerson, 2003), starting from Williamsonian TCE (Williamson, 1985). As a result, the emphasis is on how market position (Porter, 1980) is supported by governance structure choices; in other words, both strategic interaction and governance costs are related to governance structure. Although we also emphasize transaction costs and contractual choices, the thrust of our analysis is very different. Thus, we analyze transaction costs in the context of interaction (i.e., "extended rivalry"), specifically how transaction costs influence whether market participants can contract around competitive imperfections, how this influences the feasibility of strategic actions, and what managers can do in terms of influencing transaction costs to their advantage. Ours is very different from existing attempts at aligning transaction cost ideas and competitive strategy.

Future Research

Although this article builds on established and huge theoretical bodies of thought in property rights theory and strategic management, the ideas we proffer are unconventional and cast in the verbal mode. A number of our arguments therefore need further investigation, extension, and formalization.

Concerning the need to look more deeply into theoretical mechanisms, the basic idea we have proffered is that transaction costs constrain the opportunities for strategizing in an industry. These transaction costs include the costs of forming coalitions among those who are harmed by the exercise of market power, the costs of searching for and entering into agreements with potential suppliers, and the costs of monitoring agreements. This is a considerable set of transaction costs that may have different antecedents, move in different directions, etc. Among those antecedents are capabilities with respect to capturing and protecting property rights (Barzel, 1982; Hubbard, 2000), for example, the copy protection capabilities of the recording companies. Such capabilities are differentially allocated across strategizers (Foss & Foss, 2005; Hirshleifer, 1989; Umbeck, 1981), and, like other capabilities, change over time over as a result of learning. Thus, the ability to understand and react to the transaction cost environment may be a function of experience, as is the case with contract design (Argyres & Mayer, 2007; Mayer & Argyres, 2004). Relatedly, strategizers form expectations regarding other strategizers' capture and protection activities (Umbeck, 1981) and base actions on these expectations. Thus, we have pointed to farsighted contracting (Williamson, 1996) as important to understanding how coalitions of parties that potentially are harmed by monopolization can block the creation of market power. However, would-be monopolists may also exercise foresight and anticipate the creation of countervailing power. Who will win out depends on who exercises the best foresight first, establishing a link to the entrepreneurship literature (Foss & Klein, 2012).

Understanding such dynamic interaction over time is a highly important undertaking. Formal modeling may be useful in working out the specific relationships and interactions described in this article. One possible approach is to draw on formal non-cooperative game theory models to examine contests over insecure (i.e., costly to protect) property rights and how such contests dissipate value (e.g., Hirshleifer, 1989; Skaperdas, 1992; Skaperdas & Syropoulos, 1995). In this research stream, strategizers are explicitly modeled as having capture and protection functions, as well as different endowments of resources to spend on these activities. Predictions as to which player will win in contests over insecure property rights, how much value will be dissipated and how alternative kinds of social organization may reduce such dissipation can therefore be made. An alternative approach could be to link up with the emerging stream of cooperative game theory work in strategic management (Brandenburger & Stuart, 1996; Lippman & Rumelt, 2003a; MacDonald & Ryall, 2004). This modeling approach may be particularly attractive because it, like this article, considers both cooperation and competition, and, hence, includes agreements and coalitions. However, cooperative game theory does not consider the transaction costs of establishing and enforcing coalitions, or any other transaction costs for that matter. However, Brandenburger and Stuart (1996) indicate that such "frictions" could be important, and a recent contribution (Chatain & Zemsky, 2011: 2) explicitly models frictions. Specifically, sellers are constrained with respect to which buyers they can contract with, which affects rivalry and overall market efficiency. This is clearly related to our emphasis on (potential) contracting among those who may fall victim to the exercise of market power. Moreover, an outcome of their analysis is that one cannot, in general, analyze the impact of competitive forces independently, which is also a key conclusion in this paper.

Asmussen et al. (2021), which may be seen as a formal counterpart to the analysis in this chapter, examines the interaction of strategizing and economizing in driving competitive outcomes. As in this chapter, the focus is on coalitions. Thus, coalitions are formed to create more value (i.e., economizing—e.g., by means of vertical ties) and to strengthen competitive positions (i.e., strategizing). Asmussen et al. (2021) derive several unintuitive results. For example, economizing may backfire. The intuition is that the creation of additional may induce other players to strategize more aggressively. Creating countervailing power along the lines sketched in this chapter may be a double-edged sword: While it allows the coalition to appropriate more value, coalition formation can hurt coalitions members by reducing economizing investments.

Finally, we have proceeded as if the space of competitive strategy research is only occupied by economizing and strategizing approaches. In actually, important insights have also emerged from, for example, cognitive (e.g., Bogner & Barr, 2000), behavioral (Chen et al., 2002), Schumpeterian (D'Aveni, 1994; Jacobson, 1992), and competitive dynamics (MacGrath et al., 1998; Smith et al., 2001), that is, perspectives that do not fall neatly into either the economizing or the strategizing branch. However, these are highly complementary to our property rights and transaction costs perspectives. For example, Schumpeterian innovations in information and communication technology may influence the costs of contracting in ways that are detrimental to the attempts of dominant firms to monopolize an industry. Or, competitive dynamics may ensue because firms misjudge the abilities rivals and consumers to stall monopolization attempts. The behavioral economics and behavioral strategy literatures also provide insight why Coasean bargaining fails independently of transaction costs. Thus, the "endowment effect" drives a wedge between offered prices and valuations that may cause a bargaining impasse (e.g., Heath et al., 1993; Kahneman et al., 1990). We do not consider these psychological issues here, but clearly they may inform our arguments about the critical role of transaction costs. However, uncovering the many implicit transaction costs of extant strategic positioning research is logically prior to such extensions and has been the key purpose of this chapter.

References

Alchian, A. A. (1965 [1977]). Some economics of property rights. In A. A. Alchian, *Economic forces at work*. Liberty Press.

Alchian, A. A., & Demsetz, H. (1972). Production, information costs, and economic organization. *American Economic Review, 62*, 772–795.

Allen, D. W. (2000). Transaction costs. In B. Bouckeart & G. De Geest (Eds.), *Encyclopedia of law and economics* (pp. 893–926). Edward Elgar.

Argyres, N. S., & Mayer, K. J. (2007). Contract design as a firm capability: An integration of learning and transaction cost perspectives. *Academy of Management Review, 32*, 1060–1077.

Argyres, N., & Zenger, T. (2012). Capabilities, transaction costs and firm boundaries. *Organization Science, 23*, 1643–1657.

Argyres, N., Felin, T., Foss, N. J., & Zenger, T. (2012). The organizational economics of organizational capability: A research agenda. *Organization Science, 23*, 1213–1226.

Asmussen, C. G., Foss, K., Foss, N. J., & Klein, P. G. (2021). Economizing and strategizing: How coalitions and transaction costs shape value creation and appropriation. *Strategic Management Journal, 42*, 413–434.

Bain, J. S. (1956). *Barriers to new competition: Their character and consequences in manufacturing industries*. Harvard University Press.

Barney, J. B. (1986). Strategic factor markets: Expectations, luck, and business strategy. *Management Science, 32*, 1231–1241.

Barney, J. B. (1991). Firm resources and sustained competitive advantage. *Journal of Management, 17*, 99–120.

Barzel, Y. (1982). Measurement costs and the organization of markets. *Journal of Law and Economics, 25*, 27–48.

Barzel, Y. (1994). The capture of wealth by monopolists and the protection of property rights. *International Review of Law and Economics, 14*, 393–409.

Barzel, Y. (1997). *Economic analysis of property rights* (2nd ed.). Cambridge University Press.

Baumol, W. J., Panzar, J. C., & Willig, R. D. (1982). *Contestable markets and the theory of industry structure*. Harcourt Brace Jovanovich.

Benham, A., & Benham, L. (2010). The costs of exchange. In P. G. Klein & M. E. Sykuta (Eds.), *The Elgar companion to transaction cost economics* (pp. 107–119). Edward Elgar.

Bogner, W. C., & Barr, P. S. (2000). Making sense in hypercompetitive environments: A cognitive explanation for the persistence of high velocity competition. *Organization Science, 11*, 212–226.

Brandenburger, A. M., & Stuart, H. W. (1996). Value-based business strategy. *Journal of Economics and Management Strategy, 5*, 5–24.

Brousseau, E., & Glachant, J.-M. (Eds.). (2008). *New institutional economics: A guidebook*. Cambridge University Press.

Buchanan, J. M. (1969). *Cost and choice: An inquiry in economic theory*. Markham.

Capron, L., & Chatain, O. (2008). Competitors' resource-oriented strategies: Acting upon competitors' resources through interventions in factor markets and political markets. *Academy of Management Review, 33*, 97–121.

Castellblanch, R. (2003). Challenging pharmaceutical industry political power in Maine and Vermont. *Journal of Health Politics, Policy and Law, 28*, 109–132.

Caves, R., & Porter, M. E. (1977). From entry barriers to mobility barriers. *Quarterly Journal of Economics, 91*, 241–262.

Chatain, O., & Zemsky, P. (2011). Value creation and value capture with frictions. *Strategic Management Journal, 32*, 1206–1231.

Chen, M.-J., Venkataraman, S., Black, S. S., & MacMillan, I. C. (2002). The role of irreversibilities in competitive interaction: Behavioral considerations from organization theory. *Managerial and Decision Economics, 23*, 187–207.

Cheung, S. N. S. (1969). Transaction costs, risk aversion, and the choice of contractual arrangements. *Journal of Law and Economics, 12*, 23–42.

Chi, T. (1994). Trading in strategic resources: Necessary conditions, transaction cost problems, and choice of governance structures. *Strategic Management Journal, 15*, 271–290.

Christensen, H. K., & Montgomery, C. A. (1981). Corporate economic performance: Diversification strategy versus market structure. *Strategic Management Journal, 2*, 327–343.

Coase, R. H. (1937). The nature of the firm. *Economica NS4*, 386–405.

Coase, R. H. (1959). The federal communications commission. *Journal of Law & Economics, 2*, 1–40.

Coase, R. H. (1960). The problem of social cost. *Journal of Law and Economics, 3*, 1–44.

Coase, R. H. (1988). *Notes on the problem of social cost, in the firm, the market, and the law*. University of Chicago Press.

Conner, T. (1999). Customer-oriented and Market-led: A Matter of Balance. *Strategic Management Journal, 20*, 1157–1163.

Cook, M. L. (1993). Cooperatives and group action. In D. Padberg (Ed.), *Food and agricultural marketing issues for the 21st century* (pp. 154–169). Texas A&M University Press.

Cool, K., & Dierickx, I. (1993). Rivalry, strategic groups and firm profitability. *Strategic Management Journal, 14*, 47–59.

Cowling, K., & Mueller, D. C. (1978). The social costs of monopoly power. *Economic Journal, 88*, 727–748.

Cramton, P. (2002). Spectrum auctions. In M. Cave, S. Majumdar, & I. Vogelsang (Eds.), *Handbook of telecommunications economics* (pp. 605–639). Elsevier.

D'Aveni, R. A. (1994). *Hypercompetition: Managing the dynamics of strategic maneuvering*. The Free Press.

Demsetz, H. (1964). The exchange and enforcement of property rights. *Journal of Law and Economics, 7*, 11–26.

Demsetz, H. (1967). *Toward a theory of property rights.* Originally published in 1967, reprinted in *Ownership, Control, and the Firm*, idem. 1988. Basil Blackwell.

Demsetz, H. (1982). Barriers to entry. *American Economic Review, 72*, 47–57.

Dierickx, I., & Cool, K. (1989). Asset stock accumulation and the sustainability of competitive advantage. *Management Science, 35*, 1504–1511.

Edlin, A., & Farrell, J. (2011). *Freedom to trade and the competitive process.* (NBER Working Paper No. 16818). National Bureau of Economic Research.

Eggertson, T. (1990). *Economic behavior and institutions.* Cambridge University Press.

Farrell, J., & Shapiro, C. (1990). Horizontal mergers: An equilibrium analysis. *American Economic Review, 80*, 107–126.

Foss, K., & Foss, N. J. (2005). Value and transaction costs: How the economics of property rights furthers the RBV. *Strategic Management Journal, 26*, 541–553.

Foss, K., Foss, N. J., Klein, P. G., & Klein, S. K. (2007). The entrepreneurial organization of heterogeneous capital. *Journal of Management Studies, 44*, 1165–1186.

Foss, N. J., & Klein, P. G. (2012). *Entrepreneurial judgment and the theory of the firm.* Cambridge University Press.

Galbraith, J. K. (1952). *American capitalism: The concept of countervailing power.* Houghton-Mifflin.

Ghemawat, P. (1991). *Commitment.* Free Press.

Ghemawat, P. (1997). *Games businesses play.* MIT Press.

Ghosh, M., & John, G. (1999). Governance value analysis and marketing strategy. *Journal of Marketing, 63*, 131–145.

Hansen, G. S., & Wernerfelt, B. (1989). Determinants of firm performance: The relative importance of economic and organizational factors. *Strategic Management Journal, 10*, 399–411.

Heath, C., Knez, M., & Camerer, C. (1993). The strategic management of the entitlement process in the employment relationship. *Strategic Management Journal, 14*, 75–93.

High, J. (1984). Bork's Paradox: Static vs. dynamic efficiency in Antitrust analysis. *Contemporary Economic Policy, 3*, 21–34.

Hirshleifer, J. (1989). Conflict and the rent-seeking success functions. *Public Choice, 63*, 101–112.

Hoskisson, R. E., Hitt, M. A., Wan, W. P., & Yiu, D. (1999). Theory and research in strategic management: Swings of a pendulum. *Journal of Management, 25*, 417–456.

Hubbard, T. N. (2000). The demand for monitoring technologies: The case of trucking. *Quarterly Journal of Economics, 115*, 533–560.

Hueth, B., & Marcoul, P. (2003). An essay on cooperative bargaining in U.S. agricultural markets. *Journal of Agricultural & Food Industrial Organization, 1*.

Innes, R., & Sexton, R. J. (1993). Customer coalitions, monopoly price discrimination, and generic entry deterrence. *European Economic Review, 37*, 1569–1597.

Innes, R., & Sexton, R. J. (1994). Strategic buyers and exclusionary contracts. *American Economic Review, 84*, 566–584.

InternetNews.com. (2000). *Priceline Webhouse Club calls it quits*. http://www.internetnews.com/ec-news/article.php/477561/Priceline+WebHouse+Club+Calls+It+Quits.htm. Accessed 3 July 2011.

Jacobson, R. (1992). The Austrian school of strategy. *Academy of Management Review, 17*, 782–805.

Joskow, P. L., & Klevorick, A. K. (1979). *A framework for analyzing predatory pricing policy* (Faculty Scholarship Series Paper 1305). http://digitalcommons.law.yale.edu/fss_papers/1305

Kahneman, D., Knetsch, J. L., & Thaler, R. H. (1990). Experimental tests of the endowment effect and the Coase theorem. *Journal of Political Economy, 98*, 1325–1348.

Kim, J., & Mahoney, J. T. (2005). Property rights theory, transaction costs theory, and agency theory: An organizational economics approach to strategic management. *Managerial and Decision Economics, 26*, 223–242.

Kirzner, I. M. (1966). *An essay on capital*. A. M. Kelley.

Klein, B. (2003). Exclusive dealing as competition for distribution "on the merits." *George Mason Law Review, 12*, 119–162.

Klein, B., & Wright, J. D. (2007). The economics of slotting contracts. *Journal of Law & Economics, 50*, 421–454.

Klein, P. G. (2000). New institutional economics. In B. Bouckeart & G. De Geest (Eds.), *Encyclopedia of law and economics*. Edward Elgar.

Kreps, D. M., & Wilson, R. (1982). Reputation and imperfect information. *Journal of Economic Theory, 27*, 253–279.

Ladd, G. W. (1974). A model of a bargaining cooperative. *American Journal of Agricultural Economics, 56*, 509–519.

Lenk, T., & Ghemawat, P. (1990). *De Beers Consolidated Mines Ltd. (A)* (Harvard Business School Case 9-391-076). Harvard Business School Press.

Lerner, J., & Schankerman, M. (2010). *The comingled code: Open source and economic development*. MIT Press.

Lerner, J., & Tirole, J. (2002). The simple economics of open source. *Journal of Industrial Economics, 52*, 197–234.

Libecap, G. D. (1978). Economic variables and the development of the law: The case of Western mineral rights. *Journal of Economic History, 38*, 338–362.

Libecap, G. P. (1989). *Contracting for property rights*. Cambridge University Press.

Libecap, G. P. (2005). *The problem of water* (Working Paper). Department of Economics, University of Arizona.

Lippman, S. A., & Rumelt, R. P. (2003a). A Bargaining perspective on resource advantage. *Strategic Management Journal, 24*, 1069–1086.

Lippman, S. A., & Rumelt, R. P. (2003b). The payments perspective: Microfoundations of resource analysis. *Strategic Management Journal, 24*, 903–927.

Littlechild, S. C. (1981). Misleading calculations of the social cost of monopoly power. *Economic Journal, 91*, 348–363.

MacDonald, G., & Ryall, M. D. (2004). How do value creation and competition determine whether a firm appropriates value? *Management Science, 50*, 1319–1333.

MacGrath, R. G., Chen, M. J., & MacMillan, I. C. (1998). Multimarket maneuvering in uncertain spheres of influence: Resource diversion strategies. *Academy of Management Review, 23*, 724–740.

Mahoney, J. T., & Pandian, J. R. (1992). The Resource-based view within the conversation of strategic management. *Strategic Management Journal, 13*, 363–380.

Makadok, R. (2011). The four theories of profit and their joint effects. *Journal of Management, 37*, 1316–1334.

Mayer, K. J., & Argyres, N. S. (2004). Learning to contract: Evidence from the personal computer industry. *Organization Science, 15*, 394–410.

McGee, J., & Howard Thomas, H. (1986). Strategic groups: Theory, research and taxonomy. *Strategic Management Journal, 47*, 141–160.

McWilliams, A., & Smart, D. L. (1993). Efficiency v. structure-conduct-performance: Implications for strategy research and practice. *Journal of Management, 19*, 63–78.

Ménard, C., & Shirley, M. (Eds.). (2005). *Handbook of new institutional economics*. Springer.
Nickerson, J. A. (2003). *Towards a positioning-economizing theory of strategy*. Unpublished manuscript.
Nickerson, J. A., Hamilton, B. H., & Wada, T. (2001). Market position, resource profile, and governance: Linking Porter and Williamson in the context of international courier and small package services in Japan. *Strategic Management Journal, 22*, 251–273.
Nickerson, J. A., & van den Bergh, R. (1999). Economizing in a context of strategizing: Governance mode choice in Cournot competition. *Journal of Economic Behavior and Organization, 40*, 1–15.
Oi, W. (1983). Heterogeneous firms and the organization of production. *Economic Inquiry, 21*, 147–171.
Olson, M. (1965). *The logic of collective action: Public goods and the theory of groups*. Harvard University Press.
Ostrom, E. (1990). *Governing the commons: The evolution of institutions for collective action*. Cambridge University Press.
Oxley, J. (1999). Institutional environment and the mechanisms of governance: The impact of intellectual property protection on the structure of inter-firm alliances. *Journal of Economic Behavior and Organization, 38*, 283–309.
Penenberg, A. L. (2005). *Digital rights mismanagement: How Apple, Microsoft and Sony Cash in on Piracy Prevention*. http://www.slate.com/id/2130300/. Accessed July 12, 2008.
Peteraf, M. A. (1993). The cornerstones of competitive advantage: A resource-based view. *Strategic Management Journal, 14*, 179–191.
Porter, M. E. (1980). *Competitive strategy*. Free Press.
Porter, M. E. (1981). The contributions of industrial organization to strategic management. *Academy of Management Review, 6*, 609–620.
Posner, R. R. (1975). The social costs of monopoly and regulation. *Journal of Political Economy, 83*, 807–828.
Rumelt, R. P., Schendel, D., & Teece, D. J. (1991). Strategic management and economics. *Strategic Management Journal, 12*, 5–29.
Salop, S. (1979). Strategic entry deterrence. *American Economic Review, 69*, 335–338.
Salop, S. C., & Scheffman, D. (1983). Raising rivals' costs. *American Economic Review, Papers and Proceedings, 73*, 267–271.
Scheffman, D. T., & Higgins, R. S. (2003). Twenty years of raising rivals' costs: History, assessment, and future. *George Mason University Law Review, 12*, 371–387.

Scherer, F. M. (1980). *Industrial market structure and economic performance*. Houghton-Mifflin.

Shaffer, B., & Ostas, D. T. (2001). Exploring the political economy of consumer legislation: The development of automobile lemon laws. *Business and Politics, 3*, 65–76.

Shapiro, C. (1989). The theory of business strategy. *RAND Journal of Economics, 20*, 125–137.

Shapiro, C., & Varian, H. (1999). *Information rules*. Harvard Business School Press.

Sidak, G., & Teece, D. J. (2009). Dynamic competition in antitrust law. *Journal of Competition Law & Economics, 5*, 581–631.

Skaperdas, S. (1992). Cooperation, conflict and power in the absence of property rights. *American Economic Review, 82*, 720–739.

Skaperdas, S., & Syropoulos, C. (1995). *Competing for claims to property* (Working Paper No. 85). Center for Economic Studies, University of Munich.

Smith, K. G., Ferrier, W., & Ndofor, H. (2001). Competitive dynamics research: Critique and future research directions. In M. Hitt, R. E. Freeman, & J. Harrison (Eds.), *The Blackwell handbook of strategic management*. Basil Blackwell.

Snyder, C. M. (1996). Negotiation and renegotiation of optimal financial contracts under the threat of predation. *Journal of Industrial Economics, 44*, 325–343.

Spulber, D. (2004). *Management strategy*. McGraw-Hill/Irwin.

Stefanadis, C. (2003). Sunk costs, contestability, and the latent contract market. *Journal of Economics and Management Strategy, 12*, 119–138.

Stigler, G. J. (1954). The economist plays with blocs. *American Economic Review, 44*, 7–14.

Sutton, J. (1991). *Sunk cost and market structure*. MIT Press.

Teece, D. (1980). Economies of scope and the scope of the enterprise. *Journal of Economic Behavior and Organization, 1*, 223–247.

Teece, D. J. (1982). Towards an economic theory of the multiproduct firm. *Journal of Economic Behavior and Organization, 3*, 39–63.

Teece, D. J. (1986). Profiting from technological innovation. *Research Policy, 15*, 285–305.

Teece, D. J., Pisano, G., & Shuen, A. (1997). Dynamic capabilities and strategic management. *Strategic Management Journal, 18*, 509–533.

Tirole, J. (1988). *The theory of industrial organization*. MIT Press.

Umbeck, J. (1981). Might makes rights: A theory of the formation and initial distribution of property rights. *Economic Inquiry, 19*, 38–59.
Varian, H. (1989). Price discrimination. In R. D. Schmalensee & R. D. Willig (Eds.), *Handbook of industrial organization*. Elsevier.
Vickers, J. (1995). Concepts of competition. *Oxford Economic Papers, 47*, 1–23.
Wallis, J. J., & North, D. C. (1986). Measuring the transaction sector in the American economy. In S. L. Engerman & R. E. Gallman (Eds.), *Long-term factors in American economic growth* (pp. 1870–1970). University of Chicago Press.
Weigelt, K., & Camerer, C. (1988). Reputation and corporate strategy: A review of recent theory and applications. *Strategic Management Journal, 9*, 443–454.
Whitney, S. N. (1953). Errors in the concept of countervailing power. *Journal of Business, 26*, 238–253.
Williamson, O. E. (1975). *Markets and hierarchies: Analysis and antitrust implications*. Free Press.
Williamson, O. E. (1985). *The economic institutions of capitalism*. Free Press.
Williamson, O. E. (1991). Strategizing, economizing, and economic organization. *Strategic Management Journal, 12*, 75–91.
Williamson, O. E. (1996). *The mechanisms of governance*. Oxford University Press.
Williamson, O. E. (2000). The new institutional economics: Taking stock and looking ahead. *Journal of Economic Literature, 38*, 596–613.
Young, G., Smith, K. G., & Grimm, C. M. (1996). "Austrian" and industrial organization perspectives on firm-level competitive activity and performance. *Organization Science, 7*, 243–254.
Zander, I. (2007). Do you see what I mean? An entrepreneurship perspective on the nature and boundaries of the firm. *Journal of Management Studies, 44*, 1141–1164.

7

Property Rights and the Nature of the Firm

In this chapter, we move the focus from organizational strategies to the organization, or somewhat more narrowly, the profit-motivated organization, and examine firm organization from a property rights perspective. Firm organization has long been of interest in the PRE (e.g., Alchian & Demsetz, 1972; Allen & Lueck, 1998; Barzel, 1987, 2005; Barzel & Kochin, 1992; Furubotn, 2001; Jensen & Meckling, 1976, 1979). PRE is usually taken to emerge as a distinct field around 1960 with core contributions by scholars like Alchian (1958, 1961), Kessel (1958), and, of course, Coase (1960). However, the theory of the firm, or the economics of organization, is often dated to 1937 when Coase published his seminal, but for a long time neglected article, "The Nature of the Firm" (or even to 1921, the year of publication of Frank Knight's *Risk, Uncertainty, and Profit*; cf. Foss & Klein, 2012). Barzel and Kochin (1992: 25) argue that the 1937 article should be seen as part of the PRE, and point out that

> One reason Coase's theory of the firm was ignored is that until 1960, economists who wished to study the problem had to rely entirely on the 1937 piece, since Coase himself did not elaborate on "The Nature of

K. Foss and N. J. Foss, *Economic Microfoundations of Strategic Management*,
https://doi.org/10.1007/978-3-031-12910-0_7

> the Firm". Such elaboration evidently was necessary; the discussion of transaction costs in that paper is brief and cryptic, and it does not seem that economists were ready to tackle this elusive problem.
>
> In "The Problem of Social Cost" it is shown that when the cost of transacting is positive, rights are not perfectly well defined, and the Coase Theorem makes it clear that costly transacting must lower the attainable output. Thus, "The Problem of Social Cost," in pointing out a relationship between the output that can be obtained from a given set of inputs and the form of organization governing these inputs provides an elaboration useful in the study of the firm.

In other words, the analysis in the 1937 paper only made full sense (to others than Coase) in light of the analysis in the 1960 paper. We approach the 1937 paper in a similar spirit in the following. We specifically describe and discuss Coase's approach to managerial authority—which he took to be the hallmark of the firm (Coase, 1937)—placing it in the broader context of recent economics and management research on intra-firm coordination. We also bring in PRE as represented by Coase's (1960) later work on social cost by focusing on the role of managers as being about delineating property rights to assets in ways that maximize the value of production. Coase (1960) discusses the legal system and public organizations as two institutions that specialize in the delineation and enforcement of property rights. Interestingly, in the same paper, he also hints at a notion of the firm as an institution that *rearranges* previously legally defined property rights. Picking up on this idea, we consider how firms, and more specifically managers, undertake the role of delineating and rearranging property rights. We also make use of work by Coase that is less known, namely his work on opportunity costs (Buchanan & Thirlby, 1973; Coase, 1938)—work that Coase (1990) himself saw as clearly related to the work he was simultaneously doing on the theory of the firm (but did not relate to his later work on social cost).

Coase's "The Nature of the Firm"

In the usual narrative, Coase (1937) is seen as introducing a theoretical innovation in the form of identifying the need to explain the firm's existence, boundaries, and internal organization in terms of economizing on transaction costs, and providing answers that later scholars could usefully build on (e.g., Williamson, 1975, 1985). However, another contribution, and perhaps a more foundational one, is ontological, namely, conceptualizing the firm as a team of employees, coordinated by a managerial hierarchy, organizing production stages within a single legal entity.[1]

In Knight's (1921) framework, and in the later theories of Williamson (1985) and Hart (1995), the essence of the firm is the ownership relation—a firm is an entrepreneur plus an alienable asset (cf. Chapter 4). For Coase (1937), the essence of the firm is the employment relation; a firm is a manager directing a team of employees who must obey the manager's directives, within specified limits. As Coase (1937: 387) famously put it, "[i]f a workman moves from department *Y* to department *X*, he does not go because of a change in relative prices, but because he is ordered to do so." Hence Coase's treatment of managerial authority is central to his understanding of the firm. However, Coase's theory of authority and hierarchy has received much less attention than his views on transaction costs, at least until Coase (1988: 41) noted that the firm per se comes about not when there is a single employment contract, but when "the organizer has contracts with several factors whose activities he coordinates."[2]

Coase's treatment of managerial authority is significant in the history of economic thought. By the early 1930s, the "firm" in economic theory had been transformed from the rich, complex, and diverse business organization headed by merchants, entrepreneurs, and capitalists described by the classical economists, Austrians, Institutionalists, early neoclassical economists, and sociologists to what became known as the "representative firm," an abstract, mechanistic process for transforming

[1] As was common in the contemporary British research literature on industrial organization Coase (1937) uses the term "entrepreneur," not manager, to describe this coordinating agent.

[2] Other papers on Coasean authority and coordination include Masten (1988), Loasby (1999), Foss (1999), and Bylund (2014).

inputs and outputs using technologies known to all, often, wrongly, ascribed to Marshall (Foss, 1994). In the writings of Pigou, Viner, and Joan Robinson, the firm became a production function, analogous to the utility function that came to represent the consumer. Ownership, authority, delegation, incentives, monitoring, and other managerial functions are not central to the representative firm as it emerged in the 1930s; the emphasis there is on solving a constrained maximization problem in terms of combining inputs in the production of outputs in profit-maximizing manner, assuming that technical knowledge and knowledge about how to organize are costlessly available to any firm (Demsetz, 1988). The only concession to moderate realism in this picture of the firm is an acknowledgment that the managerial function is characterized by a decreasing returns' technology (Kaldor, 1994). Of course, this lack of specificity is dictated by the analytical purpose at hand, namely building an apparatus that can deal with comparative-statics issues at the market/industry level.

Coase (1937) offered a different picture, one gleaned from Coase's detailed observations of US manufacturing companies and one informed by a very different analytical purpose. In Coase's vision, firms are organizations that mobilize large numbers of workers, using shared equipment, to produce goods and services as part of a team led by professional managers. Most of what today passes as the "theory of the firm" or "organizational economics" is fundamentally Coasean in that it starts from Coase's (1937) programmatic statement of what a theory of the firm should seek to achieve, accepts the above basic ontology, and builds off from some of the key analytical insights Coase developed. However, subtle, yet important gaps remain in our understanding of what firms do. PRE has the potential to fill a number of these gaps.

Consider by now the familiar PRE notion that all assets have many different uses (attributes) and the specification of rights to use a particular asset for a particular purpose at a particular time and place constitutes a delineation of use rights to a particular attribute of an asset (Barzel, 1997; Demsetz, 1988). As we have argued this notion is essentially derived from Coase's (1960) argument that factors of production should not be conceived of as physical entities but as a circumscribed list of rights to perform certain actions. How are such assets used? Here we take our lead from Coase's (1960: 44) observation that it "would clearly be desirable if the only actions performed were those in which what was gained was worth more than what was lost." Indeed, this is an overall conceptualization of the managerial task itself. As Coase (1937) explains, managers must discover the (shadow) prices, that is, the opportunity costs of delineating and arranging property rights *within* the boundaries of the firm. This is where Coase's earlier work on opportunity costs is highly relevant (Coase, 1938). Looking back on this work, Coase (1990: 3) observed that "understanding cost accounting and opportunity costs within a firm was tied to understanding the organization of firms. The theory of the accounting system is part of the theory of the firm."

Building on this insight, we argue that just as judges or administrators in a Coasean world try to identify and compensate external effects that reduce the value of production, so do managers try to internalize externalities in firms where there are interdependencies between the various activities carried out by the firm.[3] The ability of managers to delineate rights over attributes of productive assets and arrange them in complementary combinations must often be discovered in a process of learning by doing. Firms can thus be seen as bundles of assets to which managers gradually discover and delineate property rights in a manner that enhances the value of production. Based on these ideas we sketch a Coasean coordination perspective on the firm. We focus on the coordination and production side of firms, rather than on the incentives issues that are usually in focus in the theory of economic organization.

Transaction Costs and Subjective Opportunity Costs

Much has been written on Coase's understanding of transaction costs (Allen, 2000; Benham & Benham, 2010). Transaction costs can be understood both as a cost of exchanging well-defined and well-enforced property titles (as in Coase, 1937) and as a cost of defining and enforcing

[3] Beyond the boundaries of the firm, firms that set up and manage "ecosystems" of connected firms do the same thing (Foss et al., 2022).

property titles (as in Coase, 1960). But it is rarely noticed that Coase's ideas about transaction costs emerged within a broader set of ideas about cost more generally, namely the revolutionary approach to opportunity cost that emerged at the London School of Economics in the 1930s. The idea of defining economic costs in terms of forgone alternatives was implicit in the works of Menger, Jevons, and Walras during the "marginalist revolution" of the 1870s, introduced explicitly by Wieser (1889), and developed more thoroughly by Knight, J. B. Clark, and Wicksteed. But LSE economists such as Lionel Robbins, G. F. Thirlby, Coase, and Jack Wiseman, starting in the 1930s, elaborated a much more detailed account of opportunity costs as not only marginal but also personal, subjective, forward-looking, tacit, and even ephemeral (Buchanan, 1969; Buchanan & Thirlby, 1973).

Coase explicitly treats transaction costs as subjective estimates of foregone value. "The cost of exercising a right (of using a factor of production) is always the loss which is suffered elsewhere in consequence of the exercise of that right" (Coase, 1960: 44). But starting in the 1930s, Coase recognized that while opportunity costs are subjective, entrepreneurs require cardinal numbers to estimate the benefits and costs of various potential courses of action (what Mises, 1920, referred to as the "economic calculation" problem). Entrepreneurial planning is very much an exercise in cost accounting. But contemporary cost accounting practices did not take marginal, subjective characteristics into account.

Coase elaborated on the implications of the opportunity-cost doctrine for cost accounting in a series of brief essays published in 1938. These articles, as Coase (1990: 8) later described them, argued that

> in business administration cost should be interpreted as opportunity cost and that the approach should be marginal (concerned, that is, with variations in costs and receipts). This led naturally to a critique of the practices and doctrines of cost accountants. The opportunity cost concept developed at LSE was of course derived from Knight and Wicksteed as expounded by Lionel Robbins and was also no doubt influenced by Hayek who would have added an Austrian flavor.

Cost accounting is critical in an advanced industrial economy, because the key economic question is how to allocate productive activities among potential organizational alternatives, what Williamson (1991) would later call the problem of "comparative economic organization." As Coase (1990: 11) explained, "while transaction cost considerations undoubtedly explain why firms come into existence, once most production is carried out within firms and most transactions are firm-firm transactions and not factor-factor transactions, the level of transaction costs will be greatly reduced and the dominant factor determining the institutional structure of production will in general no longer be transaction costs but the relative costs of different firms in organizing particular activities." For this reason, "[i]f economists are to study the determinants of the costs of organizing various activities within firms, they will have to call in the assistance of accountants since the costs of organizing clearly depend on the efficiency of the accounting system" (Coase, 1990: 11).

The firm's internal accounting system, Coase (1990: 11) argues, should attempt to mimic the indicators of value and cost embodied in market prices.

> Since using a resource denies its use to others, the figure for cost should represent what it would yield elsewhere in the business. In this planned society, the firms, costs do not, in the main, arise directly out of the operations of the market but are computed and provided by the accounting system. While outside the firm prices and therefore costs are explicit (because of the demands of others for resources) and are determined by the operations of the market, within the firm there are explicit costs for exactly the same reason but they are provided by the accounting system. This internal system takes the place of the pricing system of the market.

From this perspective, the limits to the size and scope of the firm can be understood in terms of accounting errors. The internal estimates of opportunity costs needed for resource allocation in the firm will tend to be less accurate than the opportunity costs reflected in real, external, market prices. As the firm expands, it internalizes more and more transactions, leading to what Rothbard (1962: 1364) called "islands of calculational chaos" that hamper efficient resource allocation. The weaknesses of internal prices, as determined by accountants, compared to external market prices, generate the ultimate limits to the firm (Klein, 1996)—a generalization of the Austrian argument that centrally planned systems cannot be economically efficient because they lack market prices (Foss, 1994; Hayek, 1945; Mises, 1920).

Just as Coase (1937) established the modern theory of the firm by reconceptualizing the problem in terms of transaction costs, Mises (1920) established the economic theory of socialism by defining the issue in terms of the socialist planner's judgments and decisions, not the planner's preferences and incentives. In a market economy, Mises argued, entrepreneurs bid for the services of productive factors based on their estimates, or "appraisements," of future marginal revenue products. The outcome of this competitive bidding process establishes the factor prices that constitute the entrepreneur's costs. Absent private ownership in resources, factor prices must be estimated according to some administrative process, resulting in prices that do not reflect underlying relative scarcities as effectively as prices generated in a competitive market process. Hayek's (1945) complementary argument added that central planners are also denied access to the tacit, dispersed knowledge that is embodied in consumer goods as well as factor-market prices.

The Austrian argument against socialism thus relies on the comparative efficiency of inter-organizational, competitive pricing processes and intra-organizational, administrative pricing systems. Of course, within an organization, some administrative pricing processes are necessary—otherwise, there would be no need to form an organization. The firm, as an "island of conscious power" (Coase, 1937: 188, quoting D. H. Robertson), substitutes subjective, administrative decisions for the "objective" decisions of the price mechanism. Coase's accounting articles explain in more detail how these subjective decisions are made, helping us see their virtues and limits.

Coase and the Firm: Coordination and Property Rights

Coase (1937) asked why the firm exists. In answering this question, he argued that the most important reason must be that the "most obvious cost of 'organizing' production through the price mechanism is that of discovering what the relevant prices are" (Coase, 1937: 21). The "relevant prices" to Coase are the prices that reflect the value that can be created through a particular use of an asset above the opportunity cost of a different use of the asset. Thus, one may interpret the process of discovering prices as one of discovering the opportunity costs of different uses of assets.

In markets the "discovery of the relevant prices" is undertaken through decentralized bargaining among owners of factors of production. It is costly to carry out such negotiations as these require that one "discover[s] who it is that one wishes to deal with, to inform people that one wishes to deal and on what terms, to conduct negotiations leading up to a bargain, to draw up the contract, to undertake the inspection needed to make sure that the terms of the contract are being observed, and so on" (Coase, 1937: 15). These search, bargaining, and ink costs involved in market transactions are relevant for explaining the introduction of long-term contracts, but not sufficient for explaining why firms come into existence.

For firms to be efficient substitutes for market transactions in discovering opportunity costs, the firm must have at its disposal different means of organizing the process of discovery compared to markets. The difference, Coase (1937) suggests, is to be found in the use of authority and managerial decisions supported by the legal structure of employment contracts. According to Coase an open-ended contract such as an employment contract is preferred "owing to the difficulty of forecasting, the longer the period of the contract is for the supply of the commodity or service, the less possible, and indeed, the less desirable it is for the person purchasing to specify what the other contracting party is expected to do" (Coase, 1937: 21). The employment contract thus allows for sequential decision regarding the best use of a particular resource or asset. However, this does not answer the question of how managers in firms discover the relevant prices. In providing an answer to this question, we suggest that the firm is conceived of as a property rights system. We suggest that such a conception of the firm provides an interesting and natural link between Coase (1937) and Coase (1960).

Property Rights and the Firm

In Chapter 5, we argued that resources have different properties and may yield different services depending on how the assets are used. For example, a plot of land can be used for building a residential house or a factory, for growing corn, for raising cattle, etc. In the absence of transaction costs, each of the properties and different uses of assets that are known could be specified and traded. Moreover, any of these uses can be subject to negotiations between anyone influenced by the particular use of the asset. More important, when legal rights are delimited there would be no problem of externalities emerging from already known types of uses of assets because all externalities would be traded (Barzel, 1997).

This is all familiar from the Coase theorem. However, Coase never specified exactly what is required for transaction costs to be zero or very low such that markets would bring about the efficient rearrangement of legal rights. One such requirement seems to be that the parties to the negotiations know each other's reservation prices or opportunity costs, effectively making full information a condition of zero transaction costs (cf. also Barzel, 1985). Thus, we can assume that the opportunity cost of any known use of an asset is known to those affected by any particular use. For example, the probable reduction of the value of crop would be known to contracting parties if a particular size of herd of cattle is raised adjacent to a particular plot of land used for growing corn. The implication is that there would not be a need for a process of discovery of the relevant prices. If new uses of assets emerged and if these new uses influenced the value that could be created from exploiting already known uses assets, a process of discovery of opportunity costs would be needed and in the absence of transaction costs this process would be costless (and therefore also instantaneous).

One could imagine that the opportunity costs of exploiting a particular use of an asset are well known, but it is costly to identify the parties with which to contract in order to rearrange legal rights. Such a case seems to be Coase's (1960: 17) discussion of the handling of smoke nuisance which "may affect a vast number of people engaged in a wide variety of activities" and has administrative costs "so high as to make any attempt to deal with the problem within the confines of a single firm impossible. In this case, "[i]nstead of instituting a legal system of rights which can be modified by transactions on the market, the government may impose regulations which state what people must or must not do and which have to be obeyed." In other words, government through regulations and restrictions influences the "list of accepted uses" of an asset. If the government faces the right incentives the delineation of rights will be efficient—that is, it will take into account the opportunity costs of different delimitations of rights. Thus, the legal system and the government act as different property rights systems (Alchian, 1965) with the legal system dealing with nuisance and being able to take into account local factors and the government ideally dealing with more global types of externalities.

Moreover, delimitation of property rights can take place within firms. In fact, Coase (1960: 16) describes government as a sort of super firm because both types of economic organizations use authority and administrative decisions to delimit and rearrange property rights: "within the firm individual bargains between the various cooperating factors of production are eliminated and for a market transaction is substituted an administrative decision." For example, an entrepreneur who owns a cattle range located next to his corn field will take into account the reduction in the value of corn produced as he increases his herd of cattle. Likewise a manager who produces two substitute products will take into account how much of each product to market in a particular geographical market taking into account the possible effects on related markets. Thus firms, like courts, deal with local factors affecting the optimal delineation of property rights. In other words, entrepreneurs have strong incentives to internalize intra-firm externalities—much stronger incentives than those of regulators and Coasean judges in dealing with social costs more generally!

Thus, according to Coase the main advantage of using firms is that they face stronger incentives to delineate property rights in ways that maximize the value of production within their local control. In "The Problem of Social Cost," Coase (1960: 17) explains that the reason for internalizing market transactions is that sometimes

> contracts are peculiarly difficult to draw up and an attempt to describe what the parties have agreed to do or not to do (e.g., the amount and kind of smell or noise that they may make or will not make) would necessitate a lengthy and highly involved document, and, whereas is probable, a long-term contract would be desirable; it would be hardly surprising if the emergence of a firm or the extension of the activities of an existing firm was not the solution adopted on many occasions to deal with the problem of harmful effects.

Interestingly, Coase does not mention the contracting problems that stem from "discovering the relevant prices," that is, identifying the opportunity costs of different delimitation of property rights. Thus, whereas in Coase (1937) firms substitute for market contracting because of the costs of discovering the relevant prices, in Coase (1960) firms seem to substitute for market contracting because of the difficulties of spelling out the kind of influence that different uses have on the value of production.

The key point here is that when transaction costs include the costs of discovering the opportunity costs of different delineations of property rights, firms and entrepreneurs play a key role in the economic system that tends to disappear from sight in the modern economics of the firm. Specifically, firms, as well as having the entrepreneurial function closely linked to the emergence and functioning of firms, are vehicles for discovering the opportunity costs of different delineations and re-combination of property rights to productive assets and for making those resource allocation decisions that are efficient in light of essentially entrepreneurial appraisal of the value and opportunity costs of rival asset uses. We elaborate on this view in the two next chapters.

Conclusions

Coase's, 1937 paper, "The Nature of the Firm," was a landmark contribution that, however, lay dormant for almost four decades. Economists' fixation on the competitive model meant that more detailed inquiry into the questions that interested Coase was for a long time outside of the vision field of the discipline. Moreover, it is arguable that economists may have felt by the tools that were at their disposal to take Coase's ideas further. However, emerging ideas of asymmetrical information, imperfect contracts, and small numbers paved the way for grappling with these ideas, and since the mid-1970s ideas on how the costs of coordination and cooperation vary with mechanisms and structures of governance have become mainstream in economics.

In this chapter, we developed a distinct PRE interpretation of firms understood as alternatives to markets. We specifically argued that the Coasian notion of firms can be viewed as a solution to problems of coordination in situations where use rights over assets cannot be perfectly specified and allocated in manners which ensures the functionality of technologies. Such situations may occur because individuals face uncertainty[4] and because they have only limited computational capacity, making it difficult for them to specify use rights in ways that solve problems of interdependencies ex-ante to a further division of labor. One of the reasons why managed coordination may be advantageous to price coordination then is that because the former reduces the costs of learning to coordinate technologically interdependent tasks.

This is arguably only part of the puzzle of why firms exist, have certain boundaries, and so on (e.g., not all firms may have the sort of interdependencies in production that motivates our focus on coordination). However, it is a hitherto unexplored part, which is distinct from existing explanations in that it, consistent with Coase (1937), does not highlight incentive conflicts as the core of the explanation. Moreover, the theory sketched here has interesting implications for our understanding of, for example, entrepreneurship, organizational learning, and innovation. In the following chapter, we elaborate on these ideas.

[4] While Coase (1937) does not explicitly suggest that uncertainty is a reason why it may be costly to discover "the relevant prices" or why managed direction may be less costly than open market transactions, uncertainty seems to play an important role in his explanation of the need of open-ended contracts such as employment contracts. According to Coase, an employment contract is preferred "… owing to the difficulty of forecasting, the longer the period of the contract is for the supply of the commodity or service, the less possible, and indeed, the less desirable it is for the person purchasing to specify what the other contracting party is expected to do" (Coase 1937: 21).

References

Alchian, A. A. (1958). Private property and the relative cost of tenure. In P. D. Bradley (Ed.), *The public stake in union power* (pp. 350–371). University of Virginia Press.

Alchian, A. A. (1961). *Some economics of property*. Rand Corporation.

Alchian, A. A. (1965 [1977]). Some economics of property rights. In A. A. Alchian (Ed.), *Economic forces at work*. Liberty Press.

Alchian, A. A., & Demsetz, H. (1972). Production, information costs, and economic organization. *American Economic Review, 62*, 772–795.

Allen, D. W. (2000). Transaction costs. In B. Bouckeart & G. De Geest (Eds.), *Encyclopedia of law and economics* (pp. 893–926). Edward Elgar.

Allen, D. W., & Lueck, D. (1998). The nature of the farm. *Journal of Law and Economics, 41*, 343–386.

Barzel, Y. (1985 [2005]). Transaction costs: Are they just costs? Reprinted in C. Mènard (Ed.), *Controversies and challenges in the new institutional economics*. Edward Elgar.

Barzel, Y. (1987). The entrepreneur's reward for self-policing. *Economic Inquiry, 25*, 103–116.

Barzel, Y. (1997). *Economic analysis of property rights* (2nd ed.). Cambridge University Press.

Barzel, Y., & Kochin, L. (1992). Ronald Coase on the nature of social cost as a key to the problem of the firm. *Scandinavian Journal of Economics, 94*, 19–31.

Benham, A., & Benham, L. (2010). The costs of exchange. In P. G. Klein & M. E. Sykuta (Eds.), *The Elgar companion to transaction cost economics* (pp. 107–119). Edward Elgar.

Buchanan, J. M. (1969). *Cost and choice: An inquiry in economic theory*. Markham.

Buchanan, J. M., & Thirlby, G. F. (1973). *LSE essays on cost*. London School of Economics and Political Science.

Bylund, P. (2014). Ronald Coase's "nature of the firm" and the argument for economic planning. *Journal of the History of Economic Thought, 36*, 305–334.

Coase, R. H. (1937). The nature of the firm. *Economica NS4*, 386–405.

Coase, R. H. (1938). Business organization and the accountant. *The Accountant, 13*, 470–472, 505–507, 537–538, 559–560, 607–608, 631–632, 665–666, 705–706, 737–739, 775–777, 814–815, 834–835.

Coase, R. H. (1960). The problem of social cost. *Journal of Law and Economics, 3*, 1–44.
Coase, R. H. (1988). The nature of the firm: Influence. *Journal of Law, Economics, and Organization, 4*, 33–47.
Coase, R. H. (1990). Accounting and the theory of the firm. *Journal of Accounting and Economics, 12*, 3–13.
Demsetz, H. (1988). A framework for the study of ownership. In H. Demsetz (Ed.), *Ownership, control, and the firm*. Basil Blackwell.
Foss, N. J. (1994). The biological analogy and the theory of the firm. *Journal of Economic Issues, 18*, 1115–1136.
Foss, N. J. (1999). The use of knowledge in firms. *Journal of Institutional and Theoretical Economics, 155*, 458–486.
Foss, N. J., & Klein, P. G. (2012). *Entrepreneurial judgment and the theory of the firm*. Cambridge University Press.
Foss, N. J., Schmidt, J., & Teece, D. J. (2022). *Ecosystem leadership as a dynamic capability*. Manuscript.
Furubotn, E. (2001). The new institutional economics and the theory of the firm. *Journal of Economic Behavior and Organization, 45*, 133–153.
Hart, O. (1995). *Firms, contracts, and financial structure*. The Clarendon Press.
Hayek, F. A. (1945). The use of knowledge in society. *American Economic Review, 35*, 519–530.
Jensen, M., & Meckling, W. (1976). Theory of the firm managerial behavior, agency costs and ownership structure. *Journal of Financial Economics, 3*, 305–360.
Jensen, M. C., & Meckling, W. (1979). Rights and production functions: An application to labor-managed firms and co-determination. *Journal of Business, 52*, 469–506.
Kaldor, N. (1994). The equilibrium of the firm. *Economic Journal, 44*, 60–76.
Kessel, R. A. (1958). Price discrimination in medicine. *Journal of Law and Economics, 1*, 20–53.
Klein, P. G. (1996). Economic calculation and the limits of organization. *Review of Austrian Economics, 9*, 51–77.
Knight, F. H. (1921). *Risk, uncertainty, and profit*. Hart, Schaffner & Marx.
Loasby, B. J. (1999). *Knowledge, institutions, and evolution in economics*. Routledge.
Masten, S. E. (1988). A legal basis for the firm. *Journal of Law, Economics, and Organization, 4*, 181–198.

Mises, Lv. (1920). Economic calculation in the socialist commonwealth. In F. A. Hayek (Ed.), *Collectivist economic planning* (p. 1935). George Routledge and Sons.

Rothbard, M. N. (1962). *Man, economy, and state*. Van Nostrand.

von Wieser, F. (1889 [1893]). *Natural value* (WilliamSmart, Ed.). Macmillan.

Williamson, O. E. (1975). *Markets and hierarchies: Analysis and antitrust implications*. Free Press.

Williamson, O. E. (1985). *The economic institutions of capitalism*. Free Press.

Williamson, O. E. (1991). Comparative economic organization: The analysis of discrete structural alternatives. *Administrative Science Quarterly, 36*, 269–296.

8

The Theory of the Firm: Specialization and Learning

Coase (1937) and much of the post-Coasian economics of organization take the costs of coordinating various tasks as well as the extent of specialization in the economy as *given* and proceeds to analyze why not all transactions among specialized agents are coordinated either in firms or in open markets. Of course, this is just a static starting point, and comparative statics can be performed by introducing, for example, technologies that influence the costs of managing within and between firms, such as the telephone (Coase, 1937), the internet (Afuah, 2003), digitization and big data analytics (Loebbecke & Picot, 2015), and artificial intelligence (Kretschmer & Khashabi, 2020). In spite of its importance to the founding of the discipline of economics (Smith, 1776), a less commonly analyzed change is the increasing division of labor, leading to higher specialization. The neglect of increasing division of labor and specialization is odd because of the obvious importance of the division of labor and specialization to firm strategy and learning at the micro-level and the emergence of industries (Stigler, 1951), industrial dynamics (Young, 1928), and indeed to the growth process (Sachs & Yang, 2008) at the more macro-level.

K. Foss and N. J. Foss, *Economic Microfoundations of Strategic Management*,
https://doi.org/10.1007/978-3-031-12910-0_8

In a series of papers (Demsetz, 1997a, 1997b, 2011), Demsetz introduced specialization as a key theme in the economics of the firm. The following quotation is typical of his reasoning (Demsetz, 2011: S10):

> Managed direction of others is not a requirement for neoclassical theory's firm to exist. Specialization of production for sale to others is the requirement. The specialist may be a multiperson institution or a single person, providing that production is for sale to others. Hence, free access to price information does not rule out neoclassical theory's firms if specialization is more productive than is self-sufficiency. The size of the firm, and the number of persons contained in the firm, will be determined by the degree of scale economies or by the productivity of managing others as opposed to freelancing it. Specialization, however, does not depend on cooperative involvement of persons or even vertical integration (although I have a great deal of difficulty conceptualizing a zero degree of vertical integration, since any task can be subdivided). Specialization basically depends for its productivity on special skills and repetitiveness of the task, not on vertical integration. Hence, zero cost of transacting does not rule out firms as these are conceived by neoclassical theory.

Demsetz' comment is an explicit critique of Coase, who defines the firm in terms of the employment contract (so that any firm must involve at least two people) and does not see specialization as an independent force in explaining the existence and boundaries of firms.

Demsetz is right that Coase's emphasis on the employment contract rules out the one-person firm. One-person firms are very important in the economy and there is no reason to abstract from them (Westall et al., 2000). He is also right that specialization has received surprisingly little attention in the post-Coasian economics of the firm, except indirectly, namely in the emphasis on specialized, relation-specific assets (Klein et al., 1978; Williamson, 1985).[1] However, the take in this chapter is very different from Demsetz's take. Demsetz' main interest seems to lie in defending the basic neoclassical model from the Coasian charge that since it abstracts from transaction costs, there cannot be a room for firms

[1] Foss (1997) links the capabilities view of the firm to the production theory of classical economics, particularly the emphasis on specialization.

(Demsetz, 2011). As Cheung (1983) argued, absent transaction costs buyers could contract directly with input suppliers; there wouldn't be any need for the intermediaries that we call firms. However, Demsetz' argument is that since specialization is productive, even in the absence of transaction costs primitive "firms" will emerge.

Our interest rather lies in linking the Coasian transaction cost theory of the firm with the themes of the division of labor and specialization. We construct a dynamic argument based on PRE that goes beyond the issue of why firms exist. We argue that an increasing division of labor introduces new, partly unforeseen coordination and cooperation problems, representing new challenges as well as new opportunities for handling increasingly specialized tasks. Handling these problems requires (managerial) experience gained through experimentation. Accumulating management knowledge through experiential learning—resulting in what some may want to call "capabilities"—reduces not only the internal costs of running the firm but also the costs of production. Different modes of economic organization such as firm and market organization influence the cost of accumulating the relevant knowledge needed to bring down costs of coordinating specialized tasks. The existence and boundaries of the firm then may be understood in terms of comparative learning costs (for related, yet different arguments, see Langlois & Robertson, 1995; Oi, 1983).

Specialization: A Property Rights Interpretation

Specialization

An increase in the division of labor in production can be described as an operation that divides the production of goods into more narrowly defined sub-tasks. The division of labor in production is, as Adam Smith (1776) pointed out in the first chapter of *The Wealth of Nations*, one of the main sources of productivity improvements. Specifically, he ascribes productivity gains to three aspects of the division of labor, namely (1) improvements in a worker's ability ("dexterity") to perform a task as it is repeated more often; (2) the time that is saved from avoiding having to switch from one task to another ("sauntering"); and (3) an improved ability of a worker to identify labor-saving innovations. As Smith indicates, the subdivision of tasks is not the only characteristic of specialization; changes in tasks as new innovations are introduced are also important characteristics of the process of the "progressive division of labor" (cf. also Young, 1928).

The division of labor and specialization in production are closely related themes. While the former refers to the subdivision of tasks involved in the production of a certain good, the latter refers to the creation of production units specialized in the production of certain goods. The two types of specialization are interconnected; thus, Yang and Ng (1995) argue that economies of specialization may arise from economies of labor specialization.[2] However, in their model, economies of division of labor do not emerge gradually. The benefits are fully known *ex ante* to any steps toward increasing the division of labor and specialization in production.

The main concern in models such as those of Yang and Ng (1995) and Becker and Murphy (1992) is to establish the equilibrium amount of specialization under different assumptions about increasing returns to division of labor. The concern here is different, since our aim is to argue that coordination and cooperation problems in complex production systems are under certain conditions best handled by the firm and that the boundaries of the firm are also influenced by a changing division of labor. In other words, the benefits from an increased division of labor reveal themselves gradually as agents improve dexterity in carrying out the tasks and as the problems of how to coordinate the more specific and interdependent tasks are gradually solved. Moreover, the division of labor can never be completed immediately, since it takes time to address, diagnose, and solve coordination and cooperation problems introduced by an ongoing process of specialization and identify costs and benefits from a

[2] Not all writers in this area distinguish between the division of labor and specialization. Adam Smith and Allyn Young did not.

further division of labor. Thus, the choice between firm and market organization of tasks change as the tasks change and as knowledge of how to coordinate the specialized tasks is accumulated and new opportunities for further division of labor is discovered.

Learning by Doing

The Smithian idea that learning by doing underlies productivity growth was reintroduced in economics by Kenneth Arrow (1962). He suggested that the growth of knowledge that underlies economic growth could partly be explained as a function of learning in production, and that technical change "… can be ascribed to experience, that is, it is the very activity of production which gives rise to problems for which favorable responses are selected over time" (1962: 156).

Moreover, Arrow argued that learning associated with repetition of tasks is subject to diminishing returns, so that continuous improvements in dexterity are dependent upon continuous changes in the tasks. Such changes may stem from innovations that may be a result of increased experience in production.

That hands-on experience in production is a source of innovativeness is also an important overall conclusion emerge from numerous studies of innovation and technological change (e.g., Epple et al., 1991; Hatch & Mowery, 1998; Rosenberg, 1976; Sahal, 1981). These studies suggest the nature of activities and the characteristics of the techniques in use tend to focus attention on certain technical problems. For example, Rosenberg (1976) argues that most incremental improvements in products and production processes are closely connected to their physical characteristics. He uses the term "technological imperatives" to indicate how some opportunities for technological development present themselves as more or less evident. Complex technologies, he argues, create internal compulsions and pressures (i.e., "focusing devices") that focus attention on the elimination of bottlenecks in productions and incompatibilities in products.

Sahal (1981) presents similar but more elaborated characterization of the sources of innovative opportunities. He argues that technological development leads to the formation of systems where the increased complexity from the mutually dependent components sets the boundaries for further development. He examines the different types of innovative activity that underlie this kind of technological development. For example, he explains how changes in the scale of a complex production system are particularly likely to create problems requiring innovative responses. These problems may be divided into three kinds: (1) problems due to uneven development in the components of the technology; (2) problems that arise because of the need for new materials; and (3) problems caused by a more complex structure of technology. Solving these problems result in innovations that change the structure of the product or the production process, introduce new materials, or combine different technologies into a new system with a more simple structure allowing for further improvements.

Three conclusions that are relevant in the present context emerge from this literature. First, productivity gains often stem from a combination of improved dexterity and innovativeness. Second, improved dexterity as well as innovativeness is a function of experience in production. Third, productivity gains from innovations in, for example, the structure of technology or materials, and reductions of bottlenecks in production are based on experience that is shaped by the nature of the activities that are undertaken, and is thus specific to those activities.

The division of labor in production influences the scope for learning by doing on the part of individuals: Their accumulation of experience in production is limited to more specialized tasks. However, there is a trade-off between the depth of learning and the scope of learning, since specialization also implies that, as tasks are repeated more often, deeper learning results. Moreover, specialization may results in faster learning of skills. Thus by focusing the attention of individuals on much a more narrow set of tasks, the division of labor may improve the rate of innovativeness with respect to the discovery of new ways of carrying out a task, or of improving tools and materials that are used.[3]

However, specialization may also create problems of bottlenecks and problems from uneven development of components. Such problems reduce the benefits from specialization, unless some mechanism for handling coordination and cooperation challenges stemming from interdependent specialized tasks is implemented. Before we turn to this, we discuss the relation between specialization, allocation of property rights, and learning by doing.

Delineating Property Rights

An important characteristic of property rights is the degree of *precision* with which they are delineated. This is a key theme in classical PRE, as externalities in asset uses are typically linked not just to whether property rights are delineated or not but also to the precision with which this is done. The extent of precision will reflect the costs of delineating right, but also the cost of enforcing rights. In the "modern" PRE (what we called "Mark II PRE" in Chapter 4), some rights can be delineated and written into contracts, that is, specific rights, while others cannot, namely, residual rights, and are exercised by those who hold ownership to assets (Hart, 1995).[4] In PRE (as well as in its agency theory offspring; Jensen & Meckling, 1976), some income rights can be written into contracts, while residual claims appear as the contractually non-specified income or pleasure a person can enjoy from using or alienating an asset (including her labor).

[3] The ability to solve technical problems may also depend on specialized technical and/or scientific knowledge. Becker and Murphy (1992) models this as exogenous defined increases in the marginal return from investments in the knowledge needed to carry out increasingly specialized tasks.

[4] The distinction between specific and residual rights is not completely clear-cut in the literature. Sometimes only the right to decide between different kinds of uses of an asset is described as residual rights while rights to decide how to use an assets in a specific way is described as discretion (Alchian & Woodward, 1988).

In any case, less-than-perfect precision in the specification of rights is the result of transaction costs (Barzel, 1997). Absent transaction costs, all rights are perfectly defined, and, furthermore, all possible uses of assets are fully known, all returns from all uses of all assets are perfectly known, all legitimate and illegitimate uses of assets are perfectly specified, and all of this is perfectly enforceable. If all rights are completely defined in this way, there cannot, by definition, arise any conflicts over the use of scarce resources or the returns from assets nor can any discoveries from learning by doing take place. All uses are already discovered and individuals do not need to have any discretion in the use of resources as all resource uses can be perfectly allocated at the outset. In actuality, all rights are far from perfectly defined.

The presence of information costs imply that transacting parties voluntarily leave rights over certain properties of an asset unspecified (Barzel, 2005). For example, to completely specify all rights of an employee to use, say, a company laptop computer requires full knowledge of all possible uses and all the different ways in which the computer may be operated, as well as a detailed listing of these uses. In addition, the employer would need to perform a tight surveillance of the users of the computer in order to enforce their ownership rights to this asset. Many rights over the computer are therefore left unspecified, and the user of the computer is then capable of exercising some discretion in his decisions on how to use or operate the computer.[5]

An interesting complication is that rights to decide between some prespecified uses of assets may be delegated to others (Aghion & Tirole, 1995; Jensen & Meckling, 1992). Rights to specify specific rights over physical assets, delegate, and otherwise transfer rights over assets follow from formal ownership over assets, and in the case of labor from voluntary agreements to transfer these rights. In the following, we use the term "specific rights" to denote only the situation where rights are delineated in ways which do not allow for discretionary behavior. If discretionary behavior occurs, this is because some rights have been imperfectly specified or enforced. The difference between having discretion and holding

[5] As long as there is incentive compatibility, in the sense that discretionary behavior does not favor one party at the expense of another, rights most likely will remain unspecified.

residual rights over assets is that the latter case includes rights to unilaterally re-define and re-allocate (by delegation or otherwise) rights over assets which are not specified in contracts.

The employment contract is left partly open because of prohibitively high costs of specifying in detail all rights and obligations of the employee in all future conceivable situations (Coase, 1937). The authority relation arises from the presence of information and transaction costs, because in the presence of such costs, incomplete contracts can give rise to conflicts and disagreements over the uses of assets (Williamson, 1985). Assigning the right to decide how assets should be used in situations that are not covered by the contract is often a low-cost way of resolving this problem.

The Division of Labor, Learning by Doing, and Property Rights

Given the above, we may now think of an increase in the division of labor in production as *a new subdivision of use rights over assets*, so that each agent engaged in production holds use rights over a more narrow set of assets or holds a more narrow set of use rights over the same assets. The latter case may imply that use rights over an asset are shared between individuals; the one kind of specialization does not preclude the other.

It should be noted that the kind of assets over which an employee holds use rights need not be the same with division of labor as without. For example, an increase in the division of labor and specialization will often be accompanied by a shift from all-purpose tools to more specialized equipment. However, the introduction of more specific equipment and tools limits rights, because these have fewer different uses. Relatedly, learning (by doing) requires the exercise of use rights over assets. The better-specified and easily monitored use rights are, the less able are those who use assets to experiment and the more constrained is their learning. Critics of Taylorists methods of production and work organization have charged that they essentially and deliberately amounted to a "deskilling" of workers (Braverman, 1974). Not only did traditional factory work organized on Taylorite principles require few skills, but they also effectively hindered workers in acquiring new skills on the job, except generic ones. Conversely, giving employees greater discretion in their use of firm assets, that is, more use rights, means greater opportunity for learning by experimenting. Such experimentation may result in labor saving innovations of the kind envisaged by Adam Smith.

However, discretionary behavior will not always result in productivity gains. Apart from the agency problem (which is likely to increase with discretionary behavior, all else being equal; Jensen & Meckling, 1992), discretionary behaviors may cause problems when there are strong technological interdependencies, so that the functional performance[6] of a technology is greatly influenced by the fit between parts and/or between activities. Discretionary behaviors may then result in bottlenecks, lack of coordination of activities, or uneven development of components. These problems arise when those who deliver parts or carry out activities are not aware of, or not motivated to heed, the need for mutual adjustment between parts and activities. In turn, these problems can be ascribed to imperfectly specified rights over assets.

PRE points out that high information and enforcement costs mean that not all rights are well specified; however, *ignorance* is another reason why rights are left unspecified.[7] Ignorance is in a sense a byproduct of an increasing division of labor in production. Thus, it may take time to discover how best to sequence or conduct various activities when subdivision of rights over assets leads to increased complexity and interdependence between tasks; this may simply not be known beforehand. Moreover, specialization and growth of markets may give way for the introduction of new kinds of specialized tools and large scale equipment which in turn may introduce new problems of how to utilize capacity

---

[6] "Functional performance of a technology" is the objectively measured performance of a technology. As examples, Sahal (1981) mentions the thermal efficiency of an electric power plant defined as the ratio of the electrical to the total thermal output of the fuel or the horse-power-hour per gallon of fuel or the horse-power-to-weight ratio of a tractor.

[7] Thus, the preciseness with which use rights are specified depend on the benefit in terms of learning from discretionary actions on the one hand and the costs that may arise due to moral hazard and a lack of coordination on the other hand. Finally, this is subject to the constraints of knowledge of the various uses and the transaction costs involved in specifying and monitoring the various tasks.

effectively (Ames & Rosenberg, 1965; Leijonhufvud, 1986). When ignorance characterizes the process of re-defining tasks and implementing new equipment, enjoying large degrees of discretion in the exercise of use rights may result in uncoordinated action.

Problems of bottlenecks and uneven development of components may arise because many of the valuable dimensions of assets only become apparent from experimenting with the use of these assets. This makes it is difficult or perhaps even impossible to specify all valued dimensions and uses of assets *prior to* an increase in the division of labor. Even if important dimensions can be specified, it may be difficult to allocate these specific rights to individuals in ways which ensure the best use of assets. This may, for example, be the case with the time and place dimension of assets where some allocations result in excess stocks of intermediate products or in idle assets.

Solving problems that arise from technological interdependencies is an important source of innovative improvements (e.g., Rosenberg, 1976; Sahal, 1981). Such problem-solving emerges from ongoing learning with respect to coordination of tasks. Much of this learning depends on the accumulation of hands-on experience from experimenting whit different ways of laying out production tasks.

What institutional set-up best provides for experimentation and accumulation of experience in the coordination of tasks? In the following section, we argue that the Coasian firm in which managers (and/or owners) direct the use of resources has the ability to reduce (relative to market organization) the transaction costs involved in setting up and conducting experiment. In situations characterized by high measurement costs and ignorance, the high costs of recontracting will make it desirable to rely on explicitly open-ended contracts rather than seemingly complete contracts. In other words, with boundedly rational agents and technological uncertainty, there may be economic gains from experimenting in coordination and such experimentation may require the flexibility afforded by an open-ended contract for the provision of labor services and possibly combined with legal ownership of physical assets.

Coordination and Experimentation in Production

The need for coordination arises as a consequence of interdependencies in consumption, between consumption and production, and between production activities. Under certain restrictive assumption, including the assumption of perfectly defined rights and zero transaction costs, prices provide sufficient information to choose between different uses of resources in a manner that at the same time optimize the utility of individuals and ensure social coordination, leaving no valuable resources idle. Firms in this stylized world simply are specialized units of production that produce for outsiders (Demsetz, 1995: 8). Their "coordination tasks" consists of selecting the profit-maximizing quantities of inputs and outputs for the specialized production tasks they each carry out. In this world, there is no need for firms to consider the question of make or buy, since with perfect price information there are no gains from organizing one more or one less specialized task within a firm.

Specialization and Coordination

Beyond the extreme neoclassical world, there will be a trade-off between the advantages from specialization and the costs of coordinating increasingly specialized tasks and motivating individuals to put effort into executing these tasks. As Coase (1937) noted real-world markets do not function as smoothly as portrayed in the basic neoclassical model. The relevance of this to our argument is that the use of real-world markets may be particularly costly when further division of labor creates new unknown technological interdependencies that result in bottlenecks and uneven development of components.

Problems of bottlenecks and uneven development of components would exist even if total self-sufficiency prevailed, since individuals producing for their own needs may be unaware of how best to carry out an activity or how to develop the technologies they use. The division of labor and specialization in production, however, is likely to magnify the problems because mutual adjustments now require awareness of what other individuals are doing.[8] If in addition the functionality of a technology is strongly dependent on the external conditions for carrying out the tasks, there may be an ongoing need for mutual adjustments. As knowledge is accumulated from learning, by doing new ways of specifying use rights will emerge. In fact, the process of discovery in a learning-by-doing fashion may itself require continuous adaptation that involve the re-definition and re-allocation of use rights between the agents.

With an extensive division of labor and strong interdependence between tasks, it may be economically efficient to rely on a centrally developed and directed experimental setup rather than on decentralized negotiations over different experimental setups. Decentralized negotiations and specialization in production make it is necessary to obtain the consent of many parties, each holding a sub-set of rights over the relevant assets needed to operate the technology in order to continually re-allocate or re-delineate rights in a way that improves the functional performance of technologies. Therefore, when further divisions of labor introduce technological independence in production, reaching coordination requires the utilization of a complementary institution to arm-length markets transactions in order to solve the problems of mutual adjustment between individuals carrying out interdependent tasks, namely the firm.

[8] The benchmark for improving coordination by re-arranging rights over human and physical assets could be the functional performance of a technology without specialization in production. However, a comparison of the functional performance of technologies in situation of specialization and no specialization is complicated by the fact that it is most likely not the same technologies which are used in both situation. A comparison between the coordination that could have been achieved in a perfect (Walrasian) market characterized by a given degree of specialization and given technologies is another possible solution. However, in a timeless world of zero transaction costs there are only very few limits to the division of labor and tasks are likely be very specialized. To derive the optimal coordination by comparing an unrealistic Walrasian market model with a real situation is to commit an error that may result in too great investments in improving coordination. All one can say then is that an investment in the improvement in coordination is efficient if the resources invested in bringing about the improvement is the best possible investment at the time at which it is contemplated.

Coase traces the reason for the existence of firms to costs of using the price mechanism and observes that "[t]he most obvious cost of 'organizing' production through the price mechanism is that of discovering what the relevant prices are" (Coase, 1937: 21). With high market cost (later termed transaction costs), the market mode of coordination is substituted by a firm mode of co-ordination based on managerial decisions. Stated in the terminology of property rights, there are high costs of specifying the valued attributes of assets in all future states; this results in some rights over valued attributes of assets being left unspecified. When the coordination between factors is subject to changes in external factors (contingencies) that cannot be specified *ex ante*, continuous redirection of resources and re-planning taking advantage of the dimensions of time and place of assets will be necessary in order to avoid bottlenecks.[9, 10] Managed direction of resources may thus substitute for price direction of resources when parties to transactions realize that contingencies of different sorts may interrupt the timing and sequencing of interdependent activities (Wernerfelt, 1997).

An arbitrageur holding stocks of assets also makes his money from superior knowledge about the value of the unspecified attributes of time and place. The employment contract could be interpreted as providing a stock of labor services that within limits could be allocated to different uses by the direction of a manager in response to unforeseen contingencies (Coase, 1937). Managers then play the role of arbitrageurs holding

[9] Bargaining as a way of determining the prices may be very costly if each contingent plan involves many interdependent tasks that require close contacts between those who carry out the activities. In the case of team effects (joint production), a pricing scheme which solves the coordination problem of time and place will be extremely complex to work out (Rosen, 1981). Moreover, "...to calculate and implement this solution requires full knowledge of the underlying technology and productivity of team members in the first place" (idem: 81). And since errors in prices can be more costly than errors in the allocation of activities and time, it may be advantageous to rely on a manager to perform the allocation of time and workers to tasks and then let the manager monitor the activities. The importance of managerial direction diminishes if the technology becomes fully known to all.

[10] In a system of production, the timing of a particular sequence of activities is a way of reducing costs of idle labor or machinery and costs due to the building up of stocks of intermediate products. The advantage to tighter integration of different steps in the process is the costs saved on stocks and idle resources. These advantages have to be measured against the cost of failure or irregularities in strongly interdependent systems. Firms therefore may hold stocks of input in order to reduce these latter costs.

stocks of labor services in order to take advantages of superior knowledge of the time and place property of labor services. Arbitrageurs only need to bear the cost of stocks if they cannot appropriate the benefits of their knowledge of time and place by selling this information. Two factors may explain why it is not always feasible to sell information about time and place dimensions of assets. First, there is the well-known problem of information as a public good which, if revealed before the transaction, cannot be protected from capture (Arrow, 1962). Secondly, negotiations may take longer time than direction by orders and because of this, the opportunity for profitable action may be gone.

However, to Coase high costs of discovering the relevant contingencies are not a sufficient factor in explaining why firms exist because for each unforeseen contingency an individual discovers, she might be able to negotiate a new contract. Therefore, firms exist only if there is also "… costs of negotiating and concluding a separate contract for each exchange transaction that takes place on a market" (ibid.: 21), which on Coase's (1937) argument can be reduced by firm organization.

Much later Coase (1991) observed that already at the time when he wrote "The Nature of the Firms," he was aware that the analogy between the employment contract and the firm could give an incomplete picture of the nature of the firm. For one thing "… a firm may imply control over another person's property as well as over their labor," an amendment which figured in a footnote of the original paper indicating that firms may also possess use rights over rented assets. Coase (1991), however, also points to a *second* amendment to the original article. He draws attention to a lecture note from 1934 in which he states that "… a full firm relationship will not come about unless several such (incomplete) contracts are made with people and for things which cooperate with one another" (Coase 1991: 64). The latter amendment can be interpreted to mean that managerial decisions fill the holes of open-ended contracts in cases where coordination of *large number of factors* that cooperate with each other is required. This is exactly the situation that comes into existence when further divisions of labor in production result in technological interdependencies between many tasks.

The inability to specify future states of the world need not be the only explanation of why managed coordination is preferred to price coordination. The importance of managed direction of interdependent assets may also be motivated by endogenously created technological uncertainty, which arises when further division of labor alters tasks and create new unknown interdependencies between tasks. For example, the complexity of technologies may make it difficult to know in advance the particular requirements for efficient coordination. In fact, with a great deal of interdependence in a complex system, the best time and place to use an asset depend on the specification for the uses of all *other* assets that are needed in the production. Managed coordination is therefore important even if there are no unforeseeable contingencies but multilateral interdependencies that require adjustment in tasks. Firms thus exist as parallel institutions to markets in order to capture the value of the unspecified attributes of assets.[11]

To sum up, firms exists if there is both high costs of "discovering the relevant prices," *and* if these costs cannot be reduced by contracting for this information. The latter may be the case where there are numerous, potentially multilateral and mutual interdependencies between owners of resources. This makes it costly to carry out the needed rearrangement of tasks to take advantage of new information about states of the world. Firms then save transaction costs by substituting *many* independently determined contingent contracts by managed directions. This may be taken to be the essence of Coase (1937). To this may be added the transaction cost that can be saved when endogenously created technological uncertainty and complexity require sequential delineation and re-allocation of rights over assets as a way of gradually improving the functional performance of technologies. The role of a managers thus are

[11] Ownership of assets, however, may also be a low-cost way of internalizing externalities. When an owner wants to enjoy the benefits of labor specialization he is required to delegate use rights to agents. If he has full knowledge of all the uses of the assets that he owns and of all the consequences of the various uses he can delegate use rights in ways that minimize the negative (economic) consequences of externalities. To avoid some of the costs of externalities which arise with interdependent activities and team production, managers may "regulate" the use of assets within firms by for example, defining strict limits of authority of decision takers or by simply forbidding certain uses of assets. To the extent that she is unaware of all the possible externalities, an owner/manager will have to conduct various experiments not only in ways of producing but also in the selective grant of authority.

different from that of an arbitrageurs since the former engage in learning activities that involve the experimentation with different allocations of use rights in order to discover profit opportunities.

For managed direction of resources to be efficient, managers must be at least as qualified in discovering the relevant prices (i.e., in this case, "shadow prices", namely the internal opportunity costs of different uses of assets) as independent contractors would be. Otherwise, costs of transacting may be saved at the expense of efficiency in the use of resources. If managers have better knowledge or information about the valuable uses of resources compared to other agents, managers have a natural ownership advantage over resources. Such an advantage explains the single person firm, but not necessarily why managers in order to take advantage of this knowledge hire employees who are prepared to take orders within certain limits.

However, managers are highly likely to acquire superior information about the opportunity costs of different use rights over assets that make up a complex technology. From the literature on incremental innovations, it is apparent that the solution to problems of bottlenecks and uneven development in components are based on experience in production and development. I shall now argue that this experience is probably more easily accumulated within the boundaries of firms.

One might expect this learning process to be less costly to organize within rather than across the boundaries of firms because managers, who hold residual rights over assets—including rights to re-define and re-allocate specific rights—are able to conduct controlled experiments without continuously having to re-negotiate contracts. Moreover, due to the uncertainty surrounding the outcome of various experimental setups, independent contractors will have different subjective valuations of different experimental strategies that can be pursued. This is likely to complicate the bargaining process.[12] In contrast, within a firm managers can unilaterally create a "controlled" experiment in which they only change some aspects of the tasks in order to trace the effects of some specific re-arrangements of rights. Finally, coordinating interdependent

[12] In this connection wage, contracts may be an efficient way of sharing risks from experimenting, putting the entire burden of risk on the shoulders of those who carry out experiments (cf. Knight, 1921).

tasks within the boundaries of a firm may provide managers with a more complete picture of the nature of interdependencies. This information is not only important in relation to eliminating bottlenecks, but also in relation to avoiding problems of uneven development of components by setting up interface standards and other more permanent solutions.

Other Determinants of the "Costs of Discovering the Relevant Prices"

In the previous section, uncertainty and complexity were seen as determinants of the costs of discovering "the relevant prices." As many contributions to the economics of organization have made clear, there may be many other reasons why there are high costs of discovering the relevant prices and some of these reasons may become more predominant with increased specialization in production. Different modern theories of the firm put emphasis on different costs of transacting—such as measurement costs, contracting costs and costs of enforcing rights over assets—in explaining the existence and boundaries of firms. This section provides a brief overview of some of the various arguments presented in the literature, and relates them to the arguments of this chapter.

Taken by themselves, high costs of discovering what the relevant prices are need not require the existence of firms. For example, high measurement costs may make it costly to determine the valued characteristics of assets and this may cause problems of excess sorting and of shirking on quality (Barzel, 1982). Managed direction of assets may not always be the most effective means of solving such problems. Other arrangements, such as product guarantees, quality classes, and investments in brand name capital are often better suited. However, specialization in production may create other kinds of problems related to high measurement costs. One of the advantages of specialization between production and consumption is the ability to take advantage of economies of scale in equipment. In order to realize such advantages, many individuals may have to cooperate in order to operate the equipment. If tasks are not perfectly specified in terms of each individual's rights to use different attributes of the equipment or if such rights cannot be enforced, it is possible that each individual will exercise discretion and try to gain at the expense of others.

If, for example, it is difficult to determine how much the operation of each individual contributes to the wear and tear of the equipment, there is a problem of common property and this implies that there is likely to be insufficient incentives for investments in maintenance.[13] Therefore according to Barzel (1997), "[a]ttributes susceptible to serious common-property problems, such as equipment lubrication, will tend to be owned by organizations created to control these problems" (p. 58). One way of controlling such problems, which involves an organization, is to use a fixed wage contract in which workers are remunerated for their time rather than their output. But workers receiving specific income for a specific amount of time have no incentives to devise ways of exercising use rights over assets that would generate utility. Thus, when fixed wage contracts are used, monitoring of effort will be needed to induce effort and managers will have to specify the tasks to be performed (Barzel, 1997).

Specialization in production creates a similar problem if there are high costs of determining the level of effort provided by individuals. In particular, where cooperation in teams is needed between different individuals in order to realize rents on their labor services from producing a given output, problems of common property may occur. This is because each individual is able to exercise discretion in providing his labor services but only bears part of the costs. The solution to such team problems is to set up an organization that will economize on metering costs and

[13] As explained by Barzel (1997), the common property problem disappears if the equipment is scaled down to fit a single operator producing an identifiable output. Some mean of coordinating individual operators is still needed but with each producing an identifiable output contracting in market may provide the coordination.

an allocation of rewards which is more in accord with the effort delivered (Alchian & Demsetz, 1972).[14] A monitor specializing[15] in metering effort and holding rights to residual income, to alter membership of the team, and to sell all their rights may provide such a solution.

A second type of explanation of why firms exist emphasizes how high information costs or uncertainty makes it difficult to enforce one's rights over assets (e.g., Hart, 1995, 1995; Klein et al., 1978; Williamson, 1975, 1985). According to this literature, there is a strong correlation between asset specificity and contracting failure, and this causes inefficiencies because valuable transactions involving investments in transaction specific assets is not completed. In particular, it is assumed that high costs of planning for all various contingencies of describing future states and of communicating these plans to a third party makes it impossible to write complete contracts. Therefore, one cannot safeguard one's investments in specific assets with the aid of a third party (typically a court).

Specialization in production may make investments in specialized equipment and in specialized knowledge which have no alternative value outside a particular relation attractive. According to incomplete contract theories, undertaking such investments requires vertical integration so that firms can take on the role of enforcer of contracts. Williamson (1985), for example, describes firms as their own ultimate court of appeal. To Hart, the physical assets over which a legitimate owner has formal residual use rights' define firms. Having residual use rights over assets provides the owner with a mean of enforcing contracts that would

[14] According to Alchian and Demsetz (1972), team production is production in which " 1) several types of resources are used and 2) the product is not a sum of separable outputs of each cooperating resource. An additional factor creates a team organization problem - not all resources used in team production belong to one person" (p. 779). The separate ownership over resource is motivated by such factors as risk aversion, the prohibition of slavery, and sunk costs investments which make short-term ownership to costly. However, the separation of ownership could also have been motivated by the possibility of realizing advantages of specialization in accumulating different complementary skills of production.

[15] Monitoring means to "… measure output performance, apportioning rewards, observing the input behavior of inputs as means of detecting or estimating their marginal productivity and giving assignments or *instruction in what to do and how to do it*" (Alchian & Demsetz, 1972: 782; my emphasis). However, the reason for the latter kind of activity is left unexplained.

not be possible if transactions took place between different owners of assets.

These different explanations of firms have in common the idea that the best uses of resources *are* already known. In one interpretation, this is because they implicitly take the standard neoclassical theory of production as sufficient for describing production, and thus assumes public knowledge of production sets and the availability of all relevant skills required for production (Langlois & Foss, 1999; Loasby, 1999). The problem is then "simply" how to provide the right incentives for efficient exploitation of or investment in the assets in question. Monitoring and incentive schemes that are more advanced than those that can be devised for re-contracting between independent individuals (with definite time horizons) help overcome such problems. However, direction by order giving is not a central element in the solution, and the possibilities of learning to coordinate tasks is limited to improving monitoring skills (Alchian & Demsetz, 1972; Oi, 1983).

Each one of the above explanations of firms surely provides important insights into factors that influence the boundaries of firms that are complementary to the specialization story told in this paper. However, they do not give any account of why the boundaries of firms may change over time. In the next section, we argue that opportunities for specialization advantages together with continuous learning in coordination within the boundaries of firms provide opportunities for continuous change in the boundary of firms.

Make or Buy Decisions: Taking Advantage of the Division of Labor

Coase (1937) explains why market and firms co-exists in a specialized economy. Having established a reason for the existence of firms, Coase goes on to apply transaction costs analysis to determine the boundaries of firms. He argues that there are increasing costs to organizing more transaction within a firm and that this explains why not all transactions are carried out in one big firm.When increasing marginal costs of management leave room for other firms to come into existence, different subsets of production tasks will be organized in different firms.

Coase (1937) did not investigate the factors that would make the costs of organizing a particular subset of tasks lower for some firms than for others. However, such an analysis is important to make or buy decisions, because these kinds of decisions are seldom a question of making a choice between either a firm or open market transactions, but of organizing a subset of production tasks within one firm *rather than another firm*. Thus, Coase (1991: 73) argues that "... if one is to explain the institutional structure of production in the system as a whole it is necessary to uncover the reasons why the costs of organizing particular activities differs among firms," and these costs "... may depend on the other activities that the firms are undertaking (p. 67)".[16]

A deeper understanding of why firms differ with respect to their costs of organizing different activities is therefore important to the analysis of the "make or buy" decisions of firms. The issue of the internal organization of the firm is intertwined with the analysis of firm boundaries, save for the case where firms are equally good at coordinating the same types of tasks. The arguments presented earlier suggest that learning by doing in production and coordination results in differential ability and thus

[16] Coase (1937) mentions "... increasing opportunity costs due to the failure of entrepreneurs to make the best use of the factor of production" (p. 23) as one of the reasons why there is a limit to the efficient size of a firm but not why some firms are more efficient in carrying out certain activities rather than other activities. Coase assumes that there are increasing opportunity costs of expanding the boundaries of a firm because "... the costs of losses through mistakes will increase with an increase in the spatial distribution of the transactions organized, in the dissimilarity of the transactions, and in the probability of changes in the relevant prices. As more transactions are organized by an entrepreneur, it would appear that the transactions would tend to be either different in kind or in different places" (p. 25). Managers, in other words, have limited capacity to "discover the relevant prices" and this increases mistakes as more and more dissimilar transactions are organized in a firm (Richardson, 1972) has a very similar argument for the boundaries of firms). Clearly, some of the problems of limited capacity of managers may be solved by delegation and selective intervention. However, as explained by Williamson (1985) there are unavoidable side effects of moving transactions into a hierarchy. According to Williamson, these costs may not be offset by gains from reduced transaction costs unless some degree of assets specificity is involved. In my opinion, the losses from integration may also be offset by the flexibility afforded by the employment contract with respect to selective intervention in activities. However, in order to efficiently delegate responsibility a manager needs experience.

different costs among firms with respect to the organization of different kinds of tasks (Demsetz, 1973). The make or buy decisions of firms reflect these endogenous changes in production and coordination costs as employees and managers learn in production and coordination.

The importance of learning in coordination tasks depends on the extent and complexity of technological interdependencies in production activities. If specialization creates strong technological interdependencies, there will be advantages from learning to coordinate which favor organization within the boundaries of firms, at least until sufficient experimentation has resulted in the delineation of specific rights in manners which deals with these interdependencies.

The costs of organizing the interdependent tasks of course also needs to be considered when deciding on make or buy. These costs consists in increasing marginal management costs and forgone opportunities for taking advantage of further specialization in other tasks until coordination costs with the already obtained degrees of labor specialization have been reduced. Since accumulation of experience in coordination is often local and not transferable (except, possibly, at high costs), firms tend to persistently differ in their capabilities and this may explain a certain path dependency in the kind of activities firms undertake. In other words, it may be difficult for firms to buy the services they produce in house cheaper from suppliers (cf. also the analysis in Langlois & Robertson, 1995).

Accumulation of experience in coordination may explain some of the cost differences between firms, but this is not the entire explanation. A different reason may be found in the fact that there are also advantages of specializing in knowledge, not just in tasks (Loasby, 1999). Managers in firms may possess different scientific and technological knowledge and therefore have different abilities to perform experiments in coordination. This line of reasoning is in line with Demsetz (1991) who argues that firms are not perfect substitutes in production of goods and services. In Demsetz' view, firms are specialized production entities, each holding a different subset of the production knowledge needed to produce a consumption good. For specialization in knowledge to be productive, specialists need to be able to take advantage of other specialists' knowledge. Within firms, coordination between specialists with different kinds of knowledge is achieved by giving orders. Following Demsetz, this is efficient because otherwise each specialist would have to learn what all other specialists already know. The boundaries of firms are shaped by the relative costs and advantages of putting specialized knowledge to use by means of order-giving or by means of selling goods accompanied by instruction on uses. The latter is advantageous when the best use of an asset does not strongly depend on it being used at a particular time and place.

Giving orders and producing goods embodying specialized knowledge are thus two different ways of economizing with the costs of transferring knowledge. This explanation indicates that a decision to make or buy must also depend on the trade-off between taking advantage of low-cost experimentation within the boundaries of a firm and taking advantage of specialized knowledge located in other firms.

Finally, socially developed norms, rules, and routines also reduce costs of coordination. Norms and routines make the behavior of others more predictable, thus reducing the need for information required for the coordination of actions. In the terminology of property rights, norms and routines can be said to act as self-enforcing constraints on use rights. Such norms and routines certainly also play a great role in determining the costs of coordination in different firms and the decision to make rather than to buy may often be grounded on superior, non-imitable, and non-transferable routines which aids coordination in production. Norms and routines are not confined to firms; they may as well evolve as means of coordinating actions between independent contractors such as, for example, two different firms. In that case, they also reduce costs of market transactions.

Firms need not have full information about all the interdependencies between tasks before they decide to buy rather than to make. Some of the experimental activities needed to improve the effective working of technologies that can be organized by means of, for example, joint ventures, strategic alliances, complex long-term contracts, etc. In some of these arrangements, the parties rely more on the use of prices and negotiations and in some more on directions as means of coordination. However, what distinguishes these arrangements from internal organization of the transactions is that they are based on agreements between legally independent agents—thus, the analysis in this chapter of the choice between firm and market applies also to the analysis of the choice between firms and interfirm arrangements. The legally independent parties to an interfirm arrangement will have to reach an agreement on the terms of corporation and this often require that they possess some knowledge/beliefs about what the proper procedures are for the experimental activities. The choice between the various arrangements therefore must depend on the knowledge/beliefs the parties have of the relevant procedures for the completion of the experimental learning process since otherwise it may be very costly to reach an agreement (if possible at all).

Conclusion

In this chapter, we expanded the Coasian view of the firm developed in the previous chapter and argued that learning in coordination within firms centers on discovering the true opportunity costs of the use of assets where prices fail to provide the proper information. There are many reasons why price information fails to indicate these opportunity cost; we have focused on one in particular, namely the increasing interdependence among various tasks which follows from increased specialization in tasks: A high degree of interdependence may make it impossible for managers *ex ante* to specify rights over assets and labor in such a way that that each sub-task fits optimally to all other tasks carried out. For example, the problem of defining an optimal sequence of task in a complex systems of production may require more calculation capacity than is available in a supercomputer (Galloway, 1996).[17] In such cases, improvements in allocation of rights require experimentation in the sequencing of tasks, which in turn requires sequential re-delineation and re-allocation of specific use rights among those carrying out the various tasks. Managed coordination is likely to be less costly relative to arm-length bargaining partly

[17] In describing the problem of scheduling batches in a 5-stage production process, Galloway (1996) writes "[t]he best schedule is the one which minimizes this idle time. Unfortunately, the only way to find the best schedule is by trial and error, and whit 20 batches there are 1.8×10^{18} possible schedules. This problem is too large even for modern computers, so a simplifying assumption is frequently used" (p. 64).

because order-taking saves bargaining costs, partly because some specialized technological knowledge may be required in order to discover the opportunity costs (or shadow prices) of various subdivisions of tasks and the respective allocation of rights.

Increasing division of labor in production influences the boundaries of firms by creating opportunities for economic gains from learning to coordinate technologically interdependent tasks. However, since there are increasing marginal costs of coordinating more specialized tasks within the boundaries of a firm it may sometime be advantageous to outsource interdependent tasks in order to take advantage of further specialization in other tasks. Finally, the knowledge acquired in experimenting with coordination together with advantages of specialization in scientific and technical knowledge may explain the relative advantages of firms in organizing some particular tasks and these advantages must also be taken into account in the make and buy decision. In the next chapter, we link this learning-based view of the firm to entrepreneurship.

References

Afuah, A. (2003). Redefining firm boundaries in the face of the internet: Are firms really shrinking? *Academy of Management Review, 28*, 34–53.

Aghion, P., & Tirole J. (1995). Real and formal authority in organizations. *Journal of Political Economy, 105*, 1–29.

Alchian, A. A., & Demsetz, H. (1972). Production, information costs, and economic organization. *American Economic Review, 62*, 772–795.

Alchian, A. A., & Woodward, S. L. (1988). The firm is dead; long live the firm: A review of Oliver E. Williamson's the economic institutions of capitalism. *Journal of Economic Literature, 26*, 65–79.

Ames, E. A., & Rosenberg, N. (1965). The progressive division and specialization of industries. *The Journal of Development Studies, 1*, 363–383.

Arrow, K. J. (1962). The economic implications of learning by doing. *The Review of Economic Studies, 29*, 155–173. Oxford Journals.

Barzel, Y. (1982). Measurement costs and the organization of markets. *Journal of Law and Economics, 25*, 27–48.

Barzel, Y. (1985 [2005]). Transaction costs: Are they just costs? Reprinted in C. Mènard (Ed.), *Controversies and challenges in the new institutional economics*. Edward Elgar.

Barzel, Y. (1997). *Economic analysis of property rights* (2nd ed.). Cambridge University Press.

Becker, G. S., & Murphy, K. M. (1992). Division of labor, coordination costs, and knowledge. *The Quarterly Journal of Economics, 107*, 1137–1160.

Braverman, H. (1974). *Labor and monopoly capital*. Monthly Review.

Cheung, S. N. S. (1983). The contractual nature of the firm. *Journal of Law and Economics, 26*, 1–26.

Coase, R. H. (1937). The nature of the firm. *Economica NS4*, 386–405.

Coase, R. H. (1991). 1991 Nobel lecture: The institutional structure of production. In O. E. Williamson & S. G. Winter, (Eds.), 1993 *The nature of the firm: Origins, evolution, and development*. Oxford University Press.

Demsetz, H. (1973). Industry structure, market rivalry, and public policy. *The Journal of Law and Economics, 16*, 1–9.

Demsetz, H. (1991). The nature of the firm revisited. In O. E. Williamson & S. G. Winter (Eds.), *The nature of the firm*. Blackwell.

Demsetz, H. (1995). *The economics of the business firm*. Cambridge University Press.

Demsetz, H. (1997a). *The economics of the business firm: Seven critical commentaries*. Cambridge University Press.

Demsetz, H. (1997b). The firm in economic theory: A quiet revolution. *American Economic Review, 87 (Papers and Proceedings)*, 426–429.

Demsetz, H. (2011). R. H. Coase and the neoclassical model of the economic system. *Journal of Law and Economics, 54*, 7–13.

Epple, D., Argote, L., & Mowery, D. C. (1991). Organizational learning curves: A method for investigating intra-plant transfer of knowledge acquired through learning by doing. *Organization Science, 2*, 58–70.

Foss, N. J. (1997). Economics, institutions, and Ludwig von Mises. *Cultural Dynamics, 9*, 77–96.

Galloway, L. (1996). *Operation management: The basics*. International Thomson Business Press.

Hart, O. (1995). *Firms, contracts, and financial structure*. The Clarendon Press.

Hatch, N. W., & Mowery, D. C. (1998). Process innovation and learning by doing in semiconductor manufacturing. *Management Science, 44*, 1461–1477.

Jensen, M., & Meckling, W. (1976). Theory of the firm managerial behavior, agency costs and ownership structure. *Journal of Financial Economics, 3*, 305–360.

Jensen, M. C., & Meckling. W. (1992). Specific and general knowledge and organizational structure. In L. Werin & H. Wijkander (Eds.), *Contract economics*. Blackwell.

Klein, B., Crawford, R. G., & Alchian, A. A. (1978). Vertical integration, appropriable rents, and the competitive contracting process. *Journal of Law and Economics, 21*, 297–326.

Knight, F. H. (1921). *Risk, uncertainty, and profit*. Hart, Schaffner & Marx.

Kretschmer, T., & Khashabi, P. (2020). Digital transformation and organization design: An integrated approach. *California Management Review, 62*, 86–104.

Langlois, R. N., & Foss, N. J. (1999). Capabilities and governance: The rebirth of production in the theory of economic organization. *Kyklos, 52*, 201–218.

Langlois, R. N., & Robertson, P. L. (1995). *Firms, markets and economic change: A dynamic theory of business institutions*. Routledge.

Leijonhufvud, A. (1986). Capitalism and the factory system. In Richard N. Langlois (Ed.), *Economics as a process: Essays in the new institutional economics*. Cambridge University Press.

Loasby, B. J. (1999). *Knowledge, institutions, and evolution in economics*. Routledge.

Loebbecke, C., & Picot, A. (2015). Reflections on societal and business model transformation arising from digitization and big data analytics: A research agenda. *Journal of Strategic Information Systems, 24*, 149–157.

Oi, W. (1983). Heterogeneous firms and the organization of production. *Economic Inquiry, 21*, 147–171.

Richardson, G. B. (1972). The organisation of industry. *The Economic Journal, 82*, 883–896.

Rosen, S. (1981). The economics of superstars. *The American Economic Review, 71*, 845–858.

Rosenberg, N. (1976). *Perspectives on technology*. Cambridge University Press.

Sachs, J., & Yang, X. (2008). *Economic development and the division of labor*. Blackwell.

Sahal, D. (1981). *Patterns of technological innovation*. Addison-Wesley.

Smith, A. (1776). *An inquiry into the nature and causes of the wealth of nations*. Oxford University Press.

Stigler, G. J. (1951). The division of labor is limited by the extent of the market. *The Journal of Political Economy, 59*, 185–193.

Wernerfelt, B. (1997). On the nature and scope of the firm: An adjustment-cost theory. *The Journal of Business, 70*, 489–514.

Westall, A., Ramsden, P., & Foley, J. (2000). *Micro-entrepreneurs: Creating enterprising communities*. New Economics Foundation.

Williamson, O. E. (1975). *Markets and hierarchies: Analysis and antitrust implications*. Free Press.

Williamson, O. E. (1985). *The economic institutions of capitalism*. Free Press.

Yang, X., & Ng, S. (1995). *Specialization and division of labor: A survey*. Centre for International Economic Studies, University of Adelaide.

Young, A. A. (1928). Increasing returns and economic progress. *The Economic Journal, 38*, 527–542.

9

Property Rights, Transaction Costs, and Entrepreneurship

On November 24th, 1874 United States Patent #157,124 was granted to Joseph Glidden of DeKalb, Illinois for improved barbed wire fencing. Glidden's patent was only the culmination of a series of nine patents for improvements to wire fencing that were granted by the U.S. Patent Office to American inventors, beginning with Michael Kelly in November 1868 and ending with Glidden's patent (McCallum, 1965) which quickly became dominant. To be sure, wire fencing had been used for a very long time. However, property rights over livestock were less secure, as wire fencing would often break under the impact of heavy livestock pressing against the fencing. This would not happen with barbed wire, and the costs at which property rights to livestock could be protected therefore fell dramatically (Anderson & Hill, 2004; Dennen, 1976).

The new fencing innovation set in motion dramatic path-dependent processes of institutional, organizational, and technological innovations throughout the Plains. Indeed, it has been argued that the emergence of barbed wire was as important a factor behind changing the life at the Plains as the rifle, telegraph, and locomotive (Hill, 1969; Webb, 1931).

K. Foss and N. J. Foss, *Economic Microfoundations of Strategic Management*,
https://doi.org/10.1007/978-3-031-12910-0_9

Arguably, barbed wire was *the* crucial factor underlying the transformation from ranching to farming, as the new fencing protected crops from livestock and meant that fields could be used as pasture after the harvest. Barbed wire ended the great cattle drives and the need for branding. Cattle could be kept at a limited area, which greatly increased the value to agricultural firms (farms) of this resource (Webb, 1931). It prompted experimentation with new more valuable resources, notably the Shorthorn, Angus, and the Hereford, as substitutes for the tougher, but less valuable Longhorn, as well as with the uses of land.

This example implies that resources (e.g., land) hold a number of potential uses, characteristics, etc., and that some of these "attributes" may not yet have been discovered. Changes in the (transaction) costs of defining and enforcing property rights, induced by technological or legal changes or brought about by entrepreneurs themselves, alert entrepreneurs to the discovery of new potentially valuable resource attributes. Such discoveries may translate into sustainable advantages. We integrate these implications with strategic management theory, providing a novel theoretical account of opportunity discovery and the competitive implications thereof. We build on the resource-based notion of firms as bundles of heterogeneous resources (Barney, 1991; Penrose, 1959), but place this notion in a dynamic context (Helfat & Peteraf, 2003). The full set of resource attributes is not known *apriori*, so these attributes must be discovered (Denrell et al., 2003; Nelson & Winter, 1982). The fundamental argument of this chapter is that *such discovery is influenced by transaction costs.*

Two mechanisms link transaction costs and opportunity discovery. The first mechanism—the "*appropriability mechanism*"—is the one implied by the above example: Transaction costs determine how well-defined and enforced property rights to resource attributes are, and this influences the value that entrepreneurial resource owners expect to appropriate, and therefore their incentives to engage in opportunity discovery (Shepherd & DeTienne, 2005). Second, entrepreneurial experience influences opportunity discovery (e.g., Shane, 2000). However, experience (also) emerges from resource learning, that is, entrepreneurs' learning about the attributes of resources—a process we began to analyze in the preceding chapter. Such learning entails transaction costs, for example, the costs of measuring the productivity potential of employees (Alchian & Demsetz, 1972; Barzel, 1982). The transaction costs that entrepreneurs face influence their resource learning, introduce path dependence in such learning (Argyres & Liebeskind, 1999; Argyres & Mayer, 2007), and therefore influence which opportunities will be discovered. We call this the "*resource learning mechanism.*" Both mechanisms imply that the level and direction of opportunity discovery is influenced by transaction costs.

Like Chapter 5, this chapter is located in the intersection of the economics of property rights (EPR) and the resource-based view (RBV). The argument that transaction costs and experience impact opportunity discovery contributes to the entrepreneurship literature (e.g., Kirzner, 1973; Shane, 2000; Shepherd & Tienne, 2005), for example, by suggesting answers to key issues in the entrepreneurship literature concerning the emergence and locus of entrepreneurial opportunities (Shane & Venkataraman, 2000). Moreover, links are forged with the strategic management literature: We explore how opportunity discovery may translate into sustained heterogeneity, and thereby respond to recent calls in the strategy literature for understanding rent-creation as a dynamic process (e.g., Helfat & Peteraf, 2003; Lippman & Rumelt, 2003a, b) and for integrating opportunity discovery with the RBV (e.g., Alvarez & Busenitz, 2001; Lippman & Rumelt, 2003b).

Opportunity Discovery and Experiential Knowledge

Opportunity Discovery

Opportunity (or entrepreneurial) discovery consists of actions initiated by individuals (Kirzner, 1973; Schumpeter, 1911; Shane, 2000) or teams (Kor, 2003; Penrose, 1959) directed at identifying a hitherto neglected opportunity. An opportunity is a situation "… in which new goods, services, raw materials, and organizing methods can be introduced and sold at a price greater than their cost of production" (Shane & Venkataraman, 2000: 220). Opportunity discovery may consist of the discovery of new resource attributes or features of organization that help to serve market needs and wants in a better way (Schumpeter, 1911). For example, individuals or firms that introduce new improved contractual designs, sorting systems, organization structures, etc. may realize an entrepreneurial return that are based on the lowering of transaction costs. Opportunity discovery may result in the formation of new firms (e.g., Knight, 1921; Ardichivili et al., 2003), may take place inside existing firms (e.g., Miller, 1983), or may not involve firms at all (Kirzner, 1973). Although entrepreneurship may have destructive consequences (Baumol, 1990), the focus is here on value-creating opportunity discovery.[1]

To some writers (notably Kirzner, 1973, 1997), the discovery of opportunities is costless, and the search, discovery, evaluation, and exploitation of opportunities are essentially one process. To us, in contrast, opportunity discovery requires significant knowledge, effort, and investment, and it makes analytical sense to distinguish different phases in the opportunity discovery process. Nevertheless, the relevant phases are strongly overlapping, as stressed in much recent creativity research (e.g., Finke et al., 1992; Runco & Chand, 1995). This overlap implies that opportunity discovery may be understood as a continuous interplay between the phases, the generation of candidate ideas constantly interacting with evaluation. Except for cases of pure arbitrage, opportunity discovery implies that entrepreneurs have to engage in speculation concerning the appropriable value that will result from the discovery (Denrell et al., 2003; Eckardt & Shane, 2003; Knight, 1921; Kaish & Gilad, 1991; Lippman & Rumelt, 2003b).

Experiential Knowledge

An influential view in the entrepreneurship literature is that opportunity discovery depends critically on the *alertness* of the entrepreneur (Busenitz, 1996; Kirzner, 1973; Shane, 2003). The recent opportunity

[1] Note that although we link up with the discovery branch of entrepreneurship, there are other, arguably more radical, notions of entrepreneurship, aptly called "creation" views by Alvarez and Barney (2007).

discovery literature concentrates on operationalizing alertness and identifying its antecedents, concentrating on expected rewards and prior, mainly experiential, knowledge (Busenitz, 1996; Gaglio & Katz, 2001; Krueger, 2000; Shane, 2000, 2003; Shane & Venkataraman, 2000; Venkataraman, 1997). In the literature, experiential knowledge is taken to include such things as "prior knowledge about markets," "prior knowledge about how to serve markets," "prior knowledge of customer problems," etc. (e.g., Shane, 2000). This emphasis harmonizes with recent firm-level work on opportunity discovery (usually conceptualized as innovativeness) and its experiential antecendents (Helfat, 1997; Helfat & Raubitschek, 2000; Lumpkin & Lichtenstein, 2005; Matsusaka, 2001; Mitchell et al., 2002; Mosakowski, 1998). However, in this literature, experiential knowledge concerns the understanding of the uses, functionalities, services, characteristics, etc. of *firm resources*, that is, knowledge of resource attributes (Foss & Foss, 2005). Such knowledge emerges from "resource learning" (Mahoney, 1995; Penrose, 1959), that is, human resources learning about the services of other (human and non-human) resources.

The outcome of resource learning is experiential knowledge that in turn influences opportunity discovery. Experiential knowledge influences opportunity discovery for the following reasons. Entrepreneurs need to categorize and describe items (specifically items that can serve as an indication of an opportunity) in a relevant information domain, in order to build a workable representation of that domain that can assist them in opportunity discovery. People who work in ill-structured decision situations—such as those that characterize opportunity discovery (Knight, 1921)—require a representation that identifies and even amplifies relevant information so as to allow them to discover discrepancies between the world and the representation that is used as an action guide (Gaglio & Katz, 2001; Walsh, 1995). Experiential knowledge shapes the building of categories and representations that assist entrepreneurs in decision-making (Abelson & Black, 1986; Day & Lord, 1992; Gaglio & Katz, 2001; Nisbett & Ross, 1980). A deep level of expertise within a certain information domain allows people to faster categorize ill-structured problems. Also, deep knowledge may provide an entrepreneur with more detailed ways of understanding and describing his or her resources (Hodgkinson & Johnson, 1994; Rensch et al., 1994), and thereby assist the discovery of new resource attributes.

Experiential knowledge from resource learning is fundamental in the initial phase of venture formation in which entrepreneurs may only be able to identify some elements of an opportunity and need to invoke imagination, and search for and process information in order to more fully identify and evaluate the opportunity (Ardichvili et al., 2003; Cohen & Levinthal, 1990). Moreover, the knowledge that entrepreneurs, or entrepreneurial teams (Kor, 2003; Penrose, 1959), acquire through resource learning may influence their knowledge structures in ways that enable them to identify opportunities faster or more consistently within a particular information domain (e.g., relating to a particular bundle of resources) than those who do not possess this particular knowledge (Dierickx & Cool, 1989; Shane, 2000). Thus, experiential knowledge from resource learning may also underlie path-dependent trajectories of discovery in established firms (Helfat, 1994; Helfat & Raubitschek, 2000), and be a source of sustained competitive advantage for such firms (Dierickx & Cool, 1989; Mahoney, 1995).

Cognition and Incentives in Opportunity Discovery

The emphasis on experiential knowledge in the entrepreneurship literature represents a cognitive focus on opportunity discovery: The main emphasis is on the discovery part, and the actual evaluation and eventual seizing of an opportunity, including the appropriation of returns, is often less emphasized (cf. Kirzner, 1973, 1997). This neglect is potentially misleading, because cognitive science implies that there is a strong and ongoing process of feedback from evaluation to discovery (cf. Finke et al., 1992; Runco & Chand, 1995). In other words, expectations of returns from opportunities influence the discovery process itself, influencing the intensity with which opportunities will be pursued and the directions in which discovery efforts will take. For example, entrepreneurs or firms may well possess the experiential knowledge that enables their scanning of certain emerging technological fields in search of discoveries. However, if expected returns in some of these fields are highly uncertain because of weak enforcement of property rights to discoveries within the field, this may negatively impact discovery efforts (Cohen & Klepper, 1996). Expected returns are influenced by assessments of the costs at which property rights to discoveries can be delineated and enforced (and possibly also exchanged). These costs are transaction costs. For example, if transaction costs are sufficiently large, they may provide a powerful disincentive to discovery. This indicates that it is worthwhile exploring the role of transaction costs and property rights in the process of opportunity discovery in order to provide a more comprehensive understanding of the antecedents of opportunity discovery,

Linking Transaction Costs and Opportunity Discovery: Appropriability and Resource Learning Mechanisms

Transaction costs have seldom been explicitly related to opportunity discovery, and there is little or no theoretical and empirical work that systematically explores the relation (but see Michael [2007] for a transaction cost analysis of the marketing side of entrepreneurial ventures). The following discussion conceptualizes the two mechanisms that link transaction costs and opportunity discovery, the "*appropriability mechanism*" and the "*resource learning mechanism.*" We make use of the economics of property rights (the EPR) to frame the discussion.

Attributes and Opportunity Discovery

A key tenet of the EPR is the notion that most resources have multiple attributes (Barzel, 1997; Cheung, 1970; Coase, 1960; Demsetz, 1988), including the different functionalities and services/uses (Penrose, 1959) that the resources can offer. For example, a copying machine is a multi-attribute resource in the sense that it can be used in different time periods, by many different persons, for many different types of copying work, can be purchased in different colors, sizes, etc. Building on the EPR, we argued in Chapter 5 that the understanding of resource value is furthered by conceptualizing resources as bundles of attributes to which property rights may be delineated, enforced, and exchanged. This builds on the recognition that it is not resources themselves that are valuable, but their attributes. Understanding attributes and the extent to which property rights can be delineated, enforced, and exchanged add increased insight into resource value and value appropriation.

Adopting an attributes perspective not only yields additional insight into resource value and value appropriation; it also links opportunity discovery and resources. Thus, opportunity discovery may be conceptualized in terms of the discovery of new valued resource attributes. Individual resources may have a multitude of *undiscovered* attributes, some of which may be associated with appropriable value (Demsetz, 1988; Denrell et al., 2003). A determinant of the appropriable value from newly discovered resource attributes is whether the discoverer can delineate and enforce property rights to his new discovery. In turn, this depends on the transaction cost of delineating and enforcing property rights.

The Appropriability Mechanism

A crucial insight of the EPR is that transactions involve the exchange of property rights rather than the exchange of goods per se (Coase, 1960, 1988). Hence, the unit of analysis is the individual property right. Property rights consist of the right to consume, obtain income from, and alienate resource attributes (Alchian, 1965). The EPR dissociates property rights from legal connotations, so that an (economic) property right is more about the actual ability of an agent to consume, obtain income from, and alienate resource attributes than to whether he is legally entitled to do so, that is, it is about effective control (cf. Barzel, 1997). (Obviously, however, such ability is likely to be influenced by the extent to which property rights are legally enforceable). In this perspective, transaction costs can be defined in a consistent manner, namely as the costs of delineating, enforcing, and exchanging property rights (Barzel, 1997; Coase, 1960). Property rights may be enforced by the state as well as by private means (Barzel, 1997), as in the case of the barbed wire example. When rights are perfectly enforced, owners can completely hinder non-payers from taking possession of, imitating, or consuming any resource attributes that they hold property rights to. That is, property rights and their enforcement influence the value entrepreneurs can appropriate from exploration of different resource attributes.

Given that discovery and evaluation of opportunities are closely intertwined processes, transaction costs influence *which attributes* will be subject to discovery. Thus, the perceived cost of delineating and enforcing property rights to newly discovered attributes are likely to influence discovery efforts in predictable directions. As a general matter, "… entrepreneurial energy and innovation are starkly biased towards the creation of those surpluses which can be *appropriated* by the innovator" (Lippman & Rumelt, 2003a: 924; our emphasis; cf. also Shepherd & DeTienne, 2005). This link between transaction costs and discovery is the "appropriability mechanism."

To illustrate, consider the barbed wire example that introduced this paper. Prior to the advent of barbed wire, the cost of enforcing property rights to cattle and land were such that ranchers did not seriously consider experimenting with introducing the Shorthorn, Angus, and Hereford on the plains. The cost of enforcing property rights to these attributes of land and cattle were prohibitive. The changing property rights' structure implied by the advent of barbed wire had the effect of drastically lowering enforcement cost, *changing the space for opportunity discovery*. As another example, the 1980 Supreme Court decision in Diamond v. Chakrabarty implied a significant removal of uncertainty with respect to what was the law in biotechnology patenting. This drastically changed the appropriability regime confronting a number of industries (Pisan, 1990), and made exploring genetic engineering and its uses in these industries substantially more attractive. The relevant space of potential opportunity discovery was expanded as a result of the delineation and enforcement of property rights to biotech research results.

Property rights to resource attributes (or bundles of attributes) are seldom perfectly enforced, as owners face transaction costs of delineating and protecting property rights to such attributes. Some resource attributes will optimally not be protected against non-payers' attempts at appropriating value generated by the attributes (Barzel, 1997). For example, resources are not likely to be completely protected against imitation; contracts may not completely safeguard against holdup; supermarkets do not monitor and price the parking spaces they offer customers (effectively inviting non-owners to capture these attributes); etc. Such imperfect protection of property rights to valuable attributes gives rise to capture by non-owners in ways that dissipate value. Capture takes many forms: While value erosion from imitation (Barney, 1991) may be the relevant mechanism of capture in the case of the biotechnology example above, the barbed wire example suggests other, more direct, kinds of capture of property rights in the form of theft. Another example is holdup (Williamson, 1996). However, the underlying logic is the same: Property rights to certain resource attributes are captured, and the "victim" is not compensated (Barzel, 1997). Note in passing that an implication of this reasoning is that the reduction of transaction costs by means of new ways of delineating (e.g., better ways of measuring attributes), protecting (e.g., improved protection of business secretes, better ways of protecting credit card information in virtual exchanges, barbed wire,), and exchanging (e.g., introducing internet trade) property rights may constitute entrepreneurial opportunities.

In sum, the appropriability mechanism implies that *transaction costs help defining the relevant space for opportunity discovery*: The transaction costs of enforcing property rights to newly discovered resource attributes moderate the relation between experiential knowledge and opportunity discovery by influencing the distribution of perceived costs and benefits in the space of discoveries.

The Resource Learning Mechanism

While experiential knowledge matters to the discovery of opportunities, building such knowledge is costly. Resource learning may imply experimenting with resources, combining and recombining them, and learning about their attributes in the process (Orr, 1996; Penrose, 1959). Thus, resource learning emerges from M&As (Matsusaka, 2001), the ramp-up and calibration of factory production (Foss, 2001; Stiglitz & Heine,

2007), interaction between employees and managers (Argote, 1999), and other processes that result in the discovery of new resource attributes. These processes are costly, and some of the relevant costs are transaction costs, such as the costs of negotiating M&As, contracting (and re-contracting) over resource uses in strategic alliances, delineating decision rights over corporate resources inside the firm, building information revelation mechanisms that can reveal the relevant types of human capital, etc. While no direct estimates of the transaction costs of resource learning appear to exist, there are reasons to believe that such costs are often substantial, think of expenses on corporate lawyers in connection with M&As or the recruitment costs of hiring new employees.

To further exemplify, consider the problem of how to design and coordinate a system of productive tasks with many task complementarities. Designers are not likely to have full knowledge *ex ante* about, for example, the optimal sequencing of tasks, even if they perfectly know the functionalities of physical resources. For example, the problem of defining an optimal sequence of tasks in a complex system of production may require more calculation capacity than is available in a supercomputer (Galloway, 1996: 64). Some kind of experimental, iterative learning process is then required to solve the problem. In a world of complete knowledge, perfect rationality, and zero transaction cost, all rights to all uses of all assets could be perfectly specified *ex ante* in contracts; there would be no need to learn about resource attributes. However, in a more realistic setting, understanding the various ways in which tasks may be sequenced, the physical equipment used, etc. requires an iterative process of specifying resource attributes and trying out solutions. Costs of defining resource uses, measuring the productivity of resources, coordinating uses, etc. are incurred. If these costs are very high, it may only pay to perform a few iterations before a solution is decided upon. Little experiential knowledge is built concerning the properties of the production system. In contrast, lower costs may lead to faster and more resource learning, and a solution that is closer to the optimum. In sum, *transaction costs directly influence resource learning processes*, because the expected gains will be balanced against the (transaction and other) costs of resource learning.

Opportunity Discovery and Sustainable Advantage: A Framework for Analysis

Benchmarks

While experiential knowledge, the appropriability mechanism, and the resource learning mechanism add insight into opportunity discovery, do they also influence how and to what extent opportunity discovery translates into sustainable advantage? Moreover, while experiential learning and the two mechanisms have so far been treated separately, it seems warranted to consider the realistic situations where they interact.

To examine these issues in greater detail, we make use of ("unrealistic") benchmark situations where the effects of experiential knowledge, the appropriability mechanism, and the resource learning mechanism on opportunity discovery and advantage are nullified. The analysis is then complicated by sequentially "switching on" experiential knowledge and the two mechanisms. The purpose of this exercise is to be able to more clearly study the effects on certain dependent variables (e.g., opportunity discovery) of certain independent variables (e.g., transaction costs), eliminating other influences. Thus, one can consider the direct effects of the independent variables as a precursor to understanding combined or interaction effects.

Such thought experiments are commonplace in economics (see Hahn [1973] for a methodological explication and defence of its use), and are also sometimes used by management scholars. For example, Barney (1991) begins his exposition of the RBV by analyzing what will happen to sustained competitive advantages in a setting where firms control identical resource bundles, then gradually introducing antecedents of sustained competitive advantage to finally arrive at the full set of jointly necessary conditions for such advantage. Thus, Barney begins from an extreme benchmark, and gradually relaxes the constraining assumptions, introducing greater realism.

We specifically ask how property rights/transaction costs and knowledge separately and interactively influence opportunity discovery and sustained advantage. The result is a clearer understanding of the operation of the mechanisms that are at work. The independent variables that we here consider as determinants of opportunity discovery and sustained advantage are property rights and transaction costs and (experiential) knowledge. We abstract from other potentially relevant independent variables, for example, risk preferences, personality traits, network position, etc.

Blueprint technology. Two analytical devices are used to characterize the benchmarks. The first one is that of "blueprint technology" (Demsetz, 1991; Robinson, 1933), that is, the assumption that knowledge that can be used by any one entrepreneur can also be used by any other entrepreneur. In the simplest versions of production theory in economics (Robinson, 1933), productive knowledge is a pure public good, that is, it is non-rivalrous in use and it is impossible to exclude any non-payers. We do not adopt this extreme assumption. As understood here, blueprint knowledge only means that the transfer of knowledge is not impeded by imperfect and differential absorptive capacity on the part of entrepreneurs. It may be possible to exclude non-payers depending on the (transaction) costs of doing so. The opposite of blueprint technology is that knowledge exchange and transfer among entrepreneurs is limited because of absorptive capacity gaps.

Zero transaction costs. The second device we make use of is that of the zero transaction cost setting introduced by Coase (1960). Coase (1988) and Barzel (1997) argue that the assumption of zero transaction costs means that property rights to all valuable resource attributes are perfectly delineated, enforced, and exchanged at zero cost. At issue, however, is what is meant by "all valuable resource attributes." Coase (1988) interprets the zero cost condition as implying omniscience, so that zero transaction costs literally mean that *all* resource attributes (including all future resource uses) are known to decision-makers. In such a setting, there is, of course, no scope for opportunity discovery (Denrell et al., 2003). However, other writers, with whom we side, argue that opportunity discovery can take place even if transaction costs are zero: That existing transactions are costless to transact does not logically imply that all potential transactions have been discovered (cf. Kirzner, 1973). Accordingly, the zero transaction cost condition does not rule out opportunity discovery that is rooted in privately held experiential knowledge (cf. Makowski & Ostroy, 2001). However, it does rule out costs of writing and enforcing contracts involving knowledge transactions. That is, only differences in absorptive capacity may impede knowledge transactions when transaction costs are zero. Moreover, in the zero transaction cost benchmark, the appropriability mechanism and the resource learning mechanism are eliminated in the sense that transaction costs cannot be antecedents of opportunity discovery under this benchmark.

Four cases The two benchmark situations can now applied to generate four cases, depending on whether we "switch on" or "switch off" transaction costs and knowledge. Specifically, we consider four combinations of the determinants of opportunity discovery and sustainable advantage. These are [zero transaction costs, blueprint knowledge], [zero transaction costs, non-blueprint knowledge], [positive transaction costs, blueprint knowledge], and [positive transaction costs, non-blueprint knowledge]. For each one of these combinations, we discuss the nature of discoverable opportunities, value creation and appropriation, the role of opportunity discovery in creating resource heterogeneity, and the organization of opportunity discovery and exploitation. We focus on these dependent variables because they are crucially important in entrepreneurship and strategic management research. See Table 9.1.

Case A: Zero Transaction Costs and Blueprint Knowledge

Opportunity discovery. Kirzner (1973) argues that even in the model of the market of economics textbooks, there is a need for the entrepreneur as an equilibrating force. This textbook model is one in which transaction costs are zero and where knowledge is blueprint. Even in this extreme case opportunity discovery can take, namely in the form of the discovery of new resource attributes and resource learning (recall that there is no assumption here that entrepreneurs are omniscient). The entrepreneur's incentives to engage in opportunity discovery and resource learning arise from the discrepancies in earnings from exploiting resource

Table 9.1 Four cases

	Opportunity discovery (OD)	Value creation and appro-priation	Path dependence and sustainable heterogeneity	Economic organization
Case A: Zero Transac-tion Costs and Blueprint Knowl-edge	All oppor-tunities will be fully exploited	The two condtbns imply that value creation will be maxi m um. Value w ill be split solely according to bargaining powers	None—as 1. All knowledge that can be profitably traded will be traded 2. All inefficiencies can be traded away	Spot market contracting can handle all transact ions/no rationale for firms
Case B: Zero Transac-tion Costs and Non-blueprint Knowl-edge	Know ledge will accumu-late differ-ently and this will impact OD. Less OD than underA	Less value creation than under A, since some knowl-edge will not be fully exploited	Yes because of. imperfect absorptive capacity	Clusters of complementary assets arise, as some knowledge cannot be traded on factor markets
Case C: Positive Transac-tion Costs and Blueprint Knowl-edge	TC of enforcing discov-eries negatively influence OD. Less OD than UnderA	TC reduce value creation. Resource ownersh-pand vertical integra-tion are means of appropria-tion	PD may stem from, e.g., sunk cost investments	Firms as governance structures emerge

(continued)

Table 9.1 (continued)

	Opportunity discovery (OD)	Value creation and appropriation	Path dependence and sustainable heterogeneity	Economic organization
Case D: Positive Transaction Costs and Non-blueprint Knowledge	OD determined jointly by TC and knowledge	Value creation less than under all other Cases	TC area source of path-dependence (sustained heterogeneity	Firm organization is chosen to foster OD "Speculative" cause of ownership

attributes that he has already discovered and exploiting newly discovered attributes. However, neither transaction costs, nor barriers to knowledge utilization will influence which resource attributes entrepreneurs discover. Property rights can be delineated and enforced at zero cost, which eliminates all concerns of capture, including capture from imitation. This nullifies the appropriability mechanism. Also, there are no transaction costs that hinder resource learning; this mechanism, too, is nullified.

Value creation and appropriation. The zero transaction cost assumption and the assumption that prior knowledge can be fully absorbed by any entrepreneur imply that any value creating discovery will be utilized to its full economic capacity (i.e., where the marginal net benefit from further utilization is zero) (Makowski & Ostroy, 2001). Over time, total value creation will be maximized because of the absence of transaction costs and barriers to knowledge absorption. While value creation will be independent of bargaining power (cf. the Coase Theorem, Coase, 1960), bargaining power will determine how much value entrepreneurs and factor owners will *appropriate*. Specifically, how much value an entrepreneur who makes a discovery can appropriate depends on the bargaining game among the entrepreneur, those who benefit from the discovery, and those who hold property rights to complementary resources that are needed to exploit the discovery (cf. Teece, 1986). There is no a priori reason to impute all or even the largest amount of the created value to the entrepreneur.

Path dependence and sustainable heterogeneity. Entrepreneurs may start out with heterogeneous bundles of resources attributes which results in heterogeneous resource learning. However, as there are no transaction costs of selling knowledge and no barriers to absorbing knowledge, no entrepreneur will be locked into a path of inferior resource learning and opportunity discovery: "Best-practice knowledge" can be purchased at factor markets. In fact, other kinds of path dependence are also ruled out by virtue of the zero transaction cost condition, as optimal solutions will always be negotiated when there are no obstacles (i.e., transaction costs) to doing so. Thus, no strategic issues relating to lock-in to inferior products or technical solutions can arise.

The other side of the coin is that long-lasting resource heterogeneity among entrepreneurs cannot be an outcome of initial knowledge endowments or opportunity discovery, because all knowledge and all discoveries will be made available on the relevant factor markets. When entrepreneurs hold secure property rights to the discoveries they make, they will be best off by letting others share in the discovery (against compensation). Factor heterogeneity stemming from initial knowledge endowments or discoveries cannot persist in this situation. Moreover, as factor markets perfectly reflect the expected value of resource attributes and of resource learning (the foundation for the discovery of new attributes), no entrepreneur can consistently outperform the market. Thus, the absence of costs or cognitive constraints on the movement of resources, including knowledge, limit the causes of sustainable heterogeneity, and therefore differential rents (Barney, 1991), to initial endowments of non-reproducible resources (e.g., location).

Economic organization. As the resource learning mechanism and the appropriability mechanisms are nullified, the process of resource learning is independent of transaction costs, and can be organized through market contracts at zero cost. Firms as governance structures have no particular advantages concerning the organization of resource learning processes (Williamson, 1996). Relatedly, the entrepreneur has no incentive to control a resource or resource bundle by means of holding ownership title; costless bargaining and contracting over resource attributes can substitute for ownership (Hart, 1995). Thus, firms will not arise as means to secure value appropriation (as in Liebeskind, 1996).

Case B: Zero Transaction Costs and Non-blueprint Knowledge

Opportunity discovery. When knowledge is non-blueprint, entrepreneurs will have less access to knowledge than in Case A (Lippman and Rumelt, 1982). The entrepreneur's own accumulated experience is an important antecedent of opportunity discovery (Shane, 2000, 2003). The non-blueprint nature of knowledge in this case is a force limiting overall opportunity discovery. However, entrepreneurs may gain by developing means of reducing buyers' knowledge requirement. For example, they may make knowledge "more tradable" by embodying it in products, equipment, or in modular components which do not require much knowledge on the part of the recipient (Demsetz, 1991). Thus, a consequence of the changing nature of knowledge is that the *nature* of the opportunity discovery process changes.

Value creation and appropriation. In terms of assumptions made, Case B perhaps best approximates the RBV (Barney, 1991; Peteraf, 1993): While the RBV pays little attention to transaction costs, differential knowledge resources are central in this view. However, the explicit introduction of opportunity discovery, a phenomenon not yet incorporated with the RBV, means that strategic challenges go beyond those traditionally identified in the RBV. Because in this case all transaction costs are zero, and property rights can therefore be costlessly protected, threats to value appropriation from imitation, opportunistic holdup and the like are non-existent. As in the RBV entrepreneurs may face potential substitutability threats; however, with ongoing opportunity discovery entrepreneurs face the threat of total value erosion, as completely different bodies of knowledge and complementary resource may serve a given market need in a new and very different way. This is a serious concern to an entrepreneur as he or she cannot insure his investments in knowledge and complementary assets against such events. No insurance markets emerge to insure against discoveries that are deemed unlikely to succeed by all except a knowledgeable entrepreneur (Knight, 1921). Strategic flexibility becomes important in this case.

Path dependence and sustainable heterogeneity. As in Case A, entrepreneurs may start out with different bundles of resource attributes which gives rise to differential accumulation of knowledge. However, in a setting in which knowledge is non-blueprint (contrary to Case A), resource heterogeneity among entrepreneurs may be sustained and perhaps even increase. The reason is that an entrepreneur's prior related knowledge provides him or her with a learning advantage and possible first mover advantages within the scope of his or her knowledge domain. Thus, the entrepreneur has an incentive to direct opportunity discovery efforts in directions that allow building on already accumulated knowledge.

Economic organization. At the same time, the entrepreneur also faces incentives to set up a productive operation by contracting with complementary resources on a longer-term basis (Alchian, 1984; Casson, 1999; Lipmann & Rumelt, 2003b). This makes economic sense to the extent that the idiosyncratic nature of the knowledge accumulated through resource learning processes makes it hard to trade on factor markets (Teece, 1982). The entrepreneur's opportunity discovery will be influenced by resource learning stemming from these complementary resources. As more knowledge that is specific to these complementary resources is accumulated, the entrepreneur will come to value this particular bundle of resources higher than entrepreneurs who do not possess the resource-specific knowledge. This may confer a factor market advantage (Barney, 1986) as the knowledgeable entrepreneur is able to take more resource attributes into account in the resource evaluation (Denrell et al., 2003). Heterogeneity is sustained because of advantages in opportunity discovery relating to the knowledge resources controlled by the entrepreneur.

Case C: Positive Transaction Costs and Blueprint Knowledge

Opportunity discovery. The presence of transaction costs "switches on" the resource learning and the appropriability mechanisms (these are not present in Case A and B). The presence of transaction costs implies that not all opportunities that would be value creating in Cases A and B will be exploited. First, transaction costs imply that property rights will be less secure and need protection. This negatively influences the net value that the entrepreneur expects to appropriate (Shepherd & DeTienne, 2005; Teece, 1986; Coff, 1997). Thus, if contracts are imperfect because of transaction costs, other agents may capture parts of the surplus from a discovery. For example, a buyer may engage in holdups (Hart, 1995; Williamson, 1996) involving complementary assets that are necessary to the production or marketing of the discovery. Second, the appropriability risk from imitation becomes a concern. Third, costs of engaging in resource learning also limit constrain the set of opportunities relative to Case A and B.

An implication of these points is that it now (in contrast to Case A and B) matters *which* entrepreneur (or firm) makes a particular discovery (even if the knowledge leading to the discovery is fully transferable). Some entrepreneurs may face transaction costs that other entrepreneurs do not face (to the same extent); for example, entrepreneurs may face differential abilities to raise capital and access complementary resources, or face different costs of protecting property rights to discoveries or costs of resource learning.

Value creation and appropriation. Overall, the presence of transaction costs harm value creation relative to Case A, first, because transaction costs dissipate value (Barzel, 1997), and, second, because many discoveries will not be made in the presence of transaction costs. The presence of transaction costs in itself may lead to opportunity discovery as entrepreneurs seek to reduce transaction costs to increase the value they can appropriate (Coase, 1988; Makowski & Ostroy, 2001). However, some transaction costs will remain. Whether the presence of transaction costs is more harmful to value creation than non-blueprint knowledge (i.e., Case B) cannot be established on *apriori* grounds.

The presence of transaction costs has several distinct strategic implications to firms in the context of opportunity discovery. First, value appropriation depends on the transaction costs firms face of delineating and enforcing property rights to resource attributes. Thus, when looking for resource attributes that may yield a competitive advantage, entrepreneurial firms must consider what are the costs of keeping these attributes rare (and non-imitable), as well as protected from other types of value capture (Chi, 1994; Foss & Foss, 2005). Second, transaction costs introduce strategic hazards in the form of externalities that negatively impact resource values. For example, low-quality producers may threaten established high-quality levels. In this situation, entrepreneurial firms may become more dependent on complementary resources that can credibly signal their intentions to important stakeholders (Akerlof, 1970; Klein & Leffler, 1981). For entrepreneurial firms that direct opportunity discovery toward the quality dimension, it is therefore a strategic challenge to acquire the relevant complementary resources and to direct opportunity discovery toward areas in which they are able to put these resources to use.

Path dependence and sustainable heterogeneity. In Case C resource heterogeneity emerges endogenously from discovery, but for reasons different from those mentioned in Case B. Transaction costs make some of the resource attributes discovered by entrepreneurs non-tradable. Some types of resource attributes are less likely to be tradable, such as new uses of capabilities, brand name capital, reputation, and culture (Dierickx & Cool, 1989); entrepreneurs face incentives to utilize these themselves by engaging in opportunity discovery in areas related to these resources (Denrell et al., 2003). This gives rise to path dependency, ultimately induced by transaction costs (cf. also Argyres & Liebeskind, 1999).

Economic organization. In a setting with transaction costs, the process of opportunity discovery will be organized in a way that minimizes transaction costs. Transaction costs create incentives for the entrepreneur to *own* resources rather than to rely on contractual delineation and enforcement of property rights to newly discovered resource attributes. Resource ownership confers a bundle of rights, including rights to *hitherto undiscovered* attributes of the relevant resource. An entrepreneur may prefer to acquire ownership of a resource rather than acquire a specified, finite list of rights to resource attributes. The reason is that resource ownership is a low-cost means of allocating the rights to resource attributes that are discovered by the entrepreneur/owner. In a well-functioning legal system, resource ownership usually implies that the courts will not interfere with an entrepreneur/owner's exploitation of new attributes. There is also an incentive effect on opportunity discovery of resource ownership: Ownership implies a legally recognized right to the income of that resource, including the right to income from discovered attributes. Moreover, resource ownership may economize with costs of enforcing property rights, because owning rather than contracting over attributes can make imitation of a discovery more costly to would-be imitators (cf. Teece, 1986; Liebeskind, 1996). Note in passing that these rationales of ownership go beyond those discussed in the economics literature (e.g., Barzel, 1982, 1997; Hart, 1995; Williamson, 1985), but makes sense in a dynamic economy in the context of opportunity discovery.

When an entrepreneur takes ownership of resources this is tantamount to forming a firm (Foss & Klein, 2005; Knight, 1921). Strictly speaking, however, it need not be the entrepreneur who sets up a firm or acquires complementary resources as, under the assumptions of the present case, the entrepreneur's knowledge may be transferred to another entrepreneur, depending on the transaction costs of doing this. Conceivably, the entrepreneur may face high transaction costs in establishing ownership to the preferred bundle of resources and in establishing a firm governance structure. For this reason, the entrepreneur may prefer to transfer the relevant knowledge of a discovery to those who have lower transaction costs of setting up a firm. Transaction costs thus determine the *organizational context of opportunity discovery*, specifically whether the entrepreneur becomes an employee or an individual contractor.

Case D: Positive Transaction Costs and Non-blueprint Knowledge

Opportunity discovery. The final, and most realistic, case is the one where both transaction costs and differential ability to absorb knowledge are allowed to influence opportunity discovery. As in Case B, firms' discovery activities will be path-dependent, because of differential accumulation of knowledge stemming from the non-blueprint nature of knowledge (Helfat, 1994; Helfat & Raubitschek, 2000). The difference is that the resource learning and the appropriability mechanisms now both contribute to shaping paths of discovery. Several different scenarios can be conceived depending on how knowledge and these two mechanisms together influence opportunity discovery. For example, firms may be very favorably positioned *vis-à-vis* opportunity discovery in terms of their control of firm-specific knowledge resources and learning; however, it may be so costly to enforce discoveries (i.e., the appropriability mechanism) that advantages are offset. Or, resource learning may be so costly (e.g., forging contractual links with outside parties to access knowledge is very costly) that it swamps benefits from low costs of enforcing property rights.

The relative contribution of knowledge and the appropriability and resource learning mechanisms with respect to shaping opportunity discovery (as well as their interaction) requires more analytical attention than can be given here. However, what influences opportunity discovery in actuality is likely to be industry-specific. Evolutionary economists and students of technological change (Cohen & Klepper, 1996; Nelson & Winter, 1982; Teece, 1986; Helfat, 1994) argue that industry-level technological change is shaped by technological opportunities and appropriability regimes and their interaction, but that these forces differ across industries. Similarly, whether knowledge or the two transaction cost mechanisms are the primary antecedents of opportunity discovery is likely to be industry-specific. For example, rather strong intellectual property rights' protection characterizes the pharmaceutical industry, and this gives the appropriability mechanism a form that is different from the form it takes in industries with weaker appropriability regimes, such as the music industry.

Value creation and appropriation. As firms discover opportunities along paths of discovery that are shaped by both firm-specific knowledge and transaction costs, the resulting heterogeneity in discovery may translate into long-lasting differences in appropriable value creation across firms. What has been said above about value creation and appropriation under Case B and C also applies here.

Path dependence and sustainable heterogeneity. Transaction costs and differential knowledge reinforce one another in the creation of resource heterogeneity and path dependency. Prior related knowledge directly constrains the learning processes, because it directs search and experimentation in certain directions as well as provides entrepreneurs with certain heuristics for problem-solving. This will produce sustained heterogeneity (when knowledge is non-blueprint). The presence of transaction costs reinforces such heterogeneity. First, as transaction costs make some opportunities unattractive (because property rights cannot be sufficiently enforced), some resource attributes will not be explored and entrepreneurs will not build knowledge relative to these. Second, transaction costs and knowledge directly interact in shaping the resource learning processes. That is, there are knowledge and transaction costs implication of organizing resource learning processes. Transaction costs exert an influence because there are costs of searching for, exploring, accessing, and combining resource attributes to try out new combinations (Kogut & Zander, 1992; Matsusaka, 2001; Teece, 1982), and these costs constrain resource learning because they constrain what resource combinations can be tried, and what resource attributes that will be examined. An implication for theory, which so far has been unexamined in strategic management, is that transaction costs play a key role in the formation and development of capabilities.

Economic organization. Transaction costs and resource learning interact in providing a rationale for ownership and firm organization. Entrepreneurs have incentives to own resources because of the costs of trading accumulated knowledge and for the "speculative" reason that resource ownership confers property rights to discovered resource attributes to the resource owner. Firms as governance structure emerge in order to reduce the costs of protecting against imitation and other types of rent capture, such as shirking and holdup (Liebeskind, 1996). However, the extent to which firms are needed in order to protect against imitation differs from Case C. In Case D, entrepreneurs have different abilities to absorb knowledge, creating a barrier to imitation. Differences among entrepreneurs with respect to their knowledge bases likewise influence their incentives to imitate competitors' resource bundles, as they do not see the same opportunities for discovery of new attributes as those who have the relevant knowledge (Denrell et al., 2003). Thus, we should expect to see not only more sustainable heterogeneity among entrepreneurs in this setting compared to Case C, but also less non-market economic organization.

A further rationale for firm organization is that firms emerge as means of lowering the transaction costs involved in resource learning. Resource learning may require that the entrepreneur have to enter into collaboration with firms who control complementary knowledge that costly to transfer. Organizing experimental processes involving combination and recombination of resource attributes across markets requires continuous costly re-negotiation among resource owners. Moreover, asset specificity may arise from such processes, giving rise to the familiar holdup problem. Given this, part of the rationale of firms is that they can organize entrepreneurial learning processes in a transaction cost-minimizing manner, as argued in the previous chapter.. Thus, contrary to Kirzner (1973), who is adamant that entrepreneurship may be exercised independently of asset ownership and firm organization, there is a logical nexus between entrepreneurship, ownership, and firms, namely when transaction costs are positive.[2]

[2] Foss and Klein (2012) pursue this further, and also criticizes the opportunity discovery approach that has informed the present chapter.

Conclusions

The key aim of this chapter has been to define a role for transaction costs and property rights along with experiential knowledge as antecedents of opportunity discovery and sustained advantage, extending the reasoning in the two previous chapters. The arguments lie in the intersection of the strategic management and entrepreneurship fields and contribute to both of these.

Consider how we contribute to the resource-based view. Because it is the source of new value creation, entrepreneurship seems central to strategic management. In general, however, entrepreneurship has not been a prominent theme in strategy research (but see, e.g., Hitt et al., 2001; Ireland et al., 2003). Although there may be deep reasons why strategy and the entrepreneurship field have lived somewhat separate lives—such as differences in levels of analysis (firm vs. the entrepreneur)—many prominent scholars have argued that understanding entrepreneurship is a pressing issue in strategic management (e.g., Denrell et al., 2003; Hitt et al., 2001; Helfat & Peteraf, 2003; Lippman & Rumelt, 2003b).

In this chapter, we have tried to overcome the schism in a number of ways. First, concerning the differences concerning levels of analysis, the analysis here suggests that what is the relevant level is *partially dependent on transaction cost considerations*: If such costs are zero, the entrepreneur is unambiguously the relevant level, as firms will not exist. However, to the extent that transaction costs cause learning and capabilities to be internalized in firms, firms become the relevant level of analysis for opportunity discovery. Second, we have linked the key entrepreneurship construct of opportunity discovery to RBV notions of resource heterogeneity and learning. While others have linked opportunity discovery to resource learning (Foss, 2001; Helfat, 1997; Helfat & Peteraf, 2003; Mahoney, 1995; Penrose, 1959; Stieglitz & Heine, 2007) and transaction costs to the RBV (e.g., Coff, 1999; Foss & Foss, 2005; Kim & Mahoney, 2006), the specific contribution of this work is to introduce transaction costs and property rights as important antecedents of opportunity discovery in the context of a resource-based view. Transaction costs moderate the relation between knowledge and opportunity discovery, and they influence the costs of engaging in resource learning. For this reason, transaction costs matter to understanding *which resource attributes* entrepreneurial firms will explore, and *which firms* will explore *which* resource attributes.

Transaction costs furthermore matter to the understanding of how heterogeneous resources emerge from resource learning, and how resource heterogeneity may be sustained—both key issues in a dynamic RBV (Helfat & Peteraf, 2003). Knowledge-based differences among entrepreneurs are likely to create long-lasting differences in entrepreneurial discovery activities when knowledge gained from resource learning possesses cumulative and path-dependent characteristics. This can lead to firm-specific trajectories of learning that result in continuous identification and exploitation of opportunities and are rent-yielding along the trajectory. Helfat (1994, 1997) describes such trajectories for the US petroleum industry. Some of the knowledge that underlies a path of resource learning is tied to a firm-specific context (Kogut & Zander, 1992), because of the high transaction costs to outsiders of accessing it. For example, it has been argued that knowledge embedded in capabilities and culture is often costly to competitors to access and imitate (Dierickx & Cool, 1989), and prohibitively costly to trade on factors markets. In other words, transaction costs may play a key role in the creation of sustained heterogeneity and therefore sustained advantage.

The analysis in this chapter also contributes to the entrepreneurship field. In an influential paper, Shane and Venkataraman (2000: 218) argued that although entrepreneurship provides research questions for many fields in management, strategy and organization scholars are fundamentally concerned with three sets of research questions, namely why, when and how (1) entrepreneurial opportunities arise; (2) certain individuals and firms and not others discover and exploit opportunities, and (3) different modes of action are used to exploit those opportunities (including the issue of "… how the exploitation of entrepreneurial opportunities are organized in the economy," p. 224). The distinctive contribution of this work is to proffer new answers informed by the EPR and the RBV to these important research questions.

With respect to the first question, how entrepreneurial opportunities arise, we have pointed to the important role of transaction costs and property rights in understanding how entrepreneurial opportunities arise. At a very fundamental level, transaction costs are at the heart of entrepreneurship: The presence of transaction costs means that there cannot be a full set of contingent forward markets, as in the full intertemporal general equilibrium model of Debreu (1959) (Radner, 1968). The intertemporal coordination of present resource uses and future consumption is undertaken by the entrepreneurial function, that is, by engaging in the discovery of intertemporal opportunities (Knight, 1921). At a simpler level, the reduction of transaction costs may in itself constitute an entrepreneurial opportunity, as when firms that come up with new contractual designs, new sorting mechanisms, etc. gain an entrepreneurial advantage (Makowski & Ostroy, 2001). However, a specific contribution of this work has been to link transaction costs to prior, mainly experiential, knowledge in opportunity discovery. Thus, transaction costs matter to opportunity discovery because, first, the experiential outcomes of processes of resource learning depend on the transaction costs of combining and recombining resource attributes, ascertaining the attributes of resources, etc., and, second, the transaction costs of enforcing property rights to discoveries influence the direction of search.

Concerning the second research question outlined by Shane and Venkatamaran, that is, why, when, and how certain individuals and firms and not others discover and exploit opportunities, this work suggests that there is an important transaction cost dimension to addressing the question. Traditionally, the entrepreneurship literature has pointed to such things as network position, personality traits, and—increasingly—prior, experiential knowledge as the critical antecedents. The literature on firm evolution and innovation similarly points to prior related knowledge as the critical antecedent. While not disagreeing with this view per se, a comprehensive understanding of the why, when, and how of opportunity discovery must include transaction costs, because resource learning and the direction of search efforts are fundamentally impacted by transaction costs.

With respect to the final research question, the why, when, and how different modes of action are used to exploit opportunities, this work has developed the point that the exploitation of opportunities is fundamentally dependent on transaction costs. In particular, firms may arise not only for the reasons familiar from the organizational economics literature (Hart, 1995; Williamson, 1996), or to protect against imitation (Liebeskind, 1996), but also because they may be superior mechanisms for coordinating resource learning processes (Foss, 2001). A specific contribution is the argument that resource ownership may arise partly for transaction cost reasons and partly for speculative reasons: Entrepreneurs will assume ownership of resources which they expect to be rich in hitherto undiscovered but potentially valuable attributes because contracting over these attributes is too costly. This differs from the view prevalent in organizational economics, namely that ownership is an instrument of bargaining power that arises to minimize dissipation of value caused by holdup threats (Hart, 1995).

Finally, let us outline a few limitations that may call for future work. As indicated by the example that introduced this chapter, there is an important "macro"-angle into opportunity discovery and resources: Changes in technologies, institutions, and legal regimes influence the matrix of property rights and transaction costs that firms face (Oxley, 1999; Teece, 1986; North, 1990; Williamson, 1996). Our analysis implies that these changes impact opportunity discovery in predictable ways and have implications for sustained advantage. In this paper, we have sidestepped this macro-angle in order to keep the analytical complexity at a manageable level. However, future work may theorize the links from macro-change to opportunity discovery. Empirical work on this may utilize both qualitative as well as event study research methodologies.

Relatedly, there is an important micro-dimension that has not been fully explored and developed. Thus, research indicates that firm organization impacts on entrepreneurship (Miller, 1983). However, as we have conflated the entrepreneur and the firm we have not dealt with this issue. Insights on property rights and transaction costs would appear to be an important part of an inquiry into these issues (for important beginning, see Alvarez & Barney [2004] and Alvarez & Parker, 2008). Other micro-issues that have not been dealt with here include the more fine-grained aspects of the appropriability and resource learning mechanisms linking transaction costs and opportunity discovery. What transaction costs are relevant here, exactly? How does experiential knowledge interact with these mechanisms (cf. Argyres & Mayer, 2007)? Additional insight into these issues likely requires extensive, mainly qualitative, research. The aim of this paper has been to outline a framework for research into how transaction costs and property rights impact opportunity discovery and sustainable advantage, thereby linking entrepreneurship and strategic management research.

References

Abelson, R. P., & Black, J. B. (1986). Introduction. In J. A. Galambos, R. P. Abelson, & J. B. Black (Eds.), *Knowledge structures*. Lawrence Erlbaum Associates.

Akerlof, G. (1970b). The market for lemons: Quality uncertainty and the market mechanism. *Quarterly Journal of Economics, 84*, 488–500.

Alchian, A. A. (1965 [1977]). Some economics of property rights. In A. A. Alchian, *Economic forces at work*. Liberty Press.

Alchian, A. A. (1984). Specificity, specialization, and coalitions. *Journal of Institutional and Theoretical Economics, 140*, 34–49.

Alchian, A. A., & Demsetz, H. (1972). Production, information costs, and economic organization. *American Economic Review, 62*, 772–795.

Alvarez, S. A., & Barney, J. B. (2004). Organizing rent generation and appropriation: Towards a theory of the entrepreneurial firm. *Journal of Business Venturing, 19*, 621–635.

Alvarez, S. A., & Barney, J. B. (2007). Discovery and creation: Alternative theories of entrepreneurial action. *Strategic Entrepreneurship Journal, 1*, 139–148.

Alvarez, S. A., & Busenitz, L. W. (2001). The entrepreneurship of resource-based theory. *Journal of Management, 27*, 755–775.

Anderson, T. L., & Hill, P. J. (2004). *The not so wild, wild west*. Stanford University Press.

Ardichvili, A., Cardozo, R., & Ray, S. (2003). A theory of entrepreneurial opportunity identification and development. *Journal of Business Venturing, 18*, 105–123.

Argote, L. (1999). *Organizational learning: Creating, retaining, and transferring knowledge*. Kluwer Academic Publishers.

Argyres, N. S., & Liebeskind, J. P. (1999). Contractual commitments, bargaining power, and governance inseparability: Incorporating history into transaction cost theory. *Academy of Management Review, 24*, 49–63.

Argyres, N. S., & Mayer, K. J. (2007). Contract design as a firm capability: An integration of learning and transaction cost perspectives. *Academy of Management Review, 32*, 1060–1077.

Barney, J. B. (1986b). Strategic factor markets: Expectations, luck, and business strategy. *Management Science, 32*, 1231–1241.

Barney, J. B. (1991). Firm resources and sustained competitive advantage. *Journal of Management, 17*, 99–120.

Barzel, Y. (1982). Measurement costs and the organization of markets. *Journal of Law and Economics, 25*, 27–48.

Barzel, Y. (1997b). *Economic analysis of property rights* (2nd ed.). Cambridge University Press.

Baumol, W. J. (1990). Entrepreneurship: Productive, unproductive and destructive. *Journal of Political Economy, 98*, 893–919.

Busenitz, L. W. (1996). Research on entrepreneurial alertness. *Journal of Small Business Management, 34*, 35–44.

Casson, M. C. (1999). The entrepreneur: An economic theory (R. Robertson, Ed., and 2nd ed.). Edward Elgar.

Cheung, S. N. S. (1970). The structure of a contract and the theory of a non-exclusive resource. *Journal of Law and Economics, 13*, 49–70.

Chi, T. (1994). Trading in strategic resources: Necessary conditions, transaction cost problems, and choice of governance structures. *Strategic Management Journal, 15*, 271–290.

Coase, R. H. (1960). The problem of social cost. *Journal of Law and Economics, 3*, 1–44.

Coase, R. H. (1988b). The nature of the firm: Influence. *Journal of Law, Economics, and Organization, 4*, 33–47.

Coff, R. (1997). Human assets and management dilemmas: Coping with hazards on the road to resource-based theory. *Academy of Management Review, 22*, 374–402.

Coff, R. (1999). When competitive advantage doesn't lead to performance: Resource-based theory and stakeholder bargaining power. *Organization Science, 10*, 119–133.

Cohen, W. M., & Klepper, S. (1996). Firm size and the nature of innovation within industries: The case of process and product R&D. *The Review of Economics and Statistics, 78*, 232–243.

Cohen, W. M., & Levinthal, D. A. (1990). Absorptive capacity: A new perspective on learning and innovation. *Administrative Science Quarterly, 35*, 128–152.

Day, D. V., & Lord, R. G. (1992). Expertise and problem categorization. The role of expert processing in organizational sense-making. *Journal of Management Studies, 29*, 35–47.

Debreu, G. (1959). *The theory of value*. Wiley.

Demsetz, H. (1988). A framework for the study of ownership. In H. Demsetz, *Ownership, control, and the firm*. Basil Blackwell.

Demsetz, H. (1991). The nature of the firm revisited. In O. E. Williamson & S. G. Winter (Eds.), *The nature of the firm*. Blackwell.

Dennen, R. T. (1976). Cattlemen's associations and property rights in land in the American West. *Explorations in Economic History, 13*(4), 423–436.

Denrell, J., Fang, C., & Winter, S. G. (2003). The economics of strategic opportunity. *Strategic Management Journal, 24*, 977–990.

Dierickx, I., & Cool, K. (1989). Asset stock accumulation and the sustainability of competitive advantage. *Management Science, 35*, 1504–1511.

Finke, R. A., Ward, T. B., & Smith, S. M. (1992). *Creative cognition: Theory, research, and applications*. MIT Press.

Foss, K. (2001). Organizing technological interdependencies: A coordination perspective on the firm. *Industrial and Corporate Change, 10*, 151–178.

Foss, K., & Foss, N. J. (2005). Value and transaction costs: How the economics of property rights furthers the RBV. *Strategic Management Journal, 26*, 541–553.

Foss, N. J., & Klein, P. G. (2005). Entrepreneurship and the economic theory of the firm: Any gains from trade? In A. Rajsree, S. A. Alvarez, & O. Sorenson (Eds.), *Handbook of entrepreneurship: Disciplinary perspectives*. Kluwer.

Foss, N. J., & Klein, P. G. (2012). *Entrepreneurial judgment and the theory of the firm*. Cambridge University Press.

Gaglio, C. M., & Katz, J. A. (2001). The psychological basis of opportunity identification: Entrepreneurial alertness. *Small Business Economics, 16*, 95–111.

Galloway, L. (1996). *Operation management: The basics*. International Thomson Business Press.

Hahn, F. H. (1973). *On the notion of equilibrium in economics*. Cambridge University Press.

Hart, O. (1995). *Firms, contracts, and financial structure*. The Clarendon Press.

Helfat, C. E., & Peteraf, M. (2003). The dynamic resource-based view: Capability lifecycles. *Strategic Management Journal, 24*, 997–1010.

Helfat, C. E., & Raubitschek, R. S. (2000). Product sequencing: Co-evolution of knowledge, capabilities and products. *Strategic Management Journal, 21*, 961–979.

Helfat, C. E. (1994). Evolutionary trajectories in petroleum firm R&D. *Management Science, 40*, 1720–1747.

Helfat, C. E. (1997). Know-how and asset complementarity and dynamic capability accumulation: The case of R&D. *Strategic Management Journal, 18*, 339–360.

Hill, J. L. (1969). *The end of the Cattle Trail*. The Pemberton Press.

Hitt, M. A., Ireland, R. D., Camp, S. M., & Sexton, D. L. (2001). Strategic entrepreneurship: Entrepreneurial strategies for wealth creation. *Strategic Management Journal, 22*, 479–492.

Hodgkinson, G. P., & Johnson, G. (1994). Exploring the mental models of competitive strategies: The case of a processual approach. *Journal of Management Studies, 31*, 525–551.

Ireland, R. D., Hitt, M. A., & Sirmon, D. G. (2003). A model of strategic entrepreneurship: The construct and its dimensions. *Journal of Management, 29*, 963–989.

Kaish, S., & Gilard, B. (1991). Characteristics of opportunities search of entrepreneurs versus executives: Sources, interests, general alertness. *Journal of Business Venturing, 6*, 54–61.

Kim, J., & Mahoney, J. T. (2006). How property rights theory furthers the resource-based view: Resources, transaction costs and entrepreneurial discovery. *International Journal of Strategic Change Management, 1*, 40–52.

Kirzner, I. M. (1973). *Competition and entrepreneurship*. University of Chicago Press.

Kirzner, I. M. (1997). Entrepreneurial discovery and the competitive market process: An Austrian approach. *Journal of Economic Literature, 35*, 60–85.

Klein, B., & Leffer, K. B. (1981). The role of market forces in assuring contractual performance. *Journal of Political Economy, 89*, 615–641.

Knight, F. H. (1921). *Risk, uncertainty, and profit*. Hart, Schaffner & Marx.

Kogut, B., & Zander, U. (1992). Knowledge of the firm, combinative capabilities, and the replication of technology. *Organization Science, 3*, 383–397.
Kor, Y. (2003). Knowledge-based top management team competence and sustained growth. *Organization Science, 14*, 707–719.
Krueger, N. F. (2000). The cognitive infrastructure of opportunity emergence. *Entrepreneurship Theory and Practice, 24*, 5–23.
Liebeskind, J. P. (1996). Knowledge, strategy, and the theory of the firm. *Strategic Management Journal, 17*(Winter Special Issue), 93–107.
Lippman, S. A., & Rumelt, R. P. (2003a). A bargaining perspective on resource advantage. *Strategic Management Journal, 24*, 1069–1086.
Lippman, S. A., & Rumelt, R. P. (2003b). The payments perspective: Microfoundations of resource analysis. *Strategic Management Journal, 24*, 903–927.
Lumpkin, G. T., & Lichtenstein, B. B. (2005). The role of organizational learning in the opportunity-recognition process. *Entrepreneurship Theory and Practice, 29*(4), 451–472.
MacCallum, H. D. (1965). *The wire that fenced the West*. University of Oklahoma Press.
Mahoney, J. T. (1995). The management of resources and the resource of management. *Journal of Business Research, 33*, 91–101.
Makowski, L., & Ostroy, J. M. (2001). Perfect competition and the creativity of markets. *Journal of Economic Literature, 39*, 479–535.
Matsusaka, J. (2001). Corporate diversification, value maximization, and organizational capabilities. *Journal of Business, 74*, 409–431.
Miller, D. (1983). The correlates of entrepreneurship in three types of firms. *Management Science, 29*, 770–791.
Michael, S. C. (2007). Transaction cost entrepreneurship. *Journal of Business Venturing, 23*, 412–426.
Mitchell, R. K., Busenitz, L., Lant, T., McDougall, P. P., Morse, E. A., & Smith, J. B. (2002). Toward a theory of entrepreneurial cognition: Rethinking the people side of entrepreneurship research. *Entrepreneurship Theory and Practice, 27*, 93–104.
Mosakowski, E. (1998). Entrepreneurial resources, organizational choices, and competitive outcomes. *Organization Science, 9*, 625–643.
Nelson, R. R., & Winter, S. G. (1982). *An evolutionary theory of economic change*. The Belknap Press.
Nisbett, R., & Ross, L. (1980). *Human inferences. Strategies and shortages of social judgment*. Prentice-Hall.

North, D. C. (1990). *Institutions, institutional change, and economic performance*. Cambridge University Press.
Orr, J. (1996). *Talking about machines: An ethnography of a modern job*. IRL Press.
Oxley, J. (1999). Institutional environment and the mechanisms of governance: The impact of intellectual property protection on the structure of inter-firm alliances. *Journal of Economic Behavior and Organization, 38*, 283–309.
Penrose, E. T. (1959). *The theory of the growth of the firm*. Oxford University Press.
Peteraf, M. A. (1993). The cornerstones of competitive advantage: A resource-based view. *Strategic Management Journal, 14*, 179–191.
Pisan, G. P. (1990). The R&D boundaries of the firm: An empirical analysis. *Administrative Science Quarterly, 35*, 153–176.
Radner, R. (1968). Competitive equilibrium under uncertainty. *Econometrica, 36*, 31–58.
Rensch, J. R., Heffner, T. S., & Duffy, L. T. (1994). What you know is what you get from experience: Team experience related to teamwork schemas. *Group & Organization Management, 19*, 450–474.
Robinson, J. (1933). *The economics of imperfect competition*. Macmillan.
Runco, M. A., & Chand, I. (1995). Cognition and creativity. *Educational Psychology Review, 7*, 243–267.
Schumpeter, J. A. (1911/1934). *The theory of economic development: An inquiry into profits, capital, credit, interest, and the business cycle*. Harvard University Press.
Shane, S., & Venkataraman, S. (2000). The promise of entrepreneurship as a field of research. *Academy of Management Review, 25*, 217–226.
Shane, S. (2000). Prior knowledge and the discovery of entrepreneurial opportunities. *Organization Science, 11*, 448–469.
Shane, S. (2003). *A general theory of entrepreneurship*. Edward Elgar.
Shepherd, D., & DeTienne, D. R. (2005). Prior knowledge, potential financial reward, and opportunity identification. *Entrepreneurship Theory and Practice, 29*(1), 91–110.
Stieglitz, N., & Heine, K. (2007). Innovations and the role of complementarities in a strategic theory of the firm. *Strategic Management Journal, 28*, 1–15.
Teece, D. J. (1982). Towards an economic theory of the multiproduct firm. *Journal of Economic Behavior and Organization, 3*, 39–63.
Teece, D. J. (1986). Profiting from technological innovation. *Research Policy, 15*, 285–305.

Venkataraman, S. (1997). The distinctive domain of entrepreneurship research. In J. Katz & R. Brockhaus (Eds.), *Advances in entrepreneurship, firm emergence, and growth*. JAI Press.

Walsh, J. P. (1995). Managerial and organizational cognition: Notes form a trip down memory lane. *Organization Science, 6*, 280–321.

Wang, N. (2003). *Measuring transaction costs: An incomplete survey* (Working Paper). Ronald Coase Institute.

Webb, W. P. (1931). *The Great Plains*. Dallas: Ginn and Company.

Williamson, O. E. (1985). *The economic institutions of capitalism*. Free Press.

Williamson, O. E. (1996). *The mechanisms of governance*. Oxford University Press.

10
Conclusions

In their 1972 review article, Furubotn and Pejovich (1972: 1156) argued that "… property rights analysis does offer a fresh and useful way of looking at economic problems. Substantial advances have already been achieved and the literature gives evidence of continuing vitality and promise of future accomplishment." 50 years has passed since the publication of that article, which was written at a time when PRE, while only a little more than a decade old then, had enjoyed very considerable success in terms of getting articles published in important journal and gaining adherents. This was a time when it made sense to self-identify as a "property rights economist" (or perhaps, given PRE's expansive ambitions, "property rights social scientist"). As we noted in Chapter 4, relatively few practicing economists nowadays would self-identify as PRE scholars. The reasons are that other competing approaches emerged on the scene (e.g., transaction cost economics, formal contract theory); PRE may have been disadvantaged by its mainly non-mathematical analytical style; and, of course, key PRE ideas got more or less smoothly absorbed into the economic mainstream.

K. Foss and N. J. Foss, *Economic Microfoundations of Strategic Management*,
https://doi.org/10.1007/978-3-031-12910-0_10

In this book, we have essentially made the case that the PRE still has much to offer, not the least to management scholars. There are several reasons for this. PRE is, as we see it, not just a set of insights but also a mode of reasoning: Its microanalytical focus means that it seeks to account for *all* margins over which individuals can make optimizing choices. In contrast, much formal model-building proceeds by suppressing some margins for the sake of tractability. While this, of course, not wrong per se, it may mean that analysis can be led astray.

The classical example is the "lighthouse in economics"—the title of Coase's (1974) account of how economists had routinely treated lighthouse services as pure public good, and argued that such services would therefore be drastically undersupplied if their production was left to the market place. However, Coase showed that bundling lighthouse services with harbor services was one way in which lighthouse services could be financed. To introduce an Austrian twist on the argument, the market is often able to innovate itself out of its alleged "failures" (Kirzner, 1997; Makowski & Ostroy, 2001). PRE theorists have typically been highly attentive to how actors seek contractual and institutional solutions to failures. In Chapter 4, we provided a concrete illustration of the contrast between PRE and modern economics in this regard when we pointed to the asymmetric treatment of, for example, enforcement issues in modern discussions of property rights (i.e., some property rights are, arbitrarily, assumed to be completely enforceable whereas others, equally arbitrarily, are assumed to not be enforceable at all).

PRE represents the economic way of thinking at its best. But it should also be recognized that its desire to take account of the creativity and entrepreneurialism of economic actors puts constraints on the extent to which it can be formalized using the tools of standard economics. Also, its preference for relatively "narrative," qualitative empirical research (e.g., Cheung, 1969a, b; Demsetz, 1967; Eggertson, 1992) isn't exactly mainstream in a discipline where causal econometric identification and experimental methods are generally seen as the proper ways of conducting empirical analysis. However, these disadvantages in the context of economics may, to some extent at least, be advantageous in the context of management research, where formal methods are still not used much and where there is considerable tolerance for qualitative research. Management scholars are certainly appreciative of the kind of rigorous verbal reasoning that PRE represents.

To illustrate the general relevance of PRE to management research, the central unit of analysis of such research (certainly its "macro" fields, such as strategy, organization theory, international business, and technology management) remains the organization. As such it is sometimes "reified" as a unitary actor. This is also how we treated the organization in Chapters 5 and 6 on firm strategy. While this may seem to be contrary to the microfoundations principles we outlined in Chapter 2, it isn't necessarily—provided we can account for firm-level decisions in terms of the decisions of firm decision-makers. We began to consider this in the subsequent chapters, where we essentially argued that many organizational phenomena directly or more indirectly involve property rights issues. The organization is fundamentally a property rights system (cf. Holmström, 1999; Miller, 1992) that serves the purpose of making individuals cooperate by delineating income rights, regulates the access to common pool resources, and in general defines boundaries around permissible behaviors. Senior managers design the overarching "institutions" at the firm level (determining budgets at lower levels, designing principles for human resource management, determining the overall goals, etc.) As we specifically argued, the function of the institution of managerial authority is to allocate resources in response to shadow process/opportunity costs in a low-cost manner. We extended this basic Coasian perspective to issues of learning and entrepreneurship to illustrate the reach and explanatory power of the PRE.

However, there are many other issues in contemporary management that we have not touched upon in this book, although property rights issues are at the heart of these issues. Consider, for example, the increasingly influential idea of stakeholder management, which exists in both normative (more parties than just shareholders should have effective control rights) and positive (firms that practice stakeholder management will perform better) versions (Foss & Klein, 2018). A key challenge is defining exactly who is, and who isn't, included in the set of relevant stakeholders. Some research follows property rights economics (Hart, 1995; Hart & Moore, 1990) in defining stakeholders with legitimate claims on firm value as those agents who make relationship-specific investments in the firm's activities (Hoskisson et al., 2017). Other approaches define the set of stakeholders more broadly, to include virtually any individuals or groups whose well-being is affected by the firm (see Aguinis & Glavas, 2012). It is clear that the definitional issue here may have serious practical implications. PRE theorists have long grappled with similar issues (e.g., research on "co-determination," as when employee representatives are placed on company boards; Jensen & Meckling, 1979; or research on coordinating owner interests; Hansmann, 1988) and PRE analysis is likely further the understanding of the implications of (alternative understandings of stakeholder management).

In general, PRE is useful for understanding all management problems that touch on issues of ownership, control, and incentives. In fact, it may even be invoked in the analysis of those "soft" organizational issues, such as issues of culture and identity that at the surface level seem very far apart from the traditional turf of PRE. However, on closer inspection such issues also involve issues of what are, for example, locally permitted uses of assets; thus, culture and identity may serve to delineate and enforce control. Our key purpose in putting this little volume together has been to illustrate the general applicability of PRE outside its traditional applications, in particular, how eminently applicable it is to the kind of issues management scholars are taken up with.

References

Aguinis, H., & Glavas, A. (2012). What we know and don't know about corporate social responsibility: A review and research agenda. *Journal of Management, 38*, 932–968.

Cheung, S. N. S. (1969a). *A theory of share tenancy*. University of Chicago Press.

Cheung, S. N. S. (1969b). Transaction costs, risk aversion, and the choice of contractual arrangements. *Journal of Law and Economics, 12*, 23–42.

Coase, R. H. (1974). The lighthouse in economics. *The Journal of Law and Economics, 17*, 357–374.

Demsetz, H. (1967). *Toward a theory of property rights.* Originally published in 1967, reprinted in *Ownership, Control, and the Firm*, idem. 1988. Basil Blackwell.

Eggertson, T. (1992). Analyzing institutional successes and failures: A millennium of common mountain pasture in Iceland. *International Review of Law and Economics, 12*, 423–437.

Foss, N. J., & Klein, P. G. (2018). Sustainability, CSR, and stakeholders: An ownership view. *Advances in Strategic Management, 38*, 17–35.

Furubotn, E., & Pejovich, S. (1972). Property rights and economic theory: A survey of recent literature. *Journal of Economic Literature, 10*, 1137–1162.

Hansmann, H. (1988). Ownership of the firm. *The Journal of Law, Economics, and Organization, 4*, 267–304.

Hart, O. (1995). *Firms, contracts, and financial structure.* The Clarendon Press.

Hart, O., & Moore, J. (1990). Property rights and the nature of the firm. *Journal of Political Economy, 98*, 1119–1158.

Holmström, B. (1999). The firm as a subeconomy. *Journal of Law, Economics, and Organization, 15*, 74–102.

Hoskisson, R., Gambetta, E., Green, C., & Li, T. (2017). Is my firm-specific investment protected? Overcoming the stakeholder investment Dilemma in the resource based view. *Academy of Management Review*, forthcoming.

Jensen, M. C., & Meckling, W. (1979). Rights and production functions: An application to labor-managed firms and co-determination. *Journal of Business, 52*, 469–506.

Kirzner, I. M. (1997). Entrepreneurial discovery and the competitive market process: An Austrian approach. *Journal of Economic Literature, 35*, 60–85.

Makowski, L., & Ostroy, J. M. (2001). Perfect competition and the creativity of the market. *Journal of Economic Literature, 34*, 479–535.

Miller, G. (1992). *Managerial Dilemmas.* Cambridge University Press.

References

Abell, P., Felin, T., & Foss, N. J. (2008). Building micro-foundations for the routines, capabilities and performance link. *Managerial and Decision Economics, 29*, 489–502.

Abelson, R. P., & Black, J. B. (1986). Introduction. In J. A. Galambos, R. P. Abelson, & J. B. Black (Eds.), *Knowledge structures*. Lawrence Erlbaum Associates.

Acemoglu, D. (2003). Why not a political Coase theorem? Social conflict, commitment, and politics. *Journal of Comparative Economics, 3*, 620–652.

Acemoglu, D., & Robinson, J. A. (2012). *Why nations fail: The origins of power, prosperity and poverty*. Crown.

Adler, P. S. (2001). Market, hierarchy, and trust: The knowledge economy and the future of capitalism. *Organization Science, 12*, 215–234.

Afuah, A. (2003). Redefining firm boundaries in the face of the internet: Are firms really shrinking? *Academy of Management Review, 28*, 34–53.

Aghion, P., & Bolton, P. (1987). Contracts as barriers to entry. *American Economic Review, 77*, 388–401.

Aghion, P., & Tirole J. (1995). Real and formal authority in organizations. *Journal of Political Economy, 105*, 1–29.

Aghion, P., Dewatripont, M., Legros, P., & Zingales, L. (2016). *The impact of incomplete contracts on economics*. Oxford University Press.

K. Foss and N. J. Foss, *Economic Microfoundations of Strategic Management*, https://doi.org/10.1007/978-3-031-12910-0

Aguinis, H., & Glavas, A. (2012). What we know and don't know about corporate social responsibility: A review and research agenda. *Journal of Management, 38*, 932–968.
Akerlof, G. (1970a [1984]). The market for lemons. In *An economic theorist's book of tales*, idem. Cambridge University Press.
Akerlof, G. (1970b). The market for lemons: Quality uncertainty and the market mechanism. *Quarterly Journal of Economics, 84*, 488–500.
Alchian, A. A. (1958). Private property and the relative cost of tenure. In P. D. Bradley (Ed.), *The public stake in union power* (pp. 350–371). University of Virginia Press.
Alchian, A. A. (1961). *Some economics of property*. Rand Corporation.
Alchian, A. A. (1965 [1977]). Some economics of property rights. In A. A. Alchian, *Economic forces at work*. Liberty Press.
Alchian, A. A. (1984). Specificity, specialization, and coalitions. *Journal of Institutional and Theoretical Economics, 140*, 34–49.
Alchian, A. A., & Allen, W. R. (1969). *Exchange and production: Theory in use*. Wadsworth.
Alchian, A. A., & Demsetz, H. (1972). Production, information costs, and economic organization. *American Economic Review, 62*, 772–795.
Alchian, A. A., & Demsetz, H. (1973). The property rights paradigm. *Journal of Economic History, 33*(1), 16–27.
Alchian, A. A., & Woodward, S. L. (1988). The firm is dead; long live the firm: A review of Oliver E. Williamson's the economic institutions of capitalism. *Journal of Economic Literature, 26*, 65–79.
Alessi, L. (1990). Development of the property rights approach. *Journal of Institutional and Theoretical Economics, 146*, 6–11.
Allen, D. W. (2000). Transaction costs. In B. Bouckeart & G. De Geest (Eds.), *Encyclopedia of law and economics* (pp. 893–926). Edward Elgar.
Allen, D. W., & Lueck, D. (1995). Risk Preferences and the economics of contracts. *American Economic Review, 85 (Papers and Proceedings)*, 447–451.
Allen, D. W., & Lueck, D. (1998). The nature of the farm. *Journal of Law and Economics, 41*, 343–386.
Alvarez, S. A., & Barney, J. B. (2004). Organizing rent generation and appropriation: Towards a theory of the entrepreneurial firm. *Journal of Business Venturing, 19*, 621–635.
Alvarez, S. A., & Barney, J. B. (2007). Discovery and creation: Alternative theories of entrepreneurial action. *Strategic Entrepreneurship Journal, 1*, 139–148.

Alvarez, S. A., & Busenitz, L. W. (2001). The entrepreneurship of resource-based theory. *Journal of Management, 27*, 755–775.

Alvarez, S. A., & Parker, S. P. (2009). Emerging firms and the allocation of control rights: A Bayesian approach. *Academy of Management Review, 34*, 209–227.

Ames, E. A., & Rosenberg, N. (1965). The progressive division and specialization of industries. *The Journal of Development Studies, 1*, 363–383.

Anderson, G. M., & Tollison, R. D. (1986). Dead men tell no tales. *Journal of the History of Economic Thought, 8*, 59–68.

Anderson, T. L., & Hill, P. J. (1990). The race for property rights. *Journal of Law and Economics, 33*, 177–197.

Anderson, T. L., & Hill, P. J. (2004). *The not so wild, wild west*. Stanford University Press.

Ardichvili, A., Cardozo, R., & Ray, S. (2003). A theory of entrepreneurial opportunity identification and development. *Journal of Business Venturing, 18*, 105–123.

Argote, L. (1999). *Organizational learning: Creating, retaining, and transferring knowledge*. Kluwer Academic Publishers.

Argyres, N. S., & Liebeskind, J. P. (1998). Privatizing the intellectual commons: Universities and the commercialization of biotechnology. *Journal of Economic Behavior and Organization, 35*, 427–454.

Argyres, N. S., & Liebeskind, J. P. (1999). Contractual commitments, bargaining power, and governance inseparability: Incorporating history into transaction cost theory. *Academy of Management Review, 24*, 49–63.

Argyres, N. S., & Mayer, K. J. (2007). Contract design as a firm capability: An integration of learning and transaction cost perspectives. *Academy of Management Review, 32*, 1060–1077.

Argyres, N. S., Felin, T., Foss, N. J., & Zenger, T. (2012). The organizational economics of organizational capability: A research agenda. *Organization Science, 23*, 1213–1226.

Argyres, N. S., & Zenger, T. (2012). Capabilities, transaction costs and firm boundaries. *Organization Science, 23*, 1643–1657.

Arrow, K. J. (1962). The economic implications of learning by doing. *The Review of Economic Studies, 29*, 155–173. Oxford Journals.

Arrow, K. J. (1969). The organization of economic activity: Issues pertinent to the choice of market versus nonmarket allocation. In *The analysis and evaluation of public expenditure, Vol. 1: The PPB system* (pp. 59–73). U.S. Joint Economic Committee, 91st Congress, Ist Session.

Asmussen, C. G., Foss, K., Foss, N. J., & Klein, P. G. (2021). Economizing and strategizing: How coalitions and transaction costs shape value creation and appropriation. *Strategic Management Journal, 42*, 413–434.

Autor, D., Dorn, D., Katz, L. F., Patterson, C., & van Reenen, J. (2020). The fall of the labor share and the rise of superstar firms. *Quarterly Journal of Economics, 135*, 645–709

Bain, J. S. (1956). *Barriers to new competition: Their character and consequences in manufacturing industries*. Harvard University Press.

Bain, J. S. (1959). *Industrial organization.* Wiley.

Barnard, C. I. (1938). *The Functions of the executive by.* Harvard University Press.

Barney, J. B. (1986). Strategic factor markets: Expectations, luck, and business strategy. *Management Science, 32*, 1231–1241.

Barney, J. B. (1991). Firm resources and sustained competitive advantage. *Journal of Management, 17*, 99–120.

Barzel, Y. (1968). Optimal timing of innovation. *Review of Economics and Statistics, 50*, 348–355.

Barzel, Y. (1982). Measurement costs and the organization of markets. *Journal of Law and Economics, 25*, 27–48.

Barzel, Y. (1985 [2005]). Transaction costs: Are they just costs? Reprinted in C. Mènard (Ed.), *Controversies and challenges in the new institutional economics.* Edward Elgar.

Barzel, Y. (1987). The entrepreneur's reward for self-policing. *Economic Inquiry, 25*, 103–116.

Barzel, Y. (1994). The capture of wealth by monopolists and the protection of property rights. *International Review of Law and Economics, 14*, 393–409.

Barzel, Y. (1997). *Economic analysis of property rights* (2nd ed.). Cambridge University Press.

Barzel, Y. (2002). *A theory of the state.* Cambridge University Press.

Barzel, Y., & Kochin, L. (1992). Ronald Coase on the nature of social cost as a key to the problem of the firm. *Scandinavian Journal of Economics, 94*, 19–31.

Bastiat, F. (1850). *The law*. Laissez-Faire Books.

Baumol, W. J. (1990). Entrepreneurship: Productive, unproductive and destructive. *Journal of Political Economy, 98*, 893–919.

Baumol, W. J., Panzar, J. C., & Willig, R. D. (1982). *Contestable markets and the theory of industry structure*. Harcourt Brace Jovanovich.

Baumol, W. J., Panzar, J. C., & Willig, R. D. (1983). Contestable markets: An uprising in the theory of industry structure. *American Economic Review, 73*, 491–496.

Becker, G. (1962). Investment in human capital: A theoretical analysis. *Journal of Political Economy, 70*, 9–49.

Becker, G. (1964). *Human capital: A theoretical and empirical analysis, with special reference to education.* The University of Chicago Press.

Becker, G. S., & Murphy, K. M. (1992). Division of labor, coordination costs, and knowledge. *The Quarterly Journal of Economics, 107*, 1137–1160.

Benham, A., & Benham, L. (2010). The costs of exchange. In P. G. Klein & M. E. Sykuta (Eds.), *The Elgar companion to transaction cost economics* (pp. 107–119). Edward Elgar.

Bennedsen, M., Pérez-González, F., & Wolfenson, J. (2015). *Estimating the value of the boss: Evidence from CEO hospitalization events* (Working Paper). https://bit.ly/3NpdSA9

Bennedsen, M., Pérez-González, F., & Wolfenzon, D. (2020). Do CEOs matter? Evidence from hospitalization events. *The Journal of Finance, 75*, 1877–1911.

Benson, B. L. (1984). Rent seeking from a property rights perspective. *Southern Economic Journal, 51*, 388–400.

Berle, A. A., & Means, G. C. (1932). *The modern corporation and private property.* Harcourt, Brace and World.

Blank, Z. (2021). *More than just route planning: How UPS drivers optimize their routes.* https://www.getstraightaway.com/blog-posts/more-than-just-route-planning-how-ups-drivers-optimize-their-routes

Bogner, W. C., & Barr, P. S. (2000). Making sense in hypercompetitive environments: A cognitive explanation for the persistence of high velocity competition. *Organization Science, 11*, 212–226.

Bolton, P., & Scharfstein, D. S. (1998). Corporate finance, the theory of the firm, and organizations. *Journal of Economic Perspectives, 12*, 95–114.

Brandenburger, A. M., & Nalebuff, B. (1996). *Co-opetition.* Harper-Collins Business.

Brandenburger, A. M., & Stuart, H. W. (1996). Value-based business strategy. *Journal of Economics and Management Strategy, 5*, 5–24.

Brandenburger, A. M., & Stuart, H. W. (2007). Biform games. *Management Science, 53*, 537–549.

Braverman, H. (1974). *Labor and monopoly capital.* Monthly Review.

Bridoux, F., & Stoelhorst, J. W. (2014). Microfoundations for stakeholder theory: Managing stakeholders with heterogeneous motives. *Strategic Management Journal, 35*, 107–125.

Brousseau, E., & Glachant, J.-M. (Eds.). (2008). *New institutional economics: A guidebook*. Cambridge University Press.

Brozen, Y. (1977). The concentration-collusion doctrine. *The Antitrust Law Journal, 46*, 826–863.

Buchanan, J. M. (1969). *Cost and choice: An inquiry in economic theory*. Markham.

Buchanan, J. M., & Thirlby, G. F. (1973). *LSE essays on cost*. London School of Economics and Political Science.

Burgelman, R. A. (1994). Fading memories: A process theory of strategic business exit in dynamic environments. *Administrative Science Quarterly, 39*, 24–56.

Busenitz, L. W. (1996). Research on entrepreneurial alertness. *Journal of Small Business Management, 34*, 35–44.

Bush, W., & Mayer, L. (1974). Some implications of anarchy for the distribution of property. *Journal of Economic Theory, 8*, 401–412.

Bylund, P. (2014). Ronald Coase's "nature of the firm" and the argument for economic planning. *Journal of the History of Economic Thought, 36*, 305–334.

Calabresi, G., Melamed, A., & Douglas, M. A. (1972). Property rules, liability rules, and inalienability: One view of the cathedral. *Harvard Law Review, 85*(6), 1089–1128.

Campbell, B. A., Kryscynski, D., & Olson, D. M. (2017). Bridging strategic human capital and employee entrepreneurship research: A labor market frictions approach. *Strategic Entrepreneurship Journal, 11*, 344–356.

Capron, L., & Chatain, O. (2008). Competitors' resource-oriented strategies: Acting upon competitors' resources through interventions in factor markets and political markets. *Academy of Management Review, 33*, 97–121.

Carlton, D., & Perloff, J. M. (1994). *Modern industrial organization*. HarperCollins.

Casson, M. C. (1999). The entrepreneur: An economic theory (R. Robertson, Ed., and 2nd ed.). Edward Elgar.

Castellblanch, R. (2003). Challenging pharmaceutical industry political power in Maine and Vermont. *Journal of Health Politics, Policy and Law, 28*, 109–132.

Caves, R., & Porter, M. E. (1977). From entry barriers to mobility barriers. *Quarterly Journal of Economics, 91*, 241–262.

Chassagnon, V., & Hollandts, X. (2014). "Who are the owners of the firm: Shareholders, employees or no one?" Post-Print halshs-01372370, HAL.

Chatain, O., & Zemsky, P. (2011). Value creation and value capture with frictions. *Strategic Management Journal, 32*, 1206–1231.

Chen, M.-J., Venkataraman, S., Black, S. S., & MacMillan, I. C. (2002). The role of irreversibilities in competitive interaction: Behavioral considerations from organization theory. *Managerial and Decision Economics, 23*, 187–207.

Chesbrough, H. (2003). *Open innovation: The new imperative for creating and profiting from technology*. Harvard Business School Press.

Cheung, S. N. S. (1968). Private property rights and sharecropping. *Journal of Political Economy, 76*, 1107–1131.

Cheung, S. N. S. (1969a). *A theory of share tenancy*. University of Chicago Press.

Cheung, S. N. S. (1969b). Transaction costs, risk aversion, and the choice of contractual arrangements. *Journal of Law and Economics, 12*, 23–42.

Cheung, S. N. S. (1970). The structure of a contract and the theory of a non-exclusive resource. *Journal of Law and Economics, 13*, 49–70.

Cheung, S. N. S. (1974). A theory of price control. *Journal of Law and Economics, 17*, 53–62.

Cheung, S. N. S. (1983). The contractual nature of the firm. *Journal of Law and Economics, 26*, 1–26.

Chi, T. (1994). Trading in strategic resources: Necessary conditions, transaction cost problems, and choice of governance structures. *Strategic Management Journal, 15*, 271–290.

Christensen, H. K., & Montgomery, C. A. (1981). Corporate economic performance: Diversification strategy versus market structure. *Strategic Management Journal, 2*, 327–343.

Clay, K., & Wright, G. (2005). Order without Law? Property rights during the California Gold Rush. *Explorations in Economic History, 42*, 155–183.

Coase, R. H. (1937). The nature of the firm. *Economica NS4*, 386–405.

Coase, R. H. (1938). Business organization and the accountant. *The Accountant, 13*, 470–472, 505–507, 537–538, 559–560, 607–608, 631–632, 665–666, 705–706, 737–739, 775–777, 814–815, 834–835.

Coase, R. H. (1959). The federal communications commission. *Journal of Law & Economics, 2*, 1–40.

Coase, R. H. (1960). The problem of social cost. *Journal of Law and Economics, 3*, 1–44.

Coase, R. H. (1974). The lighthouse in economics. *The Journal of Law and Economics, 17*, 357–374.

Coase, R. H. (1988a). *Notes on the problem of social cost, in the firm, the market, and the law*. University of Chicago Press.
Coase, R. H. (1988b). The nature of the firm: Influence. *Journal of Law, Economics, and Organization, 4*, 33–47.
Coase, R. H. (1990). Accounting and the theory of the firm. *Journal of Accounting and Economics, 12*, 3–13.
Coase, R. H. (1991). 1991 Nobel lecture: The institutional structure of production. In O. E. Williamson & S. G. Winter, (Eds.), 1993 *The nature of the firm: Origins, evolution, and development*. Oxford University Press.
Coase, R. (1992). The institutional structure of production. *American Economic Review, 82*, 713–719.
Coff, R. (1997). Human assets and management dilemmas: Coping with hazards on the road to resource-based theory. *Academy of Management Review, 22*, 374–402.
Coff, R. (1999). When competitive advantage doesn't lead to performance: Resource-based theory and stakeholder bargaining power. *Organization Science, 10*, 119–133.
Cohen, W. M., & Klepper, S. (1996). Firm size and the nature of innovation within industries: The case of process and product R&D. *The Review of Economics and Statistics, 78*, 232–243.
Cohen, W. M., & Levinthal, D. A. (1990). Absorptive capacity: A new perspective on learning and innovation. *Administrative Science Quarterly, 35*, 128–152.
Coleman, J. S. (1990). *Foundations of social theory*. University of Chicago Press.
Conner, K. R. (1991). A historical comparison of resource-based theory and five schools of thought within industrial economics: Do We have a new theory of the firm? *Journal of Management, 17*, 121–154.
Conner, T. (1999). Customer-oriented and Market-led: A matter of balance. *Strategic Management Journal, 20*, 1157–1163.
Cool, K., & Dierickx, I. (1993). Rivalry, strategic groups and firm profitability. *Strategic Management Journal, 14*, 47–59.
Cook, M. L. (1993). Cooperatives and group action. In D. Padberg (Ed.), *Food and agricultural marketing issues for the 21st century* (pp. 154–169). Texas A&M University Press.
Cooter, R. (1982). The cost of Coase. *Journal of Legal Studies, 11*, 1–33.
Cowling, K., & Mueller, D. C. (1978). The social costs of monopoly power. *Economic Journal, 88*, 727–748.

Cramton, P. (2002). Spectrum auctions. In M. Cave, S. Majumdar, & I. Vogelsang (Eds.), *Handbook of telecommunications economics* (pp. 605–639). Elsevier.

Cyert, R. M., & March, J. G. (1963). *A behavioral theory of the firm.* Prentice Hall/Pearson Education.

D'Aveni, R. A. (1994). *Hypercompetition: Managing the dynamics of strategic maneuvering*. The Free Press.

D'Aveni, R. A. (2002, November). The Empire strikes back: Counterrevolutionary strategies for industry leaders. *Harvard Business Review*, 66–74.

David, R. J., & Han, S. (2004). A systematic assessment of the empirical support for transaction cost economics. *Strategic Management Journal, 25*, 39–58.

Day, D. V., & Lord, R. G. (1992). Expertise and problem categorization. The role of expert processing in organizational sense-making. *Journal of Management Studies, 29*, 35–47.

de Avila Monteiro, G. F., & Zylbersztajn, D. (2012). A property rights approach to strategy. *Strategic Organization, 10*, 366–383.

de Avila Monteiro, G. F., & Zylbersztajn, D. (2015). Heterogeneity of property rights strategies in a global context: The case of genetically modified soybean seeds. *Global Strategy Journal, 5*(1), 69–83.

Debreu, G. (1959). *The theory of value*. Wiley.

Demsetz, H. (1964). The exchange and enforcement of property rights. *Journal of Law and Economics, 7*, 11–26.

Demsetz, H. (1967). *Toward a theory of property rights.* Originally published in 1967, reprinted in *Ownership, control, and the firm*, idem. 1988. Basil Blackwell.

Demsetz, H. (1973). Industry structure, market rivalry, and public policy. *The Journal of Law and Economics, 16*, 1–9.

Demsetz, H. (1982). Barriers to entry. *American Economic Review, 72*, 47–57.

Demsetz, H. (1988). A framework for the study of ownership. In H. Demsetz, *Ownership, control, and the firm.* Basil Blackwell.

Demsetz, H. (1991). The nature of the firm revisited. In O. E. Williamson & S. G. Winter (Eds.), *The nature of the firm.* Blackwell.

Demsetz, H. (1995). *The economics of the business firm.* Cambridge University Press.

Demsetz, H. (1997a). *The economics of the business firm: Seven critical commentaries*. Cambridge University Press.

Demsetz, H. (1997b). The firm in economic theory: A quiet revolution. *American Economic Review, 87 (Papers and Proceedings)*, 426–429.

Demsetz, H. (1998). Review of Oliver Hart, "Firms, contracts, and financial structure: Clarendon lectures in economics". *Journal of Political Economy, 106*, 446–451.

Demsetz, H. (2011). R. H. Coase and the neoclassical model of the economic system. *Journal of Law and Economics, 54*, 7–13.

Denicolò, V. (1996). Patent races and optimal patent breadth and length. *Journal of Industrial Economics, 44*, 249–265.

Dennen, R. T. (1976). Cattlemen's associations and property rights in land in the American West. *Explorations in Economic History, 13*(4), 423–436.

Denrell, J., Fang, C., & Winter, S. G. (2003). The economics of strategic opportunity. *Strategic Management Journal, 24*, 977–990.

De Soto, H. (2001). *The mystery of capital: Why capitalism triumphs in the west and fails everywhere else*. Basic Books.

Dierickx, I., & Cool, K. (1989). Asset stock accumulation and the sustainability of competitive advantage. *Management Science, 35*, 1504–1511.

Dixit, A., & Olson, M. (2000). Does voluntary participation undermine the Coase Theorem? *Journal of Public Economics, 76*, 309–335.

Eckhardt, D., & Shane, S. (2003). Opportunities and entrepreneurship. *Journal of Management, 29*, 333–349.

Edlin, A., & Farrell, J. (2011). *Freedom to trade and the competitive process.* (NBER Working Paper No. 16818). National Bureau of Economic Research.

Eggertson, T. (1990). *Economic behavior and institutions*. Cambridge University Press.

Eggertson, T. (1992). Analyzing institutional successes and failures: A millennium of common mountain pasture in Iceland. *International Review of Law and Economics, 12*, 423–437.

Elzinga, K., & Mills, D. (2001). Independent service organizations and economic efficiency. *Economic Inquiry, 39*, 549–560.

Epple, D., Argote, L., & Mowery, D. C. (1991). Organizational learning curves: A method for investigating intra-plant transfer of knowledge acquired through learning by doing. *Organization Science, 2*, 58–70.

Epstein, R. A. (2016). The economic structure of Roman property law. In P. J. Plessis, C. Ando, & K. Tuori (Eds.), *The Oxford handbook of Roman law and society*. Oxford Handbooks Online. https://bit.ly/3yIhhG7

Fama, E. (1980). Agency problems and the theory of the firm. *The Journal of Political Economy, 88*, 28–49.

Fama, E. F., & Jensen, M. C. (1983). Agency problems and residual claims. *Journal of Law and Economics, 26*, 327–349.

Farrell, J. (1987). Information and the coase theorem. *Journal of Economic Perspectives, 1*, 113–189.

Farrell, J., & Shapiro, C. (1990). Horizontal mergers: An equilibrium analysis. *American Economic Review, 80*, 107–126.

Felin, T., & Foss, N. J. (2005). Strategic organization: A field in search of micro-foundations. *Strategic Organization, 3*, 441–455.

Felin, T., Foss, N. J., & Ployhart, R. (2015). Microfoundations for management research. *Academy of Management Annals, 9*, 575–632.

Felin, T., & Hesterly, W. (2007). The knowledge-based view, nested heterogeneity, and new value creation: Philosophical considerations on the locus of knowledge. *The Academy of Management Review, 32*, 195–218.

Felin, T., & Zenger, T. (2017). The theory-based view: Economic actors as theorists. *Strategy Science, 2*, 258–271.

Finke, R. A., Ward, T. B., & Smith, S. M. (1992). *Creative cognition: Theory, research, and applications*. MIT Press.

Foss, K. (1996). Transaction costs and technological development: The case of the Danish fruit and vegetable industry. *Research Policy, 25*, 531–547.

Foss, K. (2001). Organizing technological interdependencies: A coordination perspective on the firm. *Industrial and Corporate Change, 10*, 151–178.

Foss, K., & Foss, N. J. (2000a). Competence and governance perspectives: How much do they differ? And how does it matter? In N. J. Foss & V. Mahnke (Eds.), *Competence, governance, and entrepreneurship*. Oxford University Press.

Foss, K., & Foss, N. J. (2000b). Theoretical isolation in contract economics. *Journal of Economic Methodology, 7*, 313–339.

Foss, K., & Foss, N. J. (2005). Value and transaction costs: How the economics of property rights furthers the RBV. *Strategic Management Journal, 26*, 541–553.

Foss, K., & Foss, N. J. (2008). Understanding opportunity discovery and sustainable advantage: The role of transaction costs and property rights. *Strategic Entrepreneurship Journal, 2*, 191–207.

Foss, K., Foss, N. J., Klein, P. G., & Klein, S. K. (2007). The entrepreneurial organization of heterogeneous capital. *Journal of Management Studies, 44*, 1165–1186.

Foss, N. J. (1993). More on knight and the theory of the firm. *Managerial and Decision Economics, 14*, 269–276.

Foss, N. J. (1994). The biological analogy and the theory of the firm. *Journal of Economic Issues, 18*, 1115–1136.

Foss, N. J. (1997). Economics, institutions, and Ludwig von Mises. *Cultural Dynamics, 9*, 77–96.

Foss, N. J. (1999). The use of knowledge in firms. *Journal of Institutional and Theoretical Economics, 155*, 458–486.

Foss, N. J. (2003). The strategic management and transaction cost nexus: Past debates, central questions, and future research possibilities. *Strategic Organization, 1*, 139–169.

Foss, N. J., & Hallberg, N. (2014). How symmetrical assumptions facilitate theoretical advance in strategic management: The case of the resource-based view. *Strategic Management Journal, 35*, 903–913.

Foss, N. J., & Klein, P. G. (2005). Entrepreneurship and the economic theory of the firm: Any gains from trade? In A. Rajsree, S. A. Alvarez, & O. Sorenson (Eds.), *Handbook of entrepreneurship: Disciplinary perspectives*. Kluwer.

Foss, N. J., & Klein, P. G. (2012). *Entrepreneurial judgment and the theory of the firm*. Cambridge University Press.

Foss, N. J., & Klein, P. G. (2016). Reflections on the 2016 Nobel Memorial Prize for contract theory (Oliver Hart and Bengt Holmström). *Erasmus Journal for Philosophy and Economics, 9*, 167–180.

Foss, N. J., & Klein, P. G. (2018). Sustainability, CSR, and stakeholders: An ownership view. *Advances in Strategic Management, 38*, 17–35.

Foss, N. J., Klein, P. G., Lien, L., Zellweger, T., & Zenger, T. (2021). Ownership competence. *Strategic Management Journal, 42*, 392–328.

Foss, N. J., Schmidt, J., & Teece, D. J. (2022). *Ecosystem leadership as a dynamic capability*. Manuscript.

Foss, N. J., & Weber, L. (2016). Putting opportunism in the back seat: Bounded rationality, costly conflict and hierarchical forms. *Academy of Management Review, 41*, 41–79.

Friedman, M. (1976). *Price theory*. Walter de Gruyter.

Furubotn, E. (2001). The new institutional economics and the theory of the firm. *Journal of Economic Behavior and Organization, 45*, 133–153.

Furubotn, E. G. (1991). General equilibrium models, transaction costs and the concept of efficient allocation in a capitalist economy. *Journal of Institutional and Theoretical Economics, 147*, 662–686.

Furubotn, E., & Pejovich, S. (1972). Property rights and economic theory: A survey of recent literature. *Journal of Economic Literature, 10*, 1137–1162.

Furubotn, E., & Richter, R. (2010). *Institutions and economic theory: The contributions of the new institutional economics*. University of Michigan Press.

Gaglio, C. M., & Katz, J. A. (2001). The psychological basis of opportunity identification: Entrepreneurial alertness. *Small Business Economics, 16*, 95–111.

Galbraith, J. K. (1952). *American capitalism: The concept of countervailing power*. Houghton-Mifflin.

Galloway, L. (1996). *Operation management: The basics*. International Thomson Business Press.

Gambardella, A., Panico, C., & Valentini, G. (2015). Strategic incentives to human capital. *Strategic Management Journal, 36*, 37–52.

Garnsey, P. (2009). *Thinking about property*. Cambridge University Press.

Ghemawat, P. (1991). *Commitment*. Free Press.

Ghemawat, P. (1997). *Games businesses play*. MIT Press.

Ghosh, M., & John, G. (1999). Governance value analysis and marketing strategy. *Journal of Marketing, 63*, 131–145.

Giachetti, C., Lampel, J., & Pira, S. (2017). Red Queen competitive imitation in the U.K. mobile phone industry. *Academy of Management Journal, 60*, 1882–1914.

Gibbons, R. S., & Roberts, J. (Eds.). (2012). *The handbook of organizational economics*. Princeton University Press.

Grant, R. (1991). The resource-based theory of competitive advantage: Implications for strategy formulation. *California Management Review, 33*, 114–136.

Grindley, P. (1995). *Standards, strategy, and policy*. Oxford University Press.

Grossman, S., & Hart, O. (1986). The costs and benefits of ownership: A theory of lateral and vertical integration. *Journal of Political Economy, 94*, 691–719.

Hahn, F. H. (1973). *On the notion of equilibrium in economics*. Cambridge University Press.

Hambrick, D. C., & Mason, P. A. (1984). Upper echelons: The organization as a reflection of its top managers. *Academy of Management Review, 9*, 193–206.

Hansen, G. S., & Wernerfelt, B. (1989). Determinants of firm performance: The relative importance of economic and organizational factors. *Strategic Management Journal, 10*, 399–411.

Hansmann, H. (1988). Ownership of the firm. *The Journal of Law, Economics, and Organization, 4*, 267–304.

Harsanyi, J. C. (1967). Games with incomplete information played by "Bayesian" players, I-III. part I. *The Basic Model. Management Science, 14*, 159–182.

Harsanyi, J. C. (1982). *A simplified bargaining model for the n-person cooperative game* (Papers in Game Theory, pp. 44–70). Theory and Decision Library. Springer.

Hart, O. (1995). *Firms, contracts, and financial structure*. The Clarendon Press.

Hart, O. (1996). An economist's view of authority. *Rationality and Society, 8*, 371–386.

Hart, O., & Moore, J. (1990). Property rights and the nature of the firm. *Journal of Political Economy, 98*, 1119–1158.

Hatch, N. W., & Mowery, D. C. (1998). Process innovation and learning by doing in semiconductor manufacturing. *Management Science, 44*, 1461–1477.

Hayek, F. A. (1945). The use of knowledge in society. *American Economic Review, 35*, 519–530.

Heath, C., Knez, M., & Camerer, C. (1993). The strategic management of the entitlement process in the employment relationship. *Strategic Management Journal, 14*, 75–93.

Hegel, G. W. F. (1820). *Philosophy of right*. Batoche Books.

Helfat, C. E. (1994). Evolutionary trajectories in petroleum firm R&D. *Management Science, 40*, 1720–1747.

Helfat, C. E. (1997). Know-how and asset complementarity and dynamic capability accumulation: The case of R&D. *Strategic Management Journal, 18*, 339–360.

Helfat, C. E., & Peteraf, M. (2003). The dynamic resource-based view: Capability lifecycles. *Strategic Management Journal, 24*, 997–1010.

Helfat, C. E., & Raubitschek, R. S. (2000). Product sequencing: Co-evolution of knowledge, capabilities and products. *Strategic Management Journal, 21*, 961–979.

High, J. (1984). Bork's Paradox: Static vs. dynamic efficiency in Antitrust analysis. *Contemporary Economic Policy, 3*, 21–34.

Hill, J. L. (1969). *The end of the Cattle Trail*. The Pemberton Press.

Hirshleifer, J. (1989). Conflict and the rent-seeking success functions. *Public Choice, 63*, 101–112.

Hirshleifer, J. (2001). *The dark side of the force: Economic foundations of conflict theory*. Cambridge University Press.

Hitt, M. A., Ireland, R. D., Camp, S. M., & Sexton, D. L. (2001). Strategic entrepreneurship: Entrepreneurial strategies for wealth creation. *Strategic Management Journal, 22*, 479–492.

Hodgkinson, G. P., & Johnson, G. (1994). Exploring the mental models of competitive strategies: The case of a processual approach. *Journal of Management Studies, 31*, 525–551.

Hogan, T. (2022, March 31). Will business fight back? *City Journal*. https://bit.ly/39xmiGP

Holmstrom, B. (1979). Moral hazard and observability. *The Bell Journal of Economics, 10*, 74–91.

Holmström, B. (1999). The firm as a subeconomy. *Journal of Law, Economics, and Organization, 15*, 74–102.

Holmström, B., & Milgrom, P. (1991). Multitask principal-agent analyses: Incentive contracts, asset ownership, and job design. *Journal of Law, Economics, and Organization, 7*, 24–52.

Holmström, B., & Milgrom, P. (1994). The firm as an incentive system. *American Economic Review, 84*, 972–991.

Honorè, A. M. (1961 [2013]). Ownership. *Journal of Institutional Economics, 9*, 223–255.

Hoskisson, R. E., Hitt, M. A., Wan, W. P., & Yiu, D. (1999). Theory and research in strategic management: Swings of a pendulum. *Journal of Management, 25*, 417–456.

Hoskisson, R., Gambetta, E., Green, C., & Li, T. (2017). Is my firm-specific investment protected? Overcoming the stakeholder investment Dilemma in the resource based view. *Academy of Management Review*, forthcoming.

Hubbard, T. N. (2000). The demand for monitoring technologies: The case of trucking. *Quarterly Journal of Economics, 115*, 533–560.

Hueth, B., & Marcoul, P. (2003). An essay on cooperative bargaining in U.S. agricultural markets. *Journal of Agricultural & Food Industrial Organization, 1*.

Hullinger, J. (2015, December 11). *18 secrets of UPS drivers*. Mental Floss. https://www.mentalfloss.com/article/60556/18-secrets-ups-drivers

Hume, D. (1739). *A treatise of human nature*. Penguin.

Innes, R., & Sexton, R. J. (1993). Customer coalitions, monopoly price discrimination, and generic entry deterrence. *European Economic Review, 37*, 1569–1597.

Innes, R., & Sexton, R. J. (1994). Strategic buyers and exclusionary contracts. *American Economic Review, 84*, 566–584.

InternetNews.com. (2000). *Priceline Webhouse Club calls it quits*. http://www.internetnews.com/ec-news/article.php/477561/Priceline+WebHouse+Club+Calls+It+Quits.htm. Accessed 3 July 2011.

Ireland, R. D., Hitt, M. A., & Sirmon, D. G. (2003). A model of strategic entrepreneurship: The construct and its dimensions. *Journal of Management, 29*, 963–989.

Jacobson, R. (1992). The Austrian school of strategy. *Academy of Management Review, 17*, 782–805.

Jensen, M. C., & Meckling, W. (1976). Theory of the firm managerial behavior, agency costs and ownership structure. *Journal of Financial Economics, 3*, 305–360.

Jensen, M. C., & Meckling, W. (1979). Rights and production functions: An application to labor-managed firms and co-determination. *Journal of Business, 52*, 469–506.

Jensen, M. C., & Meckling. W. (1992). Specific and general knowledge and organizational structure. In L. Werin, & H. Wijkander (Eds.), *Contract economics*. Blackwell.

Johnson, G., Whittington, R., Scholes, K., Angwin, D., & Regnér, P. (2017). *Exploring strategy*. Pearson.

Jones, G. R. (1983). Transaction costs, property rights, and organizational culture: An exchange perspective. *Administrative Science Quarterly, 28*, 454–467.

Joskow, P. L., & Klevorick, A. K. (1979). *A framework for analyzing predatory pricing policy* (Faculty Scholarship Series Paper 1305). http://digitalcommons.law.yale.edu/fss_papers/1305

Kahneman, D., Knetsch, J. L., & Thaler, R. H. (1990). Experimental tests of the endowment effect and the Coase theorem. *Journal of Political Economy, 98*, 1325–1348.

Kaish, S., & Gilard, B. (1991). Characteristics of opportunities search of entrepreneurs versus executives: Sources, interests, general alertness. *Journal of Business Venturing, 6*, 54–61.

Kaldor, N. (1994). The equilibrium of the firm. *Economic Journal, 44*, 60–76.

Kaplan, S. N., Klebanov, M. M., & Sørensen, M. (2012). Which CEO characteristics and abilities matter? *Journal of Finance, 67*, 979–107.

Kenney, R. W., & Klein, B. (1983). The economics of block booking. *Journal of Law and Economics, 26*, 497–540.

Kessel, R. A. (1958). Price discrimination in medicine. *Journal of Law and Economics, 1*, 20–53.

Khan, L., & Vaheesan, S. (2017). Market power and inequality: The antitrust counterrevolution and its discontents. *Harvard Law and Policy Review, 11*, 235–294.

Kim, J., & Mahoney, J. T. (2002). Resource-based and property rights perspectives on value creation: The case of oil field unitization. *Managerial and Decision Economics, 23*, 225–245.
Kim, J., & Mahoney, J. T. (2005). Property rights theory, transaction costs theory, and agency theory: An organizational economics approach to strategic management. *Managerial and Decision Economics, 26*, 223–242.
Kim, J., & Mahoney, J. T. (2006). How property rights theory furthers the resource-based view: Resources, transaction costs and entrepreneurial discovery. *International Journal of Strategic Change Management, 1*, 40–52.
Kim, J., & Mahoney, J. T. (2010). A strategic theory of the firm as a nexus of incomplete contracts: A property rights approach. *Journal of Management, 36*(4), 806–836.
Kirzner, I. M. (1962). Rational action and economic theory. *Journal of Political Economy, 70*, 380–385.
Kirzner, I. M. (1966). *An essay on capital*. A. M. Kelley.
Kirzner, I. M. (1997). Entrepreneurial discovery and the competitive market process: An Austrian approach. *Journal of Economic Literature, 35*, 60–85.
Klein, B. (2003). Exclusive dealing as competition for distribution "on the merits." *George Mason Law Review, 12*, 119–162.
Klein, B., Crawford, R. G., & Alchian, A. A. (1978). Vertical integration, appropriable rents, and the competitive contracting process. *Journal of Law and Economics, 21*, 297–326.
Klein, B., & Leffer, K. B. (1981). The role of market forces in assuring contractual performance. *Journal of Political Economy, 89*, 615–641.
Klein, B., & Wright, J. D. (2007). The economics of slotting contracts. *Journal of Law & Economics, 50*, 421–454.
Klein, D. B., & Robinson, J. (2011). Property: A bundle of rights? Prologue to the property symposium. *Econ Journal Watch, 8*, 193–203.
Klein, P. G. (1996). Economic calculation and the limits of organization. *Review of Austrian Economics, 9*, 51–77.
Klein, P. G. (2000). New institutional economics. In B. Bouckeart & G. De Geest (Eds.), *Encyclopedia of law and economics*. Edward Elgar.
Knight, F. H. (1921). *Risk, uncertainty, and profit*. Hart, Schaffner & Marx.
Knight, F. H. (1924). Some fallacies in the interpretation of social cost. *Quarterly Journal of Economics, 38*(4), 582–606.
Kogut, B., & Zander, U. (1992). Knowledge of the firm, combinative capabilities, and the replication of technology. *Organization Science, 3*, 383–397.
Kor, Y. (2003). Knowledge-based top management team competence and sustained growth. *Organization Science, 14*, 707–719.

Kreps, D. M. (1990). *A course in microeconomic theory*. Princeton University Press.

Kreps, D. M., & Wilson, R. (1982). Reputation and imperfect information. *Journal of Economic Theory, 27*, 253–279.

Kretschmer, T., & Khashabi, P. (2020). Digital transformation and organization design: An integrated approach. *California Management Review, 62*, 86–104.

Krueger, N. F. (2000). The cognitive infrastructure of opportunity emergence. *Entrepreneurship Theory and Practice, 24*, 5–23.

Kuhn, T. S. (1970). *The structure of scientific revolutions*. University of Chicago Press.

Kungl. Vetenskapsakademien. (1991). Press release. https://www.nobelprize.org/prizes/economic-sciences/1991/press-release/

Ladd, G. W. (1974). A model of a bargaining cooperative. *American Journal of Agricultural Economics, 56*, 509–519.

Lange, O. (1936). On the economic theory of socialism I. *The Review of Economic Studies, 4*(1), 53–71.

Langlois, R. N., & Foss, N. J. (1999). Capabilities and governance: The rebirth of production in the theory of economic organization. *Kyklos, 52*, 201–218.

Langlois, R. N., & Robertson, P. L. (1995). *Firms, markets and economic change: A dynamic theory of business institutions*. Routledge.

LaPorta, R., Lopez-de-Silanes, F., & Shleifer, A. (1999). Corporate ownership around the world. *Journal of Finance, 54*, 47.

Laursen, K., & Salter, A. (2020). Who captures value from open innovation—the firm or its employees? *Strategic Management Review*. https://leeds-faculty.colorado.edu/jere1232/Laursen%20and%20Salter.pdf

Leiblein, M. J., & Reuer, J. J. (2020). Foundations and futures of strategic management. *Strategic Management Review, 1*(1), 2.

Leiblein, M. J., Reuer, J., & Zenger, T. (2018). What makes a decision strategic? *Strategy Science, 3*, 558–573.

Leijonhufvud, A. (1986). Capitalism and the factory system. In Richard N. Langlois (Ed.), *Economics as a process: Essays in the new institutional economics*. Cambridge University Press.

Lenk, T., & Ghemawat, P. (1990). *De Beers Consolidated Mines Ltd. (A)* (Harvard Business School Case 9-391-076). Harvard Business School Press.

Lerner, J., & Schankerman, M. (2010). *The comingled code: Open source and economic development*. MIT Press.

Lerner, J., & Tirole, J. (2002). The simple economics of open source. *Journal of Industrial Economics, 52*, 197–234.

Levinthal, D. A. (2011). A behavioral approach to strategy-what's the alternative? *Strategic Management Journal, 32*(13), 1517–1523.

Libecap, G. D. (1978). Economic variables and the development of the law: The case of Western mineral rights. *Journal of Economic History, 38*, 338–362.

Libecap, G. P. (1989). *Contracting for property rights*. Cambridge University Press.

Libecap, G. P. (2005). *The problem of water* (Working Paper). Department of Economics, University of Arizona.

Liebeskind, J. P. (1996). Knowledge, strategy, and the theory of the firm. *Strategic Management Journal, 17*(Winter Special Issue), 93–107.

Lindenberg, S., & Foss, N. J. (2011). Managing motivation for joint production: The role of goal framing and governance mechanisms. *Academy of Management Review, 36*, 500–525.

Lippman, S. A., & Rumelt, R. P. (1982). Uncertain imitability: An analysis of inter-firm efficiency under competition. *Bell Journal of Economics, 13*, 418–438.

Lippman, S. A., & Rumelt, R. P. (2003a). A bargaining perspective on resource advantage. *Strategic Management Journal, 24*, 1069–1086.

Lippman, S. A., & Rumelt, R. P. (2003b). The payments perspective: Microfoundations of resource analysis. *Strategic Management Journal, 24*, 903–927.

Littlechild, S. C. (1981). Misleading calculations of the social cost of monopoly power. *Economic Journal, 91*, 348–363.

Loasby, B. J. (1999). *Knowledge, institutions, and evolution in economics*. Routledge.

Locke, J. (1698). *Two Treatises of government: In the former the False Principles and Foundation of Sir Robert Filmer and his followers, are detected and overthrown. The latter is an essay concerning the true original extent and end of civil government* (3rd ed.). Awnsham and John Churchill.

Loebbecke, C., & Picot, A. (2015). Reflections on societal and business model transformation arising from digitization and big data analytics: A research agenda. *Journal of Strategic Information Systems, 24*, 149–157.

Lueck, D. (1995). The rule of first possession and the design of the law. *Journal of Law and Economics, 38*, 393–436.

Lumpkin, G. T., & Lichtenstein, B. B. (2005). The role of organizational learning in the opportunity-recognition process. *Entrepreneurship Theory and Practice, 29*(4), 451–472.

MacCallum, H. D. (1965). *The wire that fenced the west*. University of Oklahoma Press.
MacDonald, G., & Ryall, M. D. (2004). How do value creation and competition determine whether a firm appropriates value? *Management Science, 50*, 1319–1333.
MacGrath, R. G., Chen, M. J., & MacMillan, I. C. (1998). Multimarket maneuvering in uncertain spheres of influence: Resource diversion strategies. *Academy of Management Review, 23*, 724–740.
Madhok, A. (1998). Economizing and strategizing in foreign market entry. In P. W. Beamish & J. P. Killing (Eds.), *Cooperative strategies: North American perspectives*. Lexington Books.
Mahoney, J. T. (1992a). Organizational economics within the conversation of strategic management. *Advances in Strategic Management, 8*, 103–155.
Mahoney, J. T. (1992b). The choice of organizational form: Vertical financial ownership versus other methods of vertical integration. *Strategic Management Journal, 13*, 559–584.
Mahoney, J. T. (1995). The management of resources and the resource of management. *Journal of Business Research, 33*, 91–101.
Mahoney, J. T. (2001). A resource-based theory of sustainable rents. *Journal of Management, 27*, 651–660.
Mahoney, J. T., & McGahan, A. (2007). The field of strategic management within the evolving science of strategic organization. *Strategic Organization, 5*, 79–99.
Mahoney, J. T., & Pandian, J. R. (1992). The resource-based view within the conversation of strategic management. *Strategic Management Journal, 13*, 363–380.
Makadok, R. (2003). Doing the right thing and knowing the right thing to do: Why the whole is greater than the sum of the parts. *Strategic Management Journal, 24*, 1043–1055.
Makadok, R. (2011). The four theories of profit and their joint effects. *Journal of Management, 37*, 1316–1334.
Makadok, R., & Barney, J. B. (2001). Strategic factor market intelligence: An application of information economics to strategy formulation and competitor intelligence. *Management Science, 47*, 1621–1638.
Makowski, L., & Ostroy, J. M. (2001). Perfect competition and the creativity of the market. *Journal of Economic Literature, 34*, 479–535.
March, J. G. (1962). The business firm as a political coalition. *Journal of Politics, 24*, 662–685.
March, J. G., & Simon, H. A. (1958). *Organizations*. Wiley.

Marchal, J. (1951). The construction of a new theory of profit. *American Economic Review, 41*, 549–565.
Marx, K. (2000). *Selected writings*. Oxford University Press.
Masten, S. E. (1988). A legal basis for the firm. *Journal of Law, Economics, and Organization, 4*, 181–198.
Matsusaka, J. (2001). Corporate diversification, value maximization, and organizational capabilities. *Journal of Business, 74*, 409–431.
Mayer, K. J., & Argyres, N. S. (2004). Learning to contract: Evidence from the personal computer industry. *Organization Science, 15*, 394–410.
McGee, J., & Howard Thomas, H. (1986). Strategic groups: Theory, research and taxonomy. *Strategic Management Journal, 47*, 141–160.
McGee, J. S. (1977). Why not "deregulation" for antitrust? *Antitrust Law Journal, 46*, 777–793.
McWilliams, A., & Smart, D. L. (1993). Efficiency v. structure-conduct-performance: Implications for strategy research and practice. *Journal of Management, 19*, 63–78.
Ménard, C., & Shirley, M. (Eds.). (2005). *Handbook of new institutional economics*. Springer.
Michael, S. C. (2007). Transaction cost entrepreneurship. *Journal of Business Venturing, 23*, 412–426.
Milgrom, P., & Roberts, J. (1990). Bargaining costs, influence costs, and the organization of economic activities. In D. M. Kreps (Ed.), *Perspectives on positive political economy*. Cambridge University Press.
Milgrom, P., & Roberts, J. (1992a). *Economics, organization, and management*. Prentice-Hall.
Milgrom, P., & Roberts, J. (1992b). Predation, reputation, and entry deterrence. *Journal of Economic Theory, 27*, 280–312.
Miller, D. (1983). The correlates of entrepreneurship in three types of firms. *Management Science, 29*, 770–791.
Miller, D., & Shamsie, J. (1996). The resource-based view of the firm in two environments: The Hollywood Film Studios from 1936 to 1965. *Academy of Management Journal, 39*, 519–543.
Miller, G. (1992). *Managerial dilemmas*. Cambridge University Press.
Mises, L. v. (1920). Economic calculation in the socialist commonwealth. In F. A. Hayek (Ed.), *Collectivist economic planning* (p. 1935). George Routledge and Sons.
Mises, Lv. (1936). *Socialism*. Liberty Press.
Mitchell, R. K., Busenitz, L., Lant, T., McDougall, P. P., Morse, E. A., & Smith, J. B. (2002). Toward a theory of entrepreneurial cognition: Rethinking

the people side of entrepreneurship research. *Entrepreneurship Theory and Practice, 27*, 93–104.
Monteverde, K., & Teece, D. J. (1982). Appropriable rents and quasi-vertical integration. *Journal of Law and Economics, 25*, 321–333.
Mosakowski, E. (1998). Entrepreneurial resources, organizational choices, and competitive outcomes. *Organization Science, 9*, 625–643.
Nelson, R. R., & Winter, S. G. (1982). *An evolutionary theory of economic change*. The Belknap Press.
Nickerson, J. A. (2003). *Towards a positioning-economizing theory of strategy*. Unpublished manuscript.
Nickerson, J. A., Hamilton, B. H., & Wada, T. (2001). Market position, resource profile, and governance: Linking Porter and Williamson in the context of international courier and small package services in Japan. *Strategic Management Journal, 22*, 251–273.
Nickerson, J. A., & van den Bergh, R. (1999). Economizing in a context of strategizing: Governance mode choice in Cournot competition. *Journal of Economic Behavior and Organization, 40*, 1–15.
Nisbett, R., & Ross, L. (1980). *Human inferences: Strategies and shortages of social judgment*. Prentice-Hall.
North, D. C. (1990). *Institutions, institutional change, and economic performance*. Cambridge University Press.
Oi, W. (1983). Heterogeneous firms and the organization of production. *Economic Inquiry, 21*, 147–171.
Olson, M. (1965). *The logic of collective action: Public goods and the theory of groups*. Harvard University Press.
Orr, J. (1996). *Talking about machines: An ethnography of a modern job*. IRL Press.
Ostrom, E. (1990). *Governing the commons: The evolution of institutions for collective action*. Cambridge University Press.
Oxley, J. (1999). Institutional environment and the mechanisms of governance: The impact of intellectual property protection on the structure of inter-firm alliances. *Journal of Economic Behavior and Organization, 38*, 283–309.
Pejovich, S. (1982). Karl Marx, property rights, and the process of social change. *Kyklos, 35*, 383–397.
Pejovich, S. (1990). *The economics of property rights: Towards a theory of comparative systems*. Kluwer.
Penenberg, A. L. (2005). *Digital rights mismanagement: How Apple, Microsoft and Sony Cash in on Piracy Prevention*. http://www.slate.com/id/2130300/. Accessed July 12, 2008.

Penrose, E. T. (1959). *The theory of the growth of the firm*. Oxford University Press.

Persson, T., & Tabellini, G. (2000). *Political economics: Explaining economic policy*. MIT Press.

Peteraf, M. A. (1993). The cornerstones of competitive advantage: A resource-based view. *Strategic Management Journal, 14*, 179–191.

Pigou, A. C. (1922). Empty economic boxes: A reply. *Economic Journal, 32*, 458–465.

Pigou, A. C. (1932). *The economics of welfare* (4th ed.). Macmillan and Co.

Pisan, G. P. (1990). The R&D boundaries of the firm: An empirical analysis. *Administrative Science Quarterly, 35*, 153–176.

Porter, M. E. (1980). *Competitive strategy*. Free Press.

Porter, M. E. (1981). The contributions of industrial organization to strategic management. *Academy of Management Review, 6*, 609–620.

Porter, M. E. (1985). *Competitive advantage*. Free Press.

Porter, M. E. (2008, January). The five competitive forces that shape strategy. *Harvard Business Review, 86*, 78–93.

Posner, R. R. (1975). The social costs of monopoly and regulation. *Journal of Political Economy, 83*, 807–828.

Posner, R. N. (1987). The law and economics movement. *American Economic Review (Papers & Proceedings), 77*, 1–13.

Powell, T. C., Lovallo, D., & Fox, C. (2011). Behavioral strategy. *The Strategic Management Journal, 32*, 1369–1386.

Radner, R. (1968). Competitive equilibrium under uncertainty. *Econometrica, 36*, 31–58.

Reed, R., & DeFilippi, R. (1990). Causal ambiguity, barriers to imitation and sustainable competitive advantage. *Academy of Management Review, 15*, 88–102.

Reinganum, J. (1989). The timing of innovation: Research, development, and diffusion. In R. Schmalensee & R. Willig (Eds.), *Handbook of industrial organization*. Elsevier.

Rensch, J. R., Heffner, T. S., & Duffy, L. T. (1994). What you know is what you get from experience: Team experience related to teamwork schemas. *Group & Organization Management, 19*, 450–474.

Rezabakhsh, B., Bornemann, D., Hansen, U., & Schrader, U. (2006). Consumer power: A comparison of the old economy and the internet economy. *Journal of Consumer Policy, 29*, 3–36.

Richardson, G. B. (1972). The organisation of industry. *The Economic Journal, 82*, 883–896.

Robinson, J. (1933). *The economics of imperfect competition.* Macmillan.
Rosen, S. (1981). The economics of superstars. *The American Economic Review, 71*, 845–858.
Rosenberg, N. (1976). *Perspectives on technology*. Cambridge University Press.
Rothbard, M. N. (1962). *Man, economy, and state.* Van Nostrand.
Rumelt, R. P. (1987). Theory, strategy, and entrepreneurship. In D. J. Teece (Eds.), *The competitive challenge*. Ballinger Publishing Company.
Rumelt, R. P. (2011). *Good strategy, bad strategy: The difference and why it matters.* Currency.
Rumelt, R. P., Schendel, D., & Teece, D. J. (1991). Strategic management and economics. *Strategic Management Journal, 12*, 5–29.
Rumelt, R. P., Schendel, D., & Teece, D. (1994). *Fundamental issues in strategy.* Harvard University Press.
Runco, M. A., & Chand, I. (1995). Cognition and creativity. *Educational Psychology Review, 7*, 243–267.
Sachs, J., & Yang, X. (2008). *Economic development and the division of labor.* Blackwell.
Sahal, D. (1981). *Patterns of technological innovation.* Addison-Wesley.
Salop, S. (1979). Strategic entry deterrence. *American Economic Review, 69*, 335–338.
Salop, S. C., & Scheffman, D. (1983). Raising rivals' costs. *American Economic Review, Papers and Proceedings, 73*, 267–271.
Scheffman, D. T., & Higgins, R. S. (2003). Twenty years of raising rivals' costs: History, assessment, and future. *George Mason University Law Review, 12*, 371–387.
Scheffman, D. T., & Spiller, P. T. (1992). Buyers' strategies, entry barriers, and competition. *Economic Inquiry, 30*, 418–436.
Scherer, F. M. (1980). *Industrial market structure and economic performance.* Houghton-Mifflin.
Scherer, F. M., & Ross, D. R. (1990). *Industrial market structure and economic performance*. Houghton-Mifflin.
Schumpeter, J. A. (1911 [1934]). *The theory of economic development: An inquiry into profits, capital, credit, interest, and the business cycle.* Harvard University Press.
Schumpeter, J. A. (1942). *Capitalism, socialism, and democracy*. Harper and Brothers.
Segal, I., & Whinston, M. (2012). Property rights. In R. S. Gibbons & J. Roberts (Eds.), *The handbook of organizational economics.* Princeton University Press.

Selznick, P. (1957). *Leadership in administration: A sociological interpretation.* Row, Peterson.

Shaffer, B., & Ostas, D. T. (2001). Exploring the political economy of consumer legislation: The development of automobile lemon laws. *Business and Politics, 3*, 65–76.

Shaffer, B., & Ostas, D. T. (2003). Exploring the political economy of customer legislation: The development of automobile Lemon laws. *Business and Politics, 3*, 65–76.

Shane, S. (2000). Prior knowledge and the discovery of entrepreneurial opportunities. *Organization Science, 11*, 448–469.

Shane, S. (2003). *A general theory of entrepreneurship.* Edward Elgar.

Shane, S., & Venkataraman, S. (2000). The promise of entrepreneurship as a field of research. *Academy of Management Review, 25*, 217–226.

Shapiro, C. (1989). The theory of business strategy. *RAND Journal of Economics, 20*, 125–137.

Shapiro, C., & Varian, H. (1999). *Information rules.* Harvard Business School Press.

Shepherd, D., & DeTienne, D. R. (2005). Prior knowledge, potential financial reward, and opportunity identification. *Entrepreneurship Theory and Practice, 29*(1), 91–110.

Shy, O. (2001). *The economics of network industries.* Cambridge University Press.

Sidak, G., & Teece, D. J. (2009). Dynamic competition in antitrust law. *Journal of Competition Law & Economics, 5*, 581–631.

Skaperdas, S. (1992). Cooperation, conflict and power in the absence of property rights. *American Economic Review, 82*, 720–739.

Skaperdas, S. (1994). Contest success functions. *Journal of Economic Theory, 7*, 283–290.

Skaperdas, S., & Syropoulos, C. (1995). *Competing for claims to property* (Working Paper No. 85). Center for Economic Studies, University of Munich.

Smith, A. (1776). *An inquiry into the nature and causes of the wealth of nations.* Oxford University Press.

Smith, K. G., Ferrier, W., & Ndofor, H. (2001). Competitive dynamics research: Critique and future research directions. In M. Hitt, R. E. Freeman, & J. Harrison (Eds.), *The Blackwell handbook of strategic management*. Basil Blackwell.

Snyder, C. M. (1996). Negotiation and renegotiation of optimal financial contracts under the threat of predation. *Journal of Industrial Economics, 44*, 325–343.

Spulber, D. (2004). *Management strategy*. McGraw-Hill/Irwin.

Stefanadis, C. (2003). Sunk costs, contestability, and the latent contract market. *Journal of Economics and Management Strategy, 12*, 119–138.

Stieglitz, N., & Heine, K. (2007). Innovations and the role of complementarities in a strategic theory of the firm. *Strategic Management Journal, 28*, 1–15.

Stigler, G. J. (1951). The division of labor is limited by the extent of the market. *The Journal of Political Economy, 59*, 185–193.

Stigler, G. J. (1954). The economist plays with blocs. *American Economic Review, 44*, 7–14.

Stigler, G. J. (1966). *The theory of price*. Macmillan.

Stigler, G. (1983). Nobel lecture: The process and progress of economics. *Journal of Political Economy, 91*, 529–545.

Sutton, J. (1991). *Sunk cost and market structure*. MIT Press.

Teece, D. (1980). Economies of scope and the scope of the enterprise. *Journal of Economic Behavior and Organization, 1*, 223–247.

Teece, D. J. (1982). Towards an economic theory of the multiproduct firm. *Journal of Economic Behavior and Organization, 3*, 39–63.

Teece, D. J. (1986). Profiting from technological innovation. *Research Policy, 15*, 285–305.

Teece, D. J. (2007). Explicating dynamic capabilities: The nature and microfoundations of (sustainable) enterprise performance. *Strategic Management Journal, 28*, 1319–1350.

Teece, D. J., Pisano, G., & Shuen, A. (1997). Dynamic capabilities and strategic management. *Strategic Management Journal, 18*, 509–533.

The Economist. (2020, September 12). Who owns what?

Tirole, J. (1988). *The theory of industrial organization*. MIT Press.

Tullock, G. (1980). Efficient rent-seeking. In J. M. Buchanan, R. D. Tollison, & G. Tullock (Eds.), *Toward a theory of the rent-seeking society*. Texas A&M Press.

Umbeck, J. (1977a). The California Gold Rush: A study of emerging property rights. *Explorations in Economic History, 14*, 197–226.

Umbeck, J. (1977b). A theory of contract choice and the California Gold Rush. *Journal of Law and Economics, 20*, 421–437.

Umbeck, J. (1981). Might makes rights: A theory of the formation and initial distribution of property rights. *Economic Inquiry, 19*, 38–59.

Usher, D. (1998). The Coase theorem is tautological, incoherent or wrong. *Economics Letters, 61*, 3–11.

Vanberg, V. (2000). Economic constitutions, protectionism, and competition among jurisdictions. In G. Galeotti, P. Salmon, & R. Wintrobe (Eds.), *Competition and structure: The political economy of collective decisions: Essays in honor of Albert Breton*. Cambridge University Press.

Varian, H. (1989). Price discrimination. In R. D. Schmalensee & R. D. Willig (Eds.), *Handbook of industrial organization*. Elsevier.

Venkataraman, S. (1997). The distinctive domain of entrepreneurship research. In J. Katz & R. Brockhaus (Eds.), *Advances in entrepreneurship, firm emergence, and growth*. JAI Press.

Vickers, J. (1995). Concepts of competition. *Oxford Economic Papers, 47*, 1–23.

Von Hippel, E. (1988). *The sources of innovation*. Cambridge University Press.

von Wieser, F. (1889 [1893]). *Natural value* (WilliamSmart, Ed.). Macmillan.

Vromen, J. (2010). Micro-foundations in strategic management: Squaring coleman's diagram. *Erkenntnis, 73*, 365–383.

Waldman, M. (1987). Noncooperative entry deterrence, uncertainty, and the free rider problem. *Review of Economic Studies, 54*, 301–310.

Wallis, J. J., & North, D. C. (1986). Measuring the transaction sector in the American economy. In S. L. Engerman & R. E. Gallman (Eds.), *Long-term factors in American economic growth* (pp. 1870–1970). University of Chicago Press.

Walsh, J. P. (1995). Managerial and organizational cognition: Notes form a trip down memory lane. *Organization Science, 6*, 280–321.

Wang, N. (2003). *Measuring transaction costs: An incomplete survey* (Working Paper). Ronald Coase Institute.

Webb, W. P. (1931). *The Great Plains*. Dallas: Ginn and Company.

Weber, L., Foss, N. J., & Lindenberg, S. (2022). The role of cognition and motivation in understanding Internal governance and hierarchical failure: A discriminating alignment analysis. *Academy of Management Review* (in print).

Weigelt, K., & Camerer, C. (1988). Reputation and corporate strategy: A review of recent theory and applications. *Strategic Management Journal, 9*, 443–454.

Wernerfelt, B. (1984). A resource-based theory of the firm. *Strategic Management Journal, 5*, 171–180.

Wernerfelt, B. (1997). On the nature and scope of the firm: An adjustment-cost theory. *The Journal of Business, 70*, 489–514.

Westall, A., Ramsden, P., & Foley, J. (2000). *Micro-entrepreneurs: Creating enterprising communities*. New Economics Foundation.
Whitney, S. N. (1953). Errors in the concept of countervailing power. *Journal of Business, 26*, 238–253.
Williamson, O. E. (1971). The vertical integration of production: Market failure considerations'. *American Economic Review, 61*, 112–123.
Williamson, O. E. (1975). *Markets and hierarchies: Analysis and antitrust implications*. Free Press.
Williamson, O. E. (1979). Transaction-cost economics: The governance of contractual relations. *Journal of Law and Economics, 22*, 233–261.
Williamson, O. E. (1985). *The economic institutions of capitalism*. Free Press.
Williamson, O. E. (1991a). Strategizing, economizing, and economic organization. *Strategic Management Journal, 12*, 75–91.
Williamson, O. E. (1991b). Comparative economic organization: The analysis of discrete structural alternatives. *Administrative Science Quarterly, 36*, 269–296.
Williamson, O. E. (1996). *The mechanisms of governance*. Oxford University Press.
Williamson, O. E. (2000). The new institutional economics: Taking stock and looking ahead. *Journal of Economic Literature, 38*, 596–613.
Wilson, R. (1968). The theory of syndicates. *Econometrica, 36*, 119–132.
Winter, S. G. (1964). *Economic natural selection and the theory of the firm* (Ph.D. Dissertation). Yale University.
Winter, S. G. (2003). Understanding dynamic capabilities. *Strategic Management Journal, 24*, 991–995.
Yang, X., & Ng, S. (1995). *Specialization and division of labor: A survey*. Centre for International Economic Studies, University of Adelaide.
Young, A. A. (1928). Increasing returns and economic progress. *The Economic Journal, 38*, 527–542.
Young, G., Smith, K. G., & Grimm, C. M. (1996). "Austrian" and industrial organization perspectives on firm-level competitive activity and performance. *Organization Science, 7*, 243–254.
Zander, I. (2007). Do you see what I mean? An entrepreneurship perspective on the nature and boundaries of the firm. *Journal of Management Studies, 44*, 1141–1164.
Zenger, T. R., & Hesterly, W. S. (1997). The disaggregation of corporations: Selective intervention, high-powered incentives, and molecular units. *Organization Science, 8*, 209–222.

Index

K. Foss and N. J. Foss, *Economic Microfoundations of Strategic Management*, https://doi.org/10.1007/978-3-031-12910-0

The manufacturer's authorised representative in the EU is Springer Nature Customer Service Centre GmbH, Europaplatz 3, 69115 Heidelberg, Germany. If you have any concerns regarding our products, please contact ProductSafety@springernature.com

Printed and bound by CPI Group (UK) Ltd, Croydon, CR0 4YY
01/10/2026
02225861-0005